MOTHERS & SONS

MOTHERS & SONS

Bringing up boys as a sole parent

Jo Howard

Lothian
BOOKS

Thomas C. Lothian Pty Ltd
11 Munro Street, Port Melbourne, Victoria 3207

Copyright © Jo Howard 2001
First published 2001

All rights reserved. No part of this publication may be reproduced, stored in a retrieval system or transmitted in any form by any means without the prior permission of the copyright owner. Enquiries should be made to the publisher.

National Library of Australia
Cataloguing-in-Publication data:

Howard, Jo, 1957–.
 Mothers & sons: bringing up boys as a sole parent.
 Bibliography.
 ISBN 0 7344 0186 8.

 1. Mothers and sons. 2. Child rearing. 3. Single mothers. 4. Children of single parents. 5. Sex (Psychology). I. Title. II. Title : Mothers and sons.
 649.10243

Design by Jo Waite Design
Photography Jo Howard
Printed in Australia by Griffin Press Pty Limited

Disclaimers
This book is intended as a general guide and is *not* intended to replace the services of professional counsellors and health-providers. The author and the publisher cannot be held responsible for any injury or misadventure that may result from the use of information in this book.

Every effort has been made to trace and acknowledge the front cover illustration. The author and publisher would be pleased to hear from relevant parties in order to rectify any omissions.

To my darling children, Julian and Imogen
To Steven for his integrity, courage, honesty and perseverance

Contents

Acknowledgements ix
Preface xi
Introduction 1

1 The Experience of Being a Sole Mother 5
2 Questioning Gender 27
3 Encouraging Good Communication in Boys 39
4 Talking about Feelings and Emotions 53
5 Setting Limits and Boundaries 65
6 Attention Deficit Disorder and Attention Deficit Hyperactivity Disorder 87
7 Helping Your Son with School Life 94
8 Dealing with Your Son's Anger, Understanding His Grief 107
9 Separation: Residence and Contact 125
10 Creating Connections and Negotiating New Relationships 156
11 Combining Sole Parenting with Paid Employment 173
12 Being Open about Sexuality 186

13	Dealing with Adolescent Boys	195
14	How to Recover from Domestic Violence and Prevent Child Abuse	230
15	Lesbian Mothers Raising Sons	257
16	Conclusion: Sons of Sole Mothers Speak Out	269

Helpful Contacts	279
Notes	280
Bibliography	284
Index	287

Acknowledgements

There are many people I would like to thank for making this book possible in their many different ways. First and foremost, the mothers and sons who have contributed their stories for this book. They have told their stories with much openness, and have not glossed over the sadness, angst, guilt and difficulties, yet they have also shared their hopes and joys in parenting sons, even in distressing and compromised circumstances.

Helen Wirtz, social worker and family therapist, inspired me with her wisdom and a strong and clear sense of ethics.

Other people who helped me edit the chapters and gave me direction on what to include: Ruth Chattey, social worker and family therapist; Eddie Gallagher, social worker, psychologist and family therapist; Kathy Lacey, social worker and family therapist; Lillian Nejad, psychologist; Trish Parker, social worker and family therapist — Trish also facilitates Bringing Up Boys programs; Dr Ron Schweitzer, GP and counsellor — Ron has worked tirelessly in his efforts with behavioural change programs for men who are violent, Charles Tinney, friend and lawyer, sole father; Richard

McGarvie, QC; Jane Tynan, my close friend, who is also a sole mother of two boys and a lawyer who has been steadfast in her belief that sole mothers can and do raise happy normal boys; Shane Weir, social worker and family therapist; psychiatrist David Lancaster, who refrained from making interpretations, and for his hopefulness and belief that change is possible.

Tracy, sole mother of a son, and a psychiatric nurse.

My sole-mother friends, Ann, Jane and Denise, always understood, would never hear of me accepting less than the best, and gave me a belief in a different future for myself.

My friend Meagan, who shared the experience of sole mothering in the NSW bush.

My general practitioner, Dr Severin Praszkier, has always been understanding and supportive. My workplace CEO, Kathy Wilson, and ex-manager, Robbi Chaplin, for their interest and encouragement in this project.

My children, Imogen and Julian, for their encouragement and for being delightful, exuberant, honest and open children; Julian for being a boy, and supporting the writing of this book for sole mothers.

There are many women (and some of their sons, who also contributed to this book). These include: Ann, Anne, Carla, Clare, Hannah, Ifrah, Jan, Jane, Jenny, Jo, Kaya, Kelly, Laurel, Mandy, Meagan, Melanie, Naomi, Rachel, Sara, Roslyn, Sally, Stephanie, Sue, Tracy, Ubah, Wendy, Winnie.

My thanks also to Andrew, James, Rob, Tom and David.

I would like to acknowledge the written contributions of Melanie Holland, from New Zealand. Although dealing with one of her sons' chronic illness, she took time to write extensively on the topics in this book. Thank you also to New Zealand family therapist, David Epston, who put us in touch.

Jo Howard

Preface

This book has been a long time in the making. It started with my experience of working with young Koori kids, mostly boys, and being confronted not just with age, class and gender issues but also an enormous gulf between my experience as an Anglo-Australian and that of indigenous people. Living and working with Koori people gave me an insight into other ways of parenting, and how dominant cultural assumptions can so easily undermine a mother's beliefs in her own abilities and assets.

Later still I worked with families who had experienced violence at the hands of men — including children who had been physically, sexually and emotionally abused by their step- or biological fathers, and women who had been abused by their partners. I noticed that the behaviour of their boys often prompted mothers to seek counselling.

Before my son was born, I remember having what I thought were unique and unnatural thoughts; I wondered how I might possibly cope with having a son. At the time I was working as a social worker in the areas of sexual abuse and domestic violence, and I'm sure that encouraged these thoughts. Would I be able to love my baby if it turned out to be a boy? Would I reject him? Find it impossible to form a bond? Happily, as soon as he was born and my friend said, 'It's a boy,' my heart filled with instant, overwhelming and heartfelt love. There were never, and have never been, any regrets. In fact, having a son has been a delight and a fantastic learning experience.

I thought it an important 'karmic' lesson that I did have a son (I now have a daughter too!). The experience has taken me on a steep learning curve, it has challenged many of my theoretical feminist beliefs (and shored up others!), and has given me the practical experience of parenting that matches my academic training. It has enhanced my personal life, my relationships and my professional work as a counsellor/therapist.

When I was four months' pregnant with my daughter I became a sole mother. This, in turn, brought a new range of experiences and learning, both in having a daughter and in parenting on my own. At the time I was living on a country farm, which was quite isolating and difficult. It was particularly the experience of being a sole mother and working with other sole-parent families that encouraged me to write this book. Having read and listened to the voices of many 'experts' I wanted to write a book that included not only my experience but the wisdom and voices of other sole mothers.

Some years ago I wrote a parenting manual for use by welfare practitioners working with sole mothers raising sons. This was a synthesis of the experience and expertise of sole mothers who had attended the many groups other practitioners and I had run. Many more agencies are now running these groups across Australasia. This book is written from my professional experience working with sole mothers of sons and it also includes the experiences of many women with whom I have worked and spoken.

Writing has taken time; an hour or two after the children are in bed, a Saturday afternoon when, by a rare stroke of luck, both children are visiting friends. It has meant the housework has suffered inexorably (I have since been diagnosed as 'domestically delayed'), and visitors have experienced post-traumatic stress disorder after viewing my kitchen, but then, what's so important about housework?

The mothers who were interviewed were invited to read the section of the book in which they were presented, and to add or change anything they thought important. The stories are not always happy, success stories, nor do they always include the ideological line I would prefer, but they are always stories of strength and resilience. Sole mothers are speaking out about their experience and about their successes, struggles and strengths. May they continue to do so!

Introduction

This is a book for mothers who are raising sons on their own. This may be for a number of reasons — divorce, separation, death, being a lesbian, or simply choosing to be a sole mother. Some mothers may have sons who see their father often, others irregularly, and some not at all. Mothers who are in relationships with men may still benefit from this book, although it is directed to particular sets of issues that are faced by sole mothers. It aims to highlight those issues that sole mothers say most affect their relationship with their sons. It also challenges the myth that sole mothers cannot raise well-balanced, happy and normal sons on their own. On the contrary, the premise of this book is that sole mothers can and do raise boys who grow into responsible and contributing members of society.

In 1994 Olga Silverstein and Beth Rashbaum, American family therapists, wrote a book called *The Courage to Raise Good Men*.[1] They were interested in exploring how boys are raised to be men and what boys lose in this process. They discovered in their therapeutic work that many men had experienced a sense of great loss and betrayal from their perceived rejection by their mothers, particularly around the two periods of beginning school and reaching adolescence. Mothers, on the other hand, felt that society demanded their withdrawal from their sons, and that not to do so may 'contaminate' them with their femininity.

There is little research and literature exploring the particular bond that exists between a sole mother and her son (other than in a negative way), and how social attitudes about sole mothers and how boys need to be raised impact on parenting. This book explores the relationship between sole mother and son in a way that is validating and respectful of sole mothers' experiences.

Being a boy today

Boys in today's society are grappling with a number of recently arisen issues. The structure of our society has changed markedly so that boys are not automatically assured of employment when they leave school. The feminist revolution has challenged ideas and attitudes about gender, and no longer can men expect to follow a life progression involving schooling, marriage, children and retirement at sixty. In addition women are expecting more from their relationships with men and are leaving those relationships that are unfulfilling or problematic.

Whilst girls in schools face a specific set of issues relating to their gender — such as increased reports of sexual harassment — boys are not as able to access alternatives to academic-based schooling, and may be experiencing difficulty completing their schooling. Boys in classrooms may struggle with trying to hold onto outmoded ways of being — such as being loud and disruptive — in a school culture that will not accept this.

The suicide rate for males has risen dramatically; boys lead the statistics in road accidents and substance abuse and other risk-taking behaviours. Boys in rural areas particularly struggle with finding a meaningful and positive existence,

with the suicide rate of young people 15–24 years of age having increased as much as twelve-fold in some towns with fewer than 4,000 people.[2]

The stereotyped way of being a male is no longer applicable. The pathway from boyhood to manhood is blurred and uncertain. Boys are increasingly experiencing a sense of disconnectedness — from adults, from girls and from each other. They are increasingly experiencing depression and anxiety.

In some ways boys are caught in a double bind. They have to be 'macho yet sensitive'. They have to appear to be in control, to be sure and decisive, yet also to be vulnerable and talk about their feelings. They must be open and caring, yet not too wimpy. They are caught in a time of cultural transition. The old notions of manhood are no longer applicable nor useful, but a new way for men has not fully emerged.

Most mothers raising their sons want them to be different from traditional male stereotypes. They see these stereotypes as unhelpful to boys — boys need to grow into different types of men from those of their fathers' generation if they are to be content and thrive. They want their sons to be caring and kind, not abusive and insensitive. They want their sons not to fear intimacy and to be able to communicate openly with their future partners. Mothers want their sons to share a wide range of emotions, not just their anger.

Mothers are in an excellent position to lead the transition into a new way of being for men. Such a way may emphasise those values traditionally labelled 'feminine' values that will lead future generations into co-operation rather than competitiveness, and connection rather than dislocation. Mothers can play a huge role in guiding their sons to have relationships based on respect, caring and commitment. It is my hope that mothers reading this book will be strengthened and gain confidence in rearing their sons, and that this will contribute towards social change that emphasises values that are humanistic and caring rather than competitive and distancing.

Chapter 1

The Experience of Being a Sole Mother

Sole-mothered families are the largest growing family group in today's society. By the year 2021 it is projected that one-third of 0–4-year-olds will be living with one parent. In contrast, the number of children of any age living in two-parent families is projected to decline, from 4.8 million in 1996 to between 4.1 and 4.7 million in 2021.[1] There are approximately 488,000 sole mothers with dependants under 24 years — this is 60 per cent of all family types; 16 per cent of children between the ages of 0–17 years live in sole-parent families headed by women.[2]

Probably the vast majority of sole mothers would not have chosen this path. As their stories show, most entered relationships intending they would last, and planning to build a future and solid foundation for their children with their partner. Unfortunately, stresses and lifestyle challenges mean that many relationships now end in separation. When relationships where the couple have children break down, it is more usual for children to live with their mother. In 1996 the number of female one-parent families was more than five times the number of male one-parent families.

One-parent families also result from women choosing to have children within a lesbian relationship or as sole parents. In the USA changes to in-vitro fertilisation and adoption legislation have meant that more lesbian and gay couples are becoming parents. In addition, the ability for women to be financially independent and pursue their own destiny irrespective of men has meant that some women are choosing to have children without a male partner. Sometimes this is because women reach a point in their lives where they feel they may not find a partner, so they choose to 'go it alone'.

The 'family' is a socially and historically constructed idea. What we have accepted as the 'normal' family — two heterosexual parents and two children — is now in decline. The challenge for society is to accept different types of family structures so that family members and their children feel supported and validated.

Sole mothers are bearing the brunt of social change. One newspaper survey found that the most worrying social issue cited by 78 per cent of the respondents was that 'single mothers are having children to get welfare money'.[3] Misunderstandings, prejudice and blame are a significant part of a sole mother's experience, yet these issues are rarely publicly or socially acknowledged. Mothers experience them as part of their day-to-day life, yet it is often not until they are questioned specifically that they are able to discuss these obstacles in the open.

Sole mothering is a difficult but, generally speaking, a rewarding experience. Melanie explains her experience:

> When I gave birth to each of my beautiful boys and held them for the first time, and watched as they looked up at me adoringly, it didn't enter my mind that raising them would be such a life-altering and sometimes heartbreaking task. When they were little and I read the parenting and psychology books, I thought it seemed a difficult task, but with the support of a

loving family and supportive husband it would be fulfilling and rewarding.

If I could have seen myself transported into the future, in times of isolation, with lack of support and understanding, I probably would never have gone through the experience. I never envisaged being a single parent on a social welfare benefit, pulled in many directions, away from my family, and separated from an angry, bitter and unco-operative husband.

However, having said this, I'd never be without my boys now. Each day and every tear gives me a deeper understanding of a purpose in life. I know that there are answers and encouragement in times of difficulty. Reading the right books, keeping positive, never giving up hope, even on the days when the thought of leaving the boys on someone else's doorstep enters my head.

There are many opportunities available through being on your own. You can build a relationship with the boys that doesn't include conflict with another adult who perhaps is unable or unwilling to co-operate and communicate effectively. Boys really love their Mum, and there is so much more time to get involved in their lives, sport, friendships, etc., if you're not trying to deal with an adult relationship that is not working.

In the face of adversity around parenting alone there is solace amongst the criticism, in that you can develop a caring, loving relationship with your boys. You do the best you can in your circumstances, with the resources you have at the time. It is not a perfect world, and never was meant to be, or will be. You are either parenting alone through choice for a better life for you and your boys or through no decision of your own. You are making the best of your circumstances by looking after yourself, continually assessing and reassessing your goals for yourself and the boys, and paving their way to a healthy, happy future.

As a single parent there is always the risk of losing yourself — you may even become tagged with a wide range of labels such as 'incompetent' or 'co-dependent', but it is just simply a matter of being torn in many directions, physically tired, mentally exhausted, and this is understandable. Having three boys with no man around means having to provide space for them to do the rough-and-tumble 'big' things that boys seem to like to do. It is really important for them to have a shoulder ride, roll around the floor, and do the physical things they need. With their Dad not around, I find myself doing this. At first it seemed foreign but, as I've set limits with it, it's an important part of our relationship. Pillow fights often happen in our house.

Sometimes there are too many books and too many experts. As we live in a world with vast conflict of opinion in many areas of our lives, and with such an overabundance of information from continually new sources such as the Internet there is advice coming at us from all directions on how to bring up our boys. Your gut feeling and what feels comfortable for you is the best guideline. It is up to each of us to tap into our own inner knowing/self. We're born with good sense of what's right and what's wrong for us. Parenting is a lifetime of trial and error, and learning about ourselves. Be natural; enjoy yourself, so that you can enjoy your children. Go and do things with them that you like to do. Have fun. You deserve it. They deserve it.

Despite the fact that more than half of marriages end in divorce and that more children grow up without two biological parents, it seems single mothers in particular are marginalised and isolated from participation in mainstream society. Sole mothers face many barriers in achieving full participation in society.

Financial barriers

It is estimated that income levels for women drop by two-thirds after separation, and that in general women are more likely than men to experience financial hardship after divorce.[4] This occurs for a number of reasons. On average, men earn about 10 per cent more than women. Since 1994 women's hourly rates have fallen slightly as a proportion to men's hourly rates.[5] Men are also more likely to access well-paid positions, such as in the computer industry, and as businessmen and executives. Research shows that when women have children their opportunities for employment, further education and income-earning capacity drop markedly.[6] As the custodial parent, they may need to pay a high proportion of their income for childcare, on top of the usual costs of their children's needs. Some women may retain a family property after separation, but if they are raising children on their own they may find it a constant struggle to make ends meet on a part-time wage or Centrelink benefits. Of sole-parent families with children aged 0–17 years, 56.7 per cent are renting, compared with 21 per cent of two-parent families with dependants.[7] In 1996 only 39 per cent of one-parent families owned or were buying their home, compared with 76 per cent of two-parent families.[8]

Sara says:

> My partner was supportive when we split up. But he couldn't really afford to give me much maintenance as he only worked occasionally. I had to pay a big rent, then pay for the two children. Both were at school. It seems that there are always requests for money from the school — for excursions and stalls and treats. Then there are birthday parties and things they do after school — buying football boots, and joining the cricket club. It seems to get worse as they get older.
>
> Even though I'm working and earning more now, I don't feel like I'm getting ahead at all.

Many sole mothers may spend long periods out of the workforce — only 43 per cent are employed, 23 per cent in full-time work and 20 per cent in part-time work. Children from sole-mother families are twice as likely to live in poverty as those in two-parent families.

Women report that having one income can often be a debilitating experience of living day to day and just trying to make ends meet. Even women on reasonable incomes cite financial constraints as one of the greatest stresses in sole parenting. Mothers without highly valued professional skills and training, or those who are on the sole-parent or other benefits, may experience ongoing financial stress for many years. Trying to make ends meet financially can occupy a vast proportion of a sole mother's thinking. It can feel to you as if things will never improve, that every day will be an ongoing balancing of what needs to be spent, what can be saved, and what can be put off. While everyone else seems to be buying a house or clothes, or holidaying, you may feel you are stuck at home, rationing out the money and explaining why the children can't do or have what their friends have. Mandy explains:

> It's really hard trying to explain to the children that I can't get them the fashionable runners, or why we have a car that is battered and breaks down all the time. Sometimes they get angry with me, and blame me for the situation we're in, and that really hurts. I would love so much to have a holiday or to go shopping for myself, but that just seems out of the question. I work part-time, but the kids constantly need things for school. It wasn't so bad when they were young, but now it never stops.

Sara adds:

> I try and think how lucky I am to have normal, healthy and loving kids. It is just so hard when everyone at work is planning their overseas holidays or dinner parties, and they all have houses with polished floorboards, and go and buy furniture at the weekend. Sometimes I feel embarrassed to bring them to our flat. It's like 'Wow, we live in a flat with all the other poor people'. Even my kids say that to me. I can't accept this. I try and be positive, but it eats away at me and, worse, I can't see that it will ever change. By the time the kids have left home I'll be on the pension!

Many women say that they envisage this poverty will continue until they are past middle age, especially now that children are staying at home longer than ever before. Sole mothers stand out as a group in our community whose children are brought up with their main carer's income well below the poverty line.

Attitudes of others to sole mothers

We live in a society that emphasises partnership and marriage, despite the fact that more people than ever before now live alone, and that one in three marriages end in divorce. Many sole mothers say there is suspicion from other women about their *intentions* — that somehow they are always on the lookout for a 'catch'. Sole mothers report that once they have become or are known to be single, they are excluded from couples' gatherings and are viewed with suspicion when they talk to partnered men.

Others report that other couples get nervous around them — as if separation is catching. They feel excluded — for example, when other couples go out for dinner and they are not invited, or there are social gatherings such as a school dance but it seems inappropriate to attend as a single woman. Sometimes friends of the couple may feel uncomfortable — with separation there is an assumption that family friends will need to side with one of the partners against the other.

There is a strong expectation in our society that women are supposed to hold the marriage together and take emotional responsibility for family members' wellbeing. For this reason women can be seen as having made a selfish decision to separate and placing their own interests above those of their children. People have the idea that keeping the family together 'for the sake of the children' is the most important thing. Because it is more usual for a woman to end a relationship, and because there is a stereotype that women are the emotional nurturers and carers, men can be the most sympathised with, and women can internalise a view of themselves as failures. Some sole mothers have wondered if talking about their relationship problems may remind other couples of the inadequacies or frustrations in their own relationships that they would sooner forget.

There is a pervasive and irresponsible myth that sole mothers choose to have children to receive welfare benefits. There is no logic in such an argument, and research certainly disproves this. Who on earth would hope to gain financially from receiving sole parent benefits, given what that remuneration is?

Other myths inculcated by the media project a view of sole mothers as irresponsible, uneducated, young and working class. The media sensationalising sole mothers in the name of 'current affairs' particularly perpetuates these stereotypes. This includes showing images of women in moccasins with cigarettes hanging from their mouth and four young children running around them, or young unemployed mothers who claim to be rorting the system. In fact, most sole mothers are not young teenage mothers but are in their thirties. These images are part of the misogynistic culture of mother blaming, and depict only a minute segment of the big picture. They do nothing to enhance a mother's self-worth or her belief and ability to raise children without male input.

Simone says:

> I think sole mothers can feel humiliated and looked down on by other people as inadequate. People assume that because you have children you must be in a couple relationship. Like a woman in the shoe shop who said to my son, 'You can take your new shoes home and show Dad how good they look.' That makes me feel bad.
>
> I used to feel bothered by not having a wedding ring on my finger. I'd feel people would look at me. Maybe my awareness had grown so I recognise that things are not ideal; I've been exposed to more life experiences now so it doesn't worry me as much.
>
> But even going to Centrelink was a bad experience. They were rude, and seemed to assume I was bludging off the government. I've never forgotten that feeling that 'You're just another one'!

People I'm with sometimes whinge about our taxes supporting sole mothers and I say, 'But that's me!', and they say, 'Oh, but you're different!' I'm still glad I've left the relationship with my partner. If I hadn't, I would surely have ended up with mental health problems.

Jenny talks about the difficulty of trying to be involved in the 'outside world' and of being a sole mother:

There's lots of discrimination you experience as a sole mother. If you want to rent property you are treated with great suspicion, and are always the last to get accepted when you apply. It's also really hard to get a bank loan.

It's also hard trying to be involved in community activities. I wanted to be involved and participate in my son's creche management. But the meetings were at nights. I couldn't obtain nor afford babysitting. It meant I couldn't participate.

Attitudes to children of sole mothers

There are innumerable predictions of doom and gloom for children, particularly boys, raised by sole mothers — violence, lowered academic performance, an inability to hold down a long-term relationship, a predisposition towards drug and alcohol use, and so on. A range of problems from ADD/ADHD (Attention Deficit Disorder/Attention Deficit Hyperactivity Disorder) to mental health issues and learning disabilities are attributed to growing up in a sole-mothered family. For example, an article in *Australian Family Physician* claims that 'for a boy to progress successfully, he must have an adequate and available father or other role model from six years onwards. If this does not happen, he may become "mother-bound", and turn into the kind of man who relates to women in an infantile way — such as many domestically violent men do, or men who have multiple failed marriages or who are unfaithful.'[9]

No wonder sole mothers are worried. A sole mother at my son's school told me how she had taken time off work to help in her son's gym class at school. When she arrived at the school, she was warned to expect trouble from a group of children pointed out to her because 'They're the sole-mum kids'. There is often an expectation that sole-mothered children will cause trouble, either in their approach to work and learning or on a behavioural level. Sole mothers report that, even when their children do well, it is often commented on with surprise — that, *despite* having a sole mother, her son performed well. These attitudes place an often intolerable burden on sole mothers.

Because sole mothers may be unsure of their own ability to parent, they may be more susceptible to the opinions of such 'experts' and their ideas that undermine, rather than strengthen, their parenting and feeling of self-worth.

Stress

Most mothers experience stress. There is an expectation that you should be the perfect mother, with perfect children. Motherhood is seen as something acquired naturally, and that any difficulties indicate a lack of mothering ability, an indictment that tears at every mother's feeling of self-worth. The house *should* be clean, the mother *should* look slim and attractive, and the children *should* be well behaved. Few mothers can meet this expectation, yet few feel unaffected by its demands.

For sole mothers this stress is exacerbated both by the practicalities of sole mothering, and by the marginalisation and negative and condemning attitudes towards sole mothers. There is much stress in having to be the primary caregiver, at times with little family backup and inadequate finances. Even having family support can create another form of stress, as sole mothers have reported that well-meaning family members often try to take over or give 'expert' advice.

Sole mothers who are marginalised by disability, age, isolation, or because they are from a non-English-speaking background and are dealing with a different culture in which to raise their sons, may face even greater stress.

Ubah and Ifrah are sole mothers from Somalia. They came to Australia as refugees, and both have boys whom they are raising without fathers. Ubah says:

> It is so hard being a sole mother. It takes me thirty minutes just to walk the children to school, and then I have to do the shopping. I can only do a little bit at a time because I do not have

a car. I go home and clean the house, then it's time to go back to school again. This is my life.

It is harder having boys. It will be a good thing if Yosef grows up to be like a girl and helps me in the house. He will be a better husband because he will help his wife. They ask me where their father is, and I tell them he's in Africa. It's sad for them, but that's the way it is.

Ifrah adds:

My son Hamidi is six years old. It's hard being the only parent — if you are late there is no one to pick the child up from school. It's hard also being in another culture — too many things change. In Somalia there is help from the neighbours and the family, the children can play outside — it's an easy life.

Boys are harder to have — girls listen to their mother and help, but boys don't listen. It might be hard when he is a teenager, but I will talk with him and look with him at ideas which are good. I am worried for that time because it is a new culture to us. In Somalia children respect the family and their parents, but here everything is changed. They don't accept what you say.

Stress can also arise as a result of issues relating to residence and contact, juggling the demands of work and parenting, and dealing with children through their particular developmental stages. Mothers who have retained reasonable and open relationships with their sons' fathers are at least in a position of being able to get additional support for those times when they may be ill or need backup. One of the most stressful issues for sole mothers is that there is no time out for them, little opportunity for self-nurturing or to take a breather. It can seem like a constant, unending rut, however much a mother loves her children.

Loneliness

Our society stresses the importance of friendships, partnerships and family. In some ways the portrayal of people spending time with others and being closely linked with family and friends is a myth, because communities and families are breaking down, and more people than ever experience a sense of isolation. Recreation is becoming more than ever a solitary activity — the arrival of the internet in some ways encourages this by the availability of entertainment in the solitary situation of one's own home. Longer working hours, community isolation and the breakdown of the concept of neighbourhood means people often feel cut off and alone.

Sole mothers may often experience isolation and difficulty in feeling connected with others. Jo, mother of three-year-old Max, says that:

> It's challenging being a sole mother — I had no idea what I was letting myself in for. It's totally reshaped my view of the world.
>
> As a sole parent you really find out who your friends are. I was in my mid-thirties having Max — I found childless friends wouldn't bother contacting me any more because I couldn't go out at night. People stop inviting you to places; you lose the group of people you went to bands and restaurants with.
>
> I had to create a new social circle and this was to make friends with women with children that I met through the maternal and child health centre and mothers' groups and playgroup. At least having a baby is an icebreaker.
>
> But I find you get compartmentalised. You can have a coffee with other women, but the weekends seem to be for couples only. As soon as the husband is back on the scene, you're out. Couples tend to seek out other couples — husbands want to speak with other men, not women.
>
> I've structured my time with Max to be busy during the week, but the weekends are a bit of a loss as other families are doing their own thing. My weekends are intense — there's no break at all. I'd love just an hour to be not relating to Max, just to be able to read the paper.
>
> The worst is when we're both sick at once. If it doesn't kill you, it makes you strong.

I reject being looked down upon because I'm on the pension. I could let myself be stigmatised and feel inferior, but I refuse to. I still don't like saying I'm a single parent because of the stereotype it evokes. Actually I prefer to use the words 'sole parent'; I think the word 'single' evokes that you're on the market, that you're available. The word 'sole' has more diversity in meaning.

Sole mothers may be excluded by virtue of their relationship status and are subjected to the negative attitudes of others. They may also face loneliness because they do not have the financial means to go out socially, to afford a babysitter and a dinner date with friends. It may be that the demands of work and parenting leave sole mothers exhausted or too busy to think about meeting their own needs for company, particularly as the children grow older and become more involved in extracurricular activities. Sole mothers whose confidence has been deflated by difficulties with their children or prolonged separation issues with their partners, may find it harder to brave meeting others or joining in social activities.

Anne says:

I never really thought about the difference of having a girl and a boy. I suppose I was concerned that there wasn't a man to do things with. I think Rob saw me as having difficulties doing things and would've liked to help, but there was no man to show him how.

I think he felt annoyed that his friends had lovely fathers. He missed out on a relationship and it wasn't even as if his father had died — it was that his father *chose* not to be there at all.

As my children became older I was able to tell them that their father's absence had nothing to do with them, that it was his choice. I think when Rob was little he went through hell. His Dad would ring and promise him visits, etc., and they wouldn't happen; he just wouldn't hear a thing from his father for ages.

At one stage Rob blamed me and said I'd driven his father away

— that if it weren't for me he'd still have a father. At this time he was a bit aggressive, he would stay awake at nights and cry himself to sleep. He'd ask questions about his Dad, and I'd say that he lived interstate. I think I avoided questions because I didn't really know what was going on either. I was pissed off and angry too! I tried not to convey his father in a negative light but I couldn't help it at times. Somehow you can't win either way — it was hell both with and without him (for different reasons). I remember when he moved up to the country and built a house with his new family he said to me (I still can't believe it), 'I could see more of the kids if you moved up here. There's a caravan park up the road where all the single mums live. Why don't you come up here?' He thought he'd do me the favour of seeing the kids more often!

I think Rob has had a greater understanding of what women are like. Having just one parent was probably hard, because for a while I suffered from anxiety and depression when they were little. At least we were free of the abuse and violence that would have distorted things. The children were always first, and no one else but them had priority in my life.

As a sole mother I lacked emotional support when they were young. That was the hardest. I spent a lot of time trying to come to terms with, and understand why, my relationship had broken down. I think you can be ostracised from other couples with children of the same age, just because you're single. When Noni was in grade one her schoolteacher put all the kids from single-parent families on one table because she thought they were disadvantaged. They were treated differently, and that wasn't that long ago at our local school.

You don't get invited to things where there are couples, and I couldn't afford babysitting, so you end up being alone at home watching 'Play School' with your children. The children missed out on being around other adults. Other adults were too busy to take much notice of the children. It is an isolating experience.

I'm very happy with the way that Rob turned out. He's a very independent person, motivated, level-headed, sensitive and smart. There's not one negative thing I could say about him.

Depression and anxiety

Depression and anxiety often go hand in hand in the experience of sole mothering. They may occur after the birth of a child, as in postnatal depression, or appear, almost inexplicably, just when a mother feels things are okay.

Depression and anxiety are particularly able to make their presence felt when women have experienced abuse or violence, either in their childhood or in adult relationships. Anxiety and depression thrive in a climate of fear, threats, self-doubt and guilt. Many mothers who have fled violence and abuse can feel depressed for this reason.

The effects of abuse on parenting may mean that a mother who is still living with her abusive partner is torn between being the sort of mother she would like to be and using all her energy to please her partner and avoid further abuse. At times parenting may seem like an immense burden, and this, coupled with other effects of abuse, may result in depression.

The expectation that mothers should be 'perfect' — that they should have a neat and clean house, with neat, clean and well-behaved children, and be smiling and pleasant — does not diminish with sole parenthood, but becomes more difficult to achieve (if it can be achieved at all). In our society one in ten people suffers depression and about one in eight anxiety. Women between their late thirties and early forties are particularly at risk, and women in general are more at risk than men.

Other risk factors for anxiety and depression include: having controlling or abusive parents; experiencing physical violence, either directly or witnessing it, as a child; experiencing child sexual assault; or having a controlling, violent or abusive partner.

Elements of anxiety and depression are common and normal during our lives. Sadly, they are increasing and becoming widely reported by sole mothers. It is an indictment on our society that this may be as a result of the lack of support, acceptance and encouragement our society offers to sole mothers and their children.

Guilt

Sole mothers in particular are vulnerable to the influence of guilt, both in their own lived experience and in their parenting. Sometimes guilt can be so strong that mothers find they are encouraged by the guilt to undermine their sense of confidence and self-worth. A mother may be under the influence of guilt because she has left her husband and holds the belief that a 'good' woman will keep her family intact, no matter what. The guilt may convince her that she should compensate her son for her failings by not imposing limits on him. As a result, she may not respond to his bad behaviour. In this way guilt manages to get the upper hand in her parenting. This can be particularly prevalent where the mother has strong beliefs about how mothers *should* be. These beliefs are often embedded in sociocultural expectations and stereotypes, and may be reinforced by other family members.

Mothers far more frequently blame themselves rather than the society in which they live, or her son's relationship with his father. Many sole mothers note that their son's father's absence is not commented on when things go wrong, rather the relationship between mother and son is scrutinised. At times child protection agencies may respond as if the mother is the only parent with responsibility, and may make no attempt to contact the boy's father or involve him in responsible choices.

Often guilt encourages mothers to parent to others' standards and advice, rather than relying on their own wisdom. Guilt makes it more difficult to stand strong in your own beliefs, and not take on board others' criticisms and suggestions.

A survey of mother-blaming in nine clinical journals found that two-thirds of authors attributed responsibility to mothers for negative outcomes in their children. They also found a tendency to idealise fathers, and generally the fathers' behaviour was not seen as contributing to negative outcomes in children.[10] Mothers are also often given contradictory advice — told one minute that they are overprotective of their sons, then blamed if they cannot account for their sons' every move.

Sole mothering can often feel as if it is just something that you have to do. You get up in the morning, get dressed, give your son his breakfast, etc. Sole mothering becomes routine. It just happens that you are a mother and you have a son, and you go about parenting him the best you can, with advice and support along the way if you are lucky.

Ask yourself:

- How do guilt and/or self-blame make their presence felt in your life?
- Which people or structures support guilt and self-blame?
- What do they say to you about your ability to be a successful sole parent?
- Are they helpful or unhelpful in your life?
- Are there times when you can stand up to guilt/self-blame so that their influence is lessened? How?
- Who or what is helpful in eradicating their voice?
- Suppose the influence of guilt and self-blame went away for a week, what would you be doing differently both in your life and in your parenting?
- How would you be thinking about yourself then?
- What would the absence of guilt and self-blame enable you to see and do that you are now prevented from?
- Why do you think it is that sole mothers are more easily able to fall under the influence of guilt and self-blame?

The joys of being a sole mother of a son

There are many barriers and difficulties faced by sole mothers, but there are also innumerable joys and delights. Some mothers have spoken about the sheer sense of relief in becoming a sole mother and not having to argue about decisions, particularly those that might be detrimental or harmful to their son. They speak of loving their son because he is a boy, because he is cuddly and soft, or such a 'little man', or playful or fierce, or whatever it is that makes him their special boy.

Mothers speak of feeling grateful that they have a child, of loving the experience of parenting. Along with the tiredness and lack of time, there is the joy of the first steps and words, the 'When I grow up I'm going to marry you, Mummy', the chasey in the park, the first horse ride, and so on.

James's mother, Kaya says:

> Bringing up a son was no hassle to me at all. It was great watching his progress, watching his knowledge grow with his body. I found we had to have a balance in our relationship — we talked about what was right or wrong. We started to have discussions as soon as he could talk. We'd talk about the ways a sandwich could be cut. As he got older we'd have discussions about more complex issues.
>
> He always had his own mind, and was very independent. I had to teach him some things like how to wee standing up, but he caught on quickly. It was hard at times because of the schizophrenia, I'd be hearing voices and this meant I found it extremely difficult to concentrate. James had to come to terms with me being a schizophrenic.
>
> I read a lot, and had counselling to take me through those hard times. I learnt how families should be by comparing myself to normal families. I was a bit neurotic at times. I worked part-time but that was really hard when I wasn't well. I paid people to help me; I saw a lot of private psychologists, but I didn't really feel they did help me much!

I think James has done beautifully without a father. He's independent, sensitive and intelligent. He's very easygoing — I was the emotional one. I think he got through because I did respect his feelings and encouraged him in his learning. We found some sort of balance in the relationship. I taught him it's okay to show your vulnerability, that it's okay to show your emotions. I let him know you can go into an emotional vortex and come out the other end.

Ask yourself:

- How do ideas you have heard about relationships and gender impact on how you think about the way you parent?
- What beliefs have you heard about sole mothers that might influence or get in the way of parenting your son in the way that best suits you?
- Which of these beliefs are more likely to undermine your parenting, and which to support it?
- Which of these beliefs or attitudes get in the way of parenting your son in a way that encourages the development of the sort of man you want your son to be?
- Do any of these beliefs try and push a barrier between you and your son, rather than encouraging a closeness and warmth between the two of you?
- Are there any beliefs you have had to challenge in order to be true to your way of parenting? How were you able to do that?
- What might other people — your friends, your parents, your son's father — notice about your relationship with your son and your parenting when you stand up to these beliefs and attitudes?

It is important to recognise the barriers only inasmuch as it helps you to acknowledge the realities of sole mothering as a means of validating just what sole mothering can be about, and how little such a role is appreciated. You do not need to tell your sons of your tribulations, but rather give yourself congratulations for the achievements that are rightfully yours. You can tell your son of the sweet joy of having a son, and the happiness of having someone as special as he is.

Chapter 2

Questioning Gender

The influence of gender is present in everything we say or do. The way we think about the world, the people in it, the choices we make, our aspirations and those for our children, are largely, though often not overtly, influenced by the assumptions we have about gender.

When sole mothers express their uncertainty about raising sons, they do not necessarily make the link that ideas about gender get in the way of parenting and the sort of relationship mothers want to pursue with their sons.

What is it about raising sons that mothers find difficult and complex? Why is it that mothers aren't as concerned about how to raise their daughters, despite their fears for the range of issues girls face in today's society? Why does this fear about what boys need to become 'normal' men hold so much power over the parenting practices of mothers today?

Many mothers fear that because boys are genetically different from girls and women, they need special handling, which can only be given by men. They feel that they, as women, will be ineffectual in parenting a son and giving him what he needs to become a 'real man'. Women speak of the plethora of media advice advocating that only if a male role model or mentor is available can boys grow into normal, well-adjusted men. Most of the emphasis on raising boys is on the value of men's contribution — where mothers are concerned, the advice is often 'to be careful of smothering or over-mothering your son'.

Stephanie says that:

> There are so many books and articles about sole mothers raising sons. It makes you feel that you just can't do it on your own — it makes you worried that your sons will grow up with some emotional problem or a bit crazy or dysfunctional just because you're a sole mother. And that's not good when you're trying as hard as you can to be a good parent.

It is almost as if mothers, particularly sole mothers, are in a double bind — to be the nurturing one in the family but not to get too close lest their sons be 'contaminated' by their femininity.

Some of the ideas about sole mothers raising sons include:

- Your son will grow up 'tied to his mother's apron strings'.
- Boys need a father, a male role model or mentor, in order to grow up well adjusted.
- Boys raised by women will grow up 'wusses', gay or effeminate (and that's a bad thing!).
- Mothers shouldn't get too close to their sons.
- Mothers should sacrifice themselves to their sons and give them everything.
- Boys learn to be men by dominating their mothers.
- Boys have testosterone, and that means they are naturally loud, noisy and aggressive.

Many of the proponents of ideas that suggest mothers can't 'do it all' on their own are backed up by popular parent educators. Steve Biddulph, a well-published author on a number of parenting books, wrote in *Raising Boys* that 'Boys with absent fathers are statistically likely to be violent, get hurt, get into trouble, do poorly in schools and be members of teenage gangs in adolescence.'[1] What such premonitions do not account for is that many boys who are violent often lived with fathers who were violent. It is not so much the absence of a father that has led the boy to violence, but the role modelling of a father who is violent and/or controlling. Domestic violence behaviours can be transmitted across generations — a boy who sees his father being violent, disrespectful to mothers and women in general, and using aggression to get what he wants, is more likely to follow in his father's footsteps *if he is offered no other alternatives*. Women who leave such partners are actually helping to break the cycle, both by taking a stand as a woman and by giving their sons opportunities to see other ways of behaving. Such sons, of course, may be violent — it does take a lot of hard work to change patterns of behaviour that have been entrenched from early childhood — but they can be changed.

Not having a father present is not the only variable affecting sons. Since men on average earn higher wages than women, are more likely to own property, have greater access to more highly-paid employment opportunities, and don't usually have to pay for childcare, it is highly likely that sons raised without fathers are also being raised in poverty. Poverty and sole parenthood have a whole range of associated encumbrances — isolation from well-resourced schools or educational facilities, mothers needing to work fulltime to support their children and not being as available to raise their children, and isolation from a broader, extended family.

In addition, we live in a culture that continues to judge boys' behaviours by a standard that long ago ceased to be relevant to boys growing up in modern society. For example, we still encourage boys to be leaders — to be competitive and aspire to be 'the best', although research has indicated that many men who aspire to these goals may gain financially but lose much in their physical and mental health, family relationships and quality of life.

We are still trying to push boys into a model of masculinity that has little relevance today, and, in fact, is detrimental to their wellbeing and happiness. All of these variables can have a negative impact on boys' development.

The media and 'masculinist' parent educators push the idea that boys as a group are struggling. Some boys are struggling, but many boys raised in sole-parent families are thriving. Many boys become well-adjusted adults who, because they were raised by their mothers, are more able to get in touch with the 'feminine' side of themselves — they enjoy cooking, flowers, are gentle, and are good conversationalists. They are interested in co-operative and caring relationships rather than competition, or needing to stand alone, toughing it out and being the best. Women raised millions of boys over the period of the two great wars, and no concern was ever raised for their welfare. It was expected that these mothers raising boys were helping to support their country in a time of war.

In society today it seems everyone is struggling. Middle-aged men have extremely high suicide rates (and these were men presumably raised in two-parent households), experience unemployment, depression, and high rates of heart disease and alcoholism. Women are struggling to juggle careers and parenting, and to hold onto relationships with men who have outmoded ideas on how women should be in relationships. Teenagers of both genders are struggling with the meaning of life, the pull of cyberspace, and the ever-increasing pressure to succeed academically. Society is not happy — it is split apart by an ever-widening gap between those who own the resources and those who are marginalised by their poverty. More and more we are relying on medication to address our anxiety and depression. In all of this, boys are not the only group to suffer. The issue is not one of gender or sole mothering but of the way we live our lives and the values that give rise to the society we create.

It would be ludicrous to argue that having an available, nurturing and responsible father is not worthwhile, but scare tactics will not be helpful to mothers and will only alienate and discourage them. The fact remains that more children than not are living apart from their biological fathers for the vast majority of time. It is only recently that men have begun to embrace a parenting role that encompasses more than being the provider. To tell women to enlist the support of males in order to enable their sons' healthy development is setting women up to fail and asking the near-impossible.

Many mothers feel guilt and a sense of failure that their relationship has ended — even those mothers who have experienced violence and abuse. Most societies place a great emphasis on women's role as being the provider of emotional stability and wellbeing in the family and other relationships. It is expected that women will care for and nurture other family members and sacrifice their own needs to those of other family members. They are expected to endure sadness and hardship in order to 'keep the family together' and until the children grow to adulthood. Women are held responsible for things going smoothly and for maintaining social and emotional harmony. When women take a stand against these expectations and decide to end a relationship, they are often labelled as selfish, uncaring and unfair. It is no wonder that it is mainly women who bear the emotional burden of failure, guilt and shame.

Scientists have debated for years about how much of a child's identity is formed by biology or by environmental influences. Some argue that 'biology is destiny', and that differences between male and female brains are set in concrete. Others argue that social, cultural and political influences play a larger part in men and women's ways of behaving. Whatever the mix, there is general agreement that a combination of biological and environmental influences shape a child's development.

We know that traditional ideas about how boys should be raised, and how the notion of 'masculinity' was constructed, are no longer helpful. What is needed for boys is a new and different approach to challenge these outmoded ways. We know that social and environmental influences are able to offer just this challenge. Sole mothers are in an excellent position to be able to offer their sons a range of ways of behaving, of identity choices, and of seeing and responding to the world. Mothers should never underestimate their influence nor that their influence can be positive and strengthening, something that is beneficial and helpful to their sons.

After all, 'masculinity' is not a truth, but a construct. There is no rock-solid, objective concept of 'masculinity' — it differs across time, culture, age, religion, and so on. The current Western model of masculinity has been around since the industrial revolution; at that time it suited the need for men to go off to work, to fight wars and give orders, to be strong and not complain, and to defend their families.

The Australian masculinist ethos is the butt of many jokes. We laugh at the crudity and insensitivity of Australian males. Why then do we still seek to hold such unhelpful traditions?

In Australian society it could be argued that one main stereotype of masculinity exists. Masculinity is seen as a fixed and taken-for-granted entity that should be embraced by all men, regardless of culture, age and background. It encompasses four ideas as illustrated by Brannon:[2]

1 'No sissy stuff' Any traits that are seen as feminine should be avoided at all costs. Such traits are ridiculed, and men who exhibit them are viewed as lower beings fit only to be ostracised — 'What are you mate, a girl?' Men who fail to meet these standards may also be labelled 'gay', which is seen to be the 'natural' exception to this stereotyped model. Being labelled 'gay' is also one of the worst insults a man can be given.

2 'Being a big wheel' A high value is placed on success, power, status and money. Men who are said to have achieved and been successful are those with access to money and status, such as executive directors and businessmen. These men are not allowed to show fear of failure or actual failure. Instead they conquer over all, including their partners.

3 'Being a sturdy oak' Men are expected to be cool and independent, not needing to rely on anyone, and staying rational and unemotional, even in the greatest of crises. These are the men of the emergency rescue soapies, the heroes of Australian television drama.

4 'Giving them hell' Men are expected to take greater risks, to be fearless, aggressive and a little bit crazy. They may be seen as taking risks, but this is viewed with admiration at their gameness rather than being told off for their lack of responsibility.

Although feminism has made some inroads into our ideas about masculinity and femininity, the above models still exert a major influence. The media, which both reflects and shapes our views, certainly continues to project men in these four models. The younger generation are also exposed to these stereotypical models in video clips, TV, advertisements, movies, computer games, and in the schoolyard culture. While there is some evidence that girls are challenging the constraining aspects of feminine roles, there is less evidence that boys are challenging the constraining aspects of masculine roles, and this is where they need assistance and direction.

Our society designates a range of behaviours as masculine and others as feminine. Despite the push of feminism, there are still very concrete ideas about what men and women should do. For example, most primary schoolteachers are women, as are childcare workers and nurses; however, there are more male school principals, given the ratio of male to female teachers, and the majority of politicians, pilots, company executives and computer programmers are men.

Ideas about gender are reflected in the parenting of children, both by mothers and fathers and it can be difficult to challenge those that are so ingrained. Parents who do challenge gender stereotypes may also be concerned at how doing this might negatively impact on their child. For example, you may let your son choose the colours of the clothing he wears: pink may be fine for a three-year-old, yet you may be concerned that your son would be ostracised if he wore pink when he was twelve; this concern may encourage him to choose more stereotypically gender-appropriate clothes.

Mothers find themselves caught in a double bind. On the one hand, you are wanting to encourage and help your son to experience and express his emotions. On the other hand, you are prevented by dominant ideas of masculinity that tells you how boys should be strong, and not feel or express emotions. This is implicit in common sayings that minimise and deny a boy's experience such as 'It's just a bump — get over it', 'Big boys don't cry', 'Don't be such a wuss' and 'It's nothing — just a scratch'.

It actually takes hard work and lots of energy to challenge and maintain the fight against the dominant ideas of masculinity. Of course, this does not mean that you should turn upside down all ideas about how boys should be raised. Certainly a boy's personality and individuality need to be taken into account. Some boys are loud and energetic, and love running and playing with toy cars. To try and encourage fine needlepoint work would be unfair, and probably unsuccessful. Another boy may enjoy reading or helping you cook, and this, too, is fine. Another may enjoy playing football and wrestling with his friends, and sewing and cooking.

Of course, acknowledging the influences of gender does not mean downgrading or not appreciating 'otherness'. It is fantastic for you to comment on the aspects of your son that makes him a man — his muscles, his strength in running, his leaps on the football field, his skill at repairing machinery or operating technology. What is important is that these attributes aren't stressed or emphasised over others that have been traditionally seen as 'feminine'. Your son needs to be complimented and encouraged in every way, and you are in an excellent position to do that.

By challenging ideas about gender you encourage a broad range of activities for your son to engage in.

Laurel told me:

My son's gender was much less of an issue than I expected it to be. I've never had to battle with him about respecting women. He's chosen friends with his values towards women, and he's also deeply respectful of other women and me.

I was, and am a feminist, and I talked to Sam from early childhood about relationships between men and women. He has grown up knowing strong women and not seeing men put women down. I think for a long time he thought he'd grow up to be a woman. At about six or seven years of age he realised his life would be different from mine because of our genders.

From an early age I encouraged him to express and talk about what was happening in my life. I don't mean we talked about adult concepts, but I would tell him about my experiences and feelings so he realised talking about that was an okay and normal thing to do. For example I might say, 'When you are uncooperative, I feel unhappy'.

It can be helpful for you to consider how your ideas about being a woman and relating to men might impact on your relationship with your son. For example, some women find that it can be extremely challenging raising a son once they are on their own because in their relationship with their partner they had deferred to his 'better' judgement and authority, or they had relied on him to enforce household rules and discipline. They may not have consciously acknowledged this in the relationship but it may have only become apparent once they left the relationship. In some ways a sole mother can give a boy the opportunity to see a kind of woman he may not have seen if the relationship had continued. He may see a woman who is strong, independent, able to make her own decisions, assertive and competent. This is fantastic role modelling. He can grow up with this sort of image of women, rather than having ideas that women are incompetent or passive. He will learn to relate to women with respect, and as an equal. He will learn about sharing and about valuing women's contribution to his life.

Carol Hughes and K. Weiss write that they:

> personally think that men need to be more conscious about their sense of entitlement to women's time, energy, skills and emotional support — to start valuing it or learn to live without it.[3]

Being in a sole-parent family may give a boy that specific opportunity.

Tracy, 34, is a sole mother of Samuel, now 11 years old. She says:

> Samuel was six when I separated from my husband. Samuel lives

predominantly with me, but still sees his father a lot. My parenting actually took off when I became single, being a young mum gave me more energy. When I was with Peter I abdicated my parenting and allowed him to make the decisions because he seemed more confident.

When I was pregnant I hoped for a boy, because I thought it would be easier to bring him up. I did feel alienated, because in my social circle no one else had kids, they could just get up and go off somewhere, whereas I couldn't.

I haven't let being a sole mum stop me having a life. We've both travelled overseas and have been to the outback. I want Samuel to be able to look back and see we've done some things and not been too deprived.

Now he's in his last year of primary school. I'm conscious that when he gets to secondary school he'll be lost to me. Not because I'll push him away, but because he'll start to become independent and have different interests. I don't want to mollycoddle him; I'll give him room, and I am conscious not to be an overbearing mother. I won't stop being physically affectionate, just more aware of his boundaries that he'll define for me. I will be sensitive to his signals, as I would be to a child of any gender.

I think my son feels much more comfortable discussing issues with me than with his Dad. As he gets older I censor less and less in his presence. For example, I wouldn't have used the word 'rape' a few years ago, whereas now I do. So to teach him about sex I am really just slowly incorporating more concepts relating to sex. We talk a lot over dinner — it's one thing I've insisted on maintaining. We talk about real-life things as a sounding board for exploring values and attitudes.

I want him to grow up to be emotionally mature and able to empathise with women. He gets to hear about my life's ups and downs, and puts himself in my shoes — I think he's able to transpose this to women in general. His sensitivity to women is much more heightened because he is with me alone.

I love being a sole mother of a boy, we're in tune with each other, and laugh and muck around together. It's difficult at times, but I'd never regret it. By the end of the day I feel really lucky.

Unfortunately there seems to be a recent swing back towards biological determinism. This includes a return to the ideas of gender being biologically defined. These ideas and attitudes are not particularly helpful to the possibilities of the two genders working co-operatively together. The ideas that men and women's gender development are set in concrete, rather than being socially and culturally constructed, close down, rather than open up, any space for reinterpretation or dialogue. Many women and men feel constrained by gender stereotypes and what is expected of them as men or women. Instead of letting them explore other options, such ideas are even more prescriptive and confining.

A woman who has been influenced by these ideas is possibly less likely to feel she can influence her son's development and give him options that she thinks would be more helpful and advantageous to him as a man.

The issue of gender difference is often cited as causing difficulty in the mother/son relationship. There are lots of misunderstandings about what it is to be a male living with a female. Much of these misunderstandings seem founded on fear and guilt rather than on an actual reality.

Boys are different from women — they have different needs, but they also share many of the same needs and emotions. You can appreciate and embrace this difference, but also allow for sameness and a relaxing of the boundaries of difference. Gender differences make for curiosity and wondering, rather than fear and confusion.

Chapter 3

Encouraging Good Communication in Boys

Many mothers speak about wanting to raise boys who are 'good communicators'. In some instances this desire reflects their own experience of feeling that their partners were unable to communicate well on either an emotional or conversational level. Some mothers may have attributed the breakdown of their relationship to poor communication. They may regret that the communication between their son's father and themselves was so poor, but are unclear about why this may have been.

Other mothers may be worried about how their son may communicate at school — they wonder, will he be able to speak up in class, and will he read and write okay? Mothers are keen to raise boys who can communicate clearly and openly, because they realise the importance women put on good communication, and they want their sons to be able to communicate their emotions.

Men who can communicate well do hold advantages over those who don't. For example, they are more likely to seek help or talk about their feelings if they are experiencing sadness, grief or depression. They are also more able to form a close and intimate relationship if they can express their vulnerability and talk about issues dear to them. As well they may fare better in the workplace and in society generally.

What do we mean by 'communication'?

Communication refers to the process of conversing with the world. Communication is both non-verbal and verbal, and relies on words spoken, physical gestures and body language, tone of voice, language used, and so on. The means of communicating are also increasing, and include reading and writing through a number of mediums including the electronic media. We communicate not only by what we say but also by how we say it, and what we don't say. We also communicate by how we stand or sit, or how physically close we are to those to whom we are speaking. We can also communicate by how we listen and respond to what others say and do.

Some early family-therapy literature talked about communication where the intent was different from the words actually spoken. For example, a mother may say, 'Of course I love you', but her tone of voice is actually contrary to the words she is saying. Children, as well as adults, pick up not only on what we say but how we say it.

Gendered differences in communication

There do seem to be differences in the way men and women communicate. Just how biologically and culturally influenced these are remains unclear.

Dale Spender, an Australian academic, once researched how men and women responded to each other.[1] She taped a number of dinner-party conversations, and found that much of women's conversations were about questioning the men or validating their words. The women were asking questions about the men's workplaces and their political opinions or views on world events. When the men responded, the women in the group encouraged them to talk more, saying things like 'Yes, you're right' or 'How interesting'.

Men, on the other hand, talked about themselves or asked questions of each other. They also occupied the vast majority of the conversational time.

Although this research was conducted some years ago it would probably be similar to the way men and women converse today. Men are still more inclined to give authoritative opinions or instructions, to make the decisions, while women defer to men and are reluctant to direct the conversation to talking about themselves for fear of being domineering.

Spender's research illustrates that communication differences are heavily influenced by societal expectations about how men and women should behave. Certainly there are inherent differences in the brains and physiology of boys and girls. Some research has indicated that the part of the brain responsible for language development is more developed in girls than in boys. Whether these are biologically and genetically determined, or a product of early environment and early childhood experience, is still open to debate. After all, if boys are thought to be so bad at communication, how is it that so many men have achieved fame by the myriad of ways they communicate their feelings — through art, music, poetry and other literature, sculpture and other mediums? These men have expressed their views clearly, concisely and emotively on a wide range of issues. It would be correct to assume that men are indeed capable of a deep and meaningful level of communication.

Many 'new age' books emphasise the divide between how men and women communicate. Such books argue these differences are biological, not cultural, and therefore are fixed.

Mothers who have been exposed to these ideas often feel at a loss about how to communicate with their sons. They

name a number of themes, which they say reflect difficulties or difference in communicating with their sons. These include:
- Boys are less cerebral — they like to act first, then talk, whereas girls do the opposite.
- You need to approach boys gently and choose your timing about when to bring up 'tricky' issues.
- Boys can be overpowering — they have loud voices, and an overbearing manner.
- You need to nag them to get them to help.
- Boys 'bottle' things up, and don't talk about their feelings.
- Boys express their feelings in an action-orientated way.

- Boys are good at expressing anger, but not any other feelings.

Many mothers express confusion about whether boys are inherently 'bad' communicators, or whether it is something that boys have learnt (or not learnt, as the case may be). They may wonder whether they can shape their sons' ability to communicate, or if they just have to expect silences or one-word answers from their sons. At the same time, they believe that good and effective communication will be an asset to their sons' journey through life, and it is something they wish to nurture in them.

It seems that some mothers, particularly those who have been in relationships where they have not been valued or respected, confuse poor communication with aggression and abuse. A son swearing at his mother, punching walls, and 'standing over' you so you feel you are 'walking on eggshells' so as not to upset him, is not lacking communication skills. This behaviour is about violence, control, power and intimidation. It is very important that you separate the two.

If mothers are used to putting men first, they may also feel they have to defer to their sons' views. Some mothers may believe that boys need to feel their views are more important than their mothers' in order to grow up with good self-esteem. But good communication for boys involves learning to argue and debate without necessarily winning, and with having the good grace to still enjoy and appreciate the argument and the intelligence of someone else, including that of women.

Ask yourself:

- What aspects of our conversations replicate existing gender stereotypes that I do not aspire to?
- What aspects of our conversations create and open up space for a 'new' and different kind of relating and communication between men and women?

- How will the way we communicate encourage him to respect women and enjoy their company?
- How can I encourage him to challenge sexist ways but still feel okay about being a male?

What is good communication for boys?

Helping boys be good communicators necessitates thinking about how ideas on men's and women's communication might get in the way of teaching your son good communication. Good communication for boys involves:

- respect for others
- interest in hearing the other's viewpoint
- giving equal time to other conversationalists
- being able to listen actively
- being assertive, and not passive or aggressive
- not using threats or bullying
- being able to express vulnerability
- being aware of the tone and volume of their voice
- taking responsibility for what they say
- being able to exert control over what they say and how they say it
- being aware of both their and others' non-verbal cues.

It seems a lot to ask, but if you are able to keep this in mind from an early age most boys will grow into being good communicators. You also need to think about how you communicate. Think about how you communicate with men. Do you defer to them? Are you shy? Is it difficult to be assertive? Do you tend to be more or less domineering? Do you find it similar to communicating with women?

Sons will model the way that people they are close to communicate. Unfortunately, this may mean that, if your son sees you and his father arguing loudly, he may use the same tone of voice with you. If he sees you speaking with other mothers at school or having friends over and talking and laughing with them, he will pick up more socially acceptable communication skills. It is helpful for him to spend time with you when you are talking with other people so that he can observe and practise how people communicate. If he sees his father, he may also get the opportunity to do that with his father's friends or new family.

Communication and self-esteem

The way you communicate to your son can also build his feelings of self-worth. If you can take the time to be genuinely interested in what your son has to say, to hear his opinions, his experiences and his feelings, he will grow up to believe that what he has to say is important and worth hearing. If he is used to being listened to in an interested and attentive way, he will be more likely to listen in the same way to others.

Attentive listening means concentrating on what he has to say, rather than continuing to do other tasks or watch the TV. It includes facing him and asking him leading questions, which will continue, rather than end, the conversation. It also includes giving him feedback: 'I was really interested to hear about that science test. It sounded really hard, but I like that you tried to answer those tricky questions and didn't just give up'.

Many parents unintentionally use shaming language with their sons that they do not use with their daughters, for example, 'I thought a big boy like you wouldn't have worried about that' or 'What will Vanessa think of her big brother now?' It is important to find ways to talk to your son that he can respond to. Be careful to avoid judging your son or advising him. Instead use 'wondering' language and language that indicates you have a belief in his ability to find a solution and make the right choices. For example, if he performs poorly at a test at school you might respond by asking him how he feels about it, and wondering what might be helpful for him and for you to do to improve his results next time, or simply acknowledge that he did his best.

Encouraging good communication

Boys can be taught to communicate well from an early age. The main thing is to talk to them from the time they are very young, not to think they are too little to understand or appreciate communication. Newborn babies respond to the sound of other voices, and babies are never too young to be spoken to or to hear the sound of their mother's voice.

You can describe things to your son as they happen, for example: 'Oh, there's a big black cow, and she's walking over to the fence to see her friend. See the grass she's eating, and her long tail for swishing away the flies.' Young children can easily incorporate their mother's words into their own everyday language, once they have learnt to speak.

Cuddle your little toddler, point things out to him, encourage him to touch and explore the world around him — all this is the beginnings of communication.

Ideas to encourage good communication

- Choose your time for meaningful communication, such as making a special time when your son is in bed or early on a Sunday morning (if you don't work at the weekend). He can look forward to this special time together with you, and it means a working mother has this opportunity as well.
- When talking with a smaller boy, squat or kneel so that you are at his eye-level and are able to make eye contact with him.
- Touch your child or say his name to gain his attention.
- Make sure your tone of voice matches the words you are saying.
- Make sure you speak with him in the same room, rather than having to shout from another.
- It can be helpful to talk while you are doing things together, such as running, or cooking, or playing ball, to make talking time a fun time.

- Take what he says seriously — it can be easy to laugh or tease him, but this does not lead to trust. Be discreet, and respect his experience, privacy and confidentiality.
- As well as asking him about his day, tell him about yours. Share your life with him — he will be interested in what you do.
- Encourage good manners and respect in communication. This means teaching him not to interrupt, to say 'Please', 'Pardon' and 'Thank you', and to listen attentively.
- Don't focus on the negative things he does, but communicate what you like about him: 'I really liked the way you wiped the bench down', 'I appreciate you making me a cup of tea', 'The game was exciting — I love watching you play.'
- Use 'owning' language, like sentences that begin with 'I', rather than 'You'. For example, say 'I would like you to clean up your cars now' rather than 'You have to clean up your cars before you go to bed.'
- Ask open-ended rather than closed-ended questions. The standard 'What did you do at school today?' may yield a 'Nothing'. Asking him 'What was the best thing you did at school today?' may yield a totally different response.

Reading

Boys tend to both read less than girls, and have more difficulty in learning to read. Whereas girls seem to take 'naturally' to books, boys may seem to shun them or want to play action games rather than to be quiet and read.

Reading is something that can be encouraged, learnt and appreciated. It is helpful to start reading to children when they are very young, long before they can read themselves. Children who are avid readers are often those whose parents read to them nightly and encouraged a love of literature. When you are reading to your son, ask him what he thinks might happen next, who he likes best in the book, what he thinks the character likes for breakfast? Engage him in a conversation so that he gets to participate actively in the event of reading.

Reading can also be a calming activity for energetic boys. It can help them to impose self-discipline and be grounded. Many mothers ensure that at least half an hour a day is spent as a quiet time in reading, even if it is just looking at pictures. If this habit is established early in life it will assist your son in continuing his reading and enjoying it as well.

Writing

As with reading, learning to write can start for your son at an early age by giving him crayons or pencils to draw with, by letting him get familiar with paper and holding a writing implement. As he gets older, encourage him to sign his name on cards for other people or to write simple messages such as thankyou notes following his birthday or other celebration. Have fun making up poems together or playing word-games like Scrabble.

Melanie shares her ideas about communicating with boys:

> Helping to teach your boys effective communication techniques is not greatly different from any adult communication enhancement program. The effectiveness of communication is dependent on the participants using assertive and constructive communication, rather than other styles such as aggressive, destructive or passive techniques. We need to encourage clear and open communication.
>
> Boys love you to play rough-and-tumble games with them. They love playful pillow fights (not to be confused with pillow punching sometimes recommended for expressing anger) and wrestling games, that is, a controlled, non-aggressive form of physical contact with limits and boundaries. At first I found this foreign, and thought that it was my duty to stop them from doing this, but I now enjoy it because I realise that it is a part of their development and they get so much out of it. I see it as

people contact, and a part of their communication development. I guess the main issue is setting limits and boundaries and knowing when to stop, and how to wind down afterwards. It's important for teaching them when enough is enough and when to stop, and also that some people will not want to participate in this game, and that is fine also. This can help them with their relationships with women when they are older.

Being part of teaching boys how to respect women is a very important part of their development. This is much easier than if you have a male partner who is disrespectful towards you, so it can be a blessing to be teaching this alone. Especially if they have no sisters or girl cousins, take some time out to help them to understand girls. Some of their friends may have sisters, or there may be a girl in the neighbourhood they can befriend. A neighbour's little girl loves to come over, as she is the only child in her family. She joins in the chasing and pillow fighting, and sometimes I intervene and the boys make clear rules when she is playing. She says she doesn't really like boys, but she just keeps coming over all the same.

We have a ritual of candlelit dinners with wineglasses (containing water). Setting the right environment for good communication is very important. Enjoying a meal together is a perfect opportunity for sharing what has happened during the day. With busy families, and especially as they get older, this may be the only time the whole family is together, so make it an important, special occasion every day. If a person (whether it is you or one of the children) has gone to the trouble of cooking a meal, then it deserves to be enjoyed and made an occasion. Eating dinner in front of the television is not interactive, and does not pave the way for good conversation.

Not becoming isolated as a sole mother is very important. Sometimes you can become so busy keeping your head above water and become so independent that you can spend night after night on your own. Keeping people calling over and modelling good communication between adults is very good for the boys as well as you.

Pets are a wonderful part of the communication process.

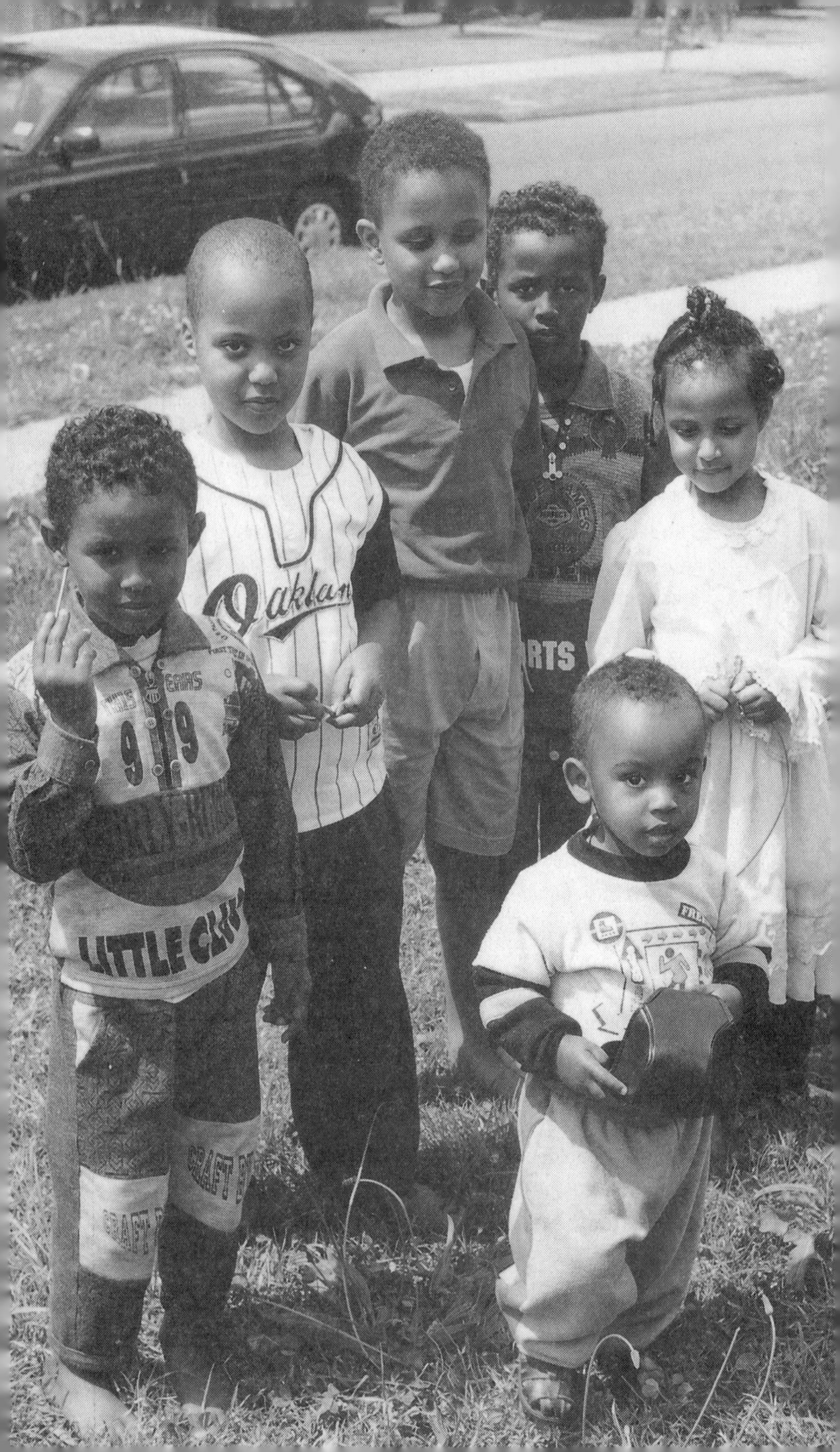
Oaklan
LITTLE CLU
RTS

Caring for them, calling them, training them, nurturing them and disciplining them are all really helpful as part of your boy's development. Patting and stroking pets is also therapeutic.

Some boys prefer to communicate while they are doing something. They may feel under pressure and not as relaxed if they are approached while they are in their rooms or sitting at the table doing their homework. So it can be easier to go bike riding, play ball or go for a walk together when you want to talk about something that may be a bit 'touchy'.

Ask your son:
- What was the best thing about school today?
- Why did you like that so much?
- What was the thing you did that you most enjoyed?
- What were the games you played at lunchtime?
- Which of your friends did you play with today?
- What do you think your teacher would say about the work you did today?
- How did you decide what to draw for art?
- What are the colours you like to use most of all?
- How exactly did you design that model?
- Where did you get the idea to do it that way?
- What do you think you'll need to do to improve on that?
- What part of the soccer game made you most proud of yourself?
- How were you able to score that goal?
- Which was the best part of the movie you saw?

Communication is the cornerstone to a boy's healthy development. How you communicate with him will influence his experience of your setting limits and boundaries. It will influence his ability to identify and express emotions, his relationships with others and his view of himself. You are well placed to teach your son the so-called 'feminine' ways of communicating that have barred men from expressing themselves and being open and sharing. You can teach your son that being open is something to be embraced, not feared. By doing this, you can contribute substantially to securing your son's stable emotional future.

Chapter 4

Talking about Feelings and Emotions

One of the biggest complaints women have about their male partners is that they do not seem to be in touch with their feelings and emotions. Women say they wonder what men's emotional responses are, or whether in fact they do emotionally connect, as at times it seems they do not have feelings at all. At times they say their partners tell them they do have feelings but find it difficult to express them. Other men can easily show feelings of anger, jealousy, hurt and betrayal, but not other more nurturing feelings like love and caring.

Many relationships end because women say they have lost any sense of an emotional connection with their partner. They find it is their female friends with whom they share precious moments and gain comfort. Because they feel shut off from their partners, they, in turn, stop trying, and close down their own communication. This can escalate, with the resultant couple breakdown.

Many books which focus on emotions often have a biological focus. They argue that men are genetically different and that women and men have to be *more* aware of these differences and behave accordingly in their interactions with each other. In this way they actually legitimate such differences, and present them as fixed and unchangeable. This, of course, does nothing to change the gendered way in which our society works, nor address the related issues with which boys are struggling.

Mothers want to encourage their sons to name and express their feelings. Some mothers report that their sons appear 'locked up' and unable to talk about their feelings and emotions. When they try to entice their sons to communicate, they are met with an 'I don't know' or 'Stop hassling me.' Mothers wonder if this is because boys are genetically made this way, or whether it is something about our culture that encourages this in boys from an early age.

Gender stereotyping begins from birth, when boy babies are dressed in blue and girls in pink. Studies have shown that boy babies are left to cry much longer than girl babies. Girl babies are hugged and fussed over more than boys. Boy babies spend much longer physically apart from their mothers than girl babies. They are more likely to be breast-fed for a shorter period of time.

When babies are born, their thinking and responses are far from fully developed. The brain is open to a myriad of experiences, which in turn formulate how the brain grows and develops. The baby's brain is wired to accommodate developmental interactions that further shape the nervous system after birth, with profound consequences for lifelong functioning.[1] This means that how we respond to baby boys and young sons will determine if they will have a healthy emotional start in life and will affect their style of behaviour in the future.

The capacity to use language, to tolerate distress, and to show and name feelings is affected by the emotional environment created for boys in early childhood. Although biology and male hormones such as testosterone play a role in a boy's development, they are equalled by the role played by caring adults in his early years. These adults influence his formative years, how he sees the world and his place in it, how he experiences love, trust, cuddling and expression. These early environmental experiences also impact on his brain's development. Modern science has demonstrated how easily nurture becomes nature; there is no rigid dichotomy between the two. Both have vital roles to play.

When mothers are questioned about how they want their sons to grow up, almost all state that they hope their sons develop into men who are articulate and open about their feelings. Sole mothers, in particular, seem to avert their distress as they watch this process of blocking out occurring in their sons. Many feel powerless to stand up to this process in the face of peer and societal pressure. They question their own involvement and connection with their son. Perhaps they are being too protective, too nurturing, too involved?

Also, girls are raised to be the carers and nurturers. They are taught to act as a conduit for males to voice their feelings. It is girls and women who take on the social and emotional responsibilities in the family — to cook meals for family friends, to comfort the children, to write cards of condolences when someone dies, to do the birthday and Christmas shopping, and to keep the peace. From an early age girls are encouraged to write letters to others, to make gifts, to give Daddy a hug because he is tired — in short, to take notice of, and look after others' feelings. Because this caring is seen as such a 'feminine' thing to do, it is not questioned when boys are not part of this. If boys are not involved, both by their physical presence and emotional contribution, in these rituals and gatherings, they will not see it as part of their future role.

In many cultures there are no such hang-ups for men — in Asia men freely hold hands, or massage each other's shoulders; in European countries it is common for men to cry, or embrace each other. Cultural norms develop over time, and can be challenged and changed. Some Australian historians have argued that ways of behaving are part of a historical development from the early days of white invasion in Australia where men were brutalised and where survival depended on being tough and macho. Now men no longer need to be this way; in fact, being this way is detrimental to boys' and men's wellbeing. The women's movement was in the forefront in challenging gender roles and stereotypes, and men perhaps now need to challenge those ideas that are unhelpful and limiting to them.

It can be tough work for a mother to take on this challenge. You may wonder if, in fact, you are doing your son a disservice by encouraging him to cry or express deeper emotions. But many men in our society are suffering the effects of not expressing their emotions. Their relationships are falling apart, they are experiencing a greater amount of stress, and depression and anxiety among men is rising dramatically. The suicide rate for young Australian men is alarming: in Australia in 1998 there were 446 deaths from suicide in the 15–24 year age group. Young males comprised 364 of these deaths. Suicide is one of the three leading causes of death among people aged 15–34.[2] Many parents of young men who have taken their own lives say, 'If only he had told us something was wrong'.

One of the first steps in challenging how society expects boys to be is to challenge our own beliefs about boys. If mothers believe boys are victims of testosterone — impulsive, tough, uncaring, and a hassle — then boys will grow up with this template already imposed on them. If mothers challenge these ideas and see that boys are not born this way but are very much created by the ideas and attitudes we have about them, then we will be freed up to explore other ways of relating with our sons.

Ask yourself:

- Do you think it is more of a hindrance or a help for a boy to express caring emotions?

- Why might it be that women report men have no difficulty showing their anger, but may have difficulty expressing other more 'vulnerable' feelings?

- What role, if any, do women, particularly mothers, have in helping men to express their feelings?

- How might it be helpful to a man if he were honestly, openly and respectfully able to communicate his feelings?

- How can you help your son to learn to express his feelings?

Ways to help your son identify and express his feelings

Babies, of course, have no vocabulary to express their emotions. They smile and cry, then slowly begin to adopt other behaviours that indicate how they are feeling. For example, at about eighteen months toddlers start having anger tantrums, which may be so intense that they hold their breath or bang their heads.

Gradually children are able to identify a few basic feelings — they may say they are happy or mad or sad. Often they will describe other things in terms of judging a feeling attached to that thing. For example, your son may say 'Naughty mummy' or 'Bad puppy'. As he gets older you can continue to help him identify other feelings, both positive and negative, so that he develops a wide vocabulary of feeling words.

One way of teaching about feelings is to put a 'feeling face' chart on the fridge. This page of different little faces illustrate numerous feelings, including feeling miserable, mischievous, exhilarated, thoughtful, frightened, ecstatic, sublime, anxious, determined, guilty, interested, and so on. You can use these feeling faces in a number of ways:

- **Help your son identify his feelings**

School-aged children can identify feelings by using feeling faces. When your son has an emotional experience, ask him to identify the face that best suits the feeling. If he points to the 'confident' face, you can say, 'Oh, so you are feeling confident. Would that be right — that when you played that game of cricket you felt confident?', or if he pointed to 'jealous' face you could say, 'You told me that Michael got a new computer. Do you feel that it's not fair that you don't have one or is it a different feeling?' He may not seem to pick a face that goes with the feeling, but you can still explore this with him. For example, he may point to a 'happy' face after his dog was run over. You can explore with him, how he feels inside, what he is thinking, and ask perhaps, if another face better matches that feeling.

Alternatively you can ask him to draw or paint or use plasticine to express his feelings. Ask which colour represents the way he feels right now, or ask what feelings he would draw? Even if a young boy is just sitting doodling you can ask with curiosity, 'If you were going to draw a happy feeling what would it look like?' 'What about an angry feeling, how would that be?'

- **Locate feelings in the body**

Even as adults we are often out of touch with our feelings. We may feel them on an emotional level, but are disconnected from the way they physically impact on us. This can mean that we are less able to control the impact of feelings on us, which can lead to problems like panic attacks, anxiety and depression. One of the first steps in taking control over these problems is learning to identify where they are experienced in the body.

When your son experiences a strong feeling, you can help

him explore where he feels it. Ask him, 'You are so, so sad. Does it almost seem to hurt your body? Whereabouts do you feel it?' or 'You said you were so scared when that car nearly hit you. How did you notice that fear in your body? Was your tummy all churned up or were your legs shaking?'

Helping a boy identify feelings in his body means that he can also learn to exhibit self-control over feelings that may be destructive, such as anger. He can learn to observe the patterns where feelings build up, and can therefore learn how to bring those feelings back under control through breathing or talking about them.

- **Involve your son in conversations about feelings**

Include conversations about feelings from the time your son is very young. He will then assume that it is quite a natural and normal part of everyday conversation to describe feelings.

You can do this type of questioning with real people or by using people on the TV: 'How do you think Jake felt when his dog died?' 'Why do you think he felt that?' 'Have you ever felt that way about something?' 'What do you think he could do to let other people know how he felt?'

Help your child name a feeling by guessing what it could be: 'It sounds like you feel really frustrated' or 'That must have felt really lonely' or 'I bet you were absolutely exhilarated when that happened.' It doesn't matter if you use feeling words that he doesn't understand. When you use them in your everyday language he will pick them up and use them too, just as he does with other new vocabulary.

It is also helpful to assist your son to identify specific, rather than general, feelings. A young son may at first only differentiate between 'sad' and 'happy' feelings. You can help him expand his feeling vocabulary by asking, 'Do you mean sad like lonely, or sad like frustrated, or sad like jealous, or another kind of sad?' Or with 'happiness', 'Do you feel happy like peaceful, or loved, or pleased with yourself, or some other feeling?' This will help him build a vocabulary of words about feelings.

- **Let him know that feelings are important**

Some mothers worry that they may overindulge their sons, spoil them and consequently turn them into 'wusses', 'sissies' or 'mummy's boys'. There are no equivalent terms that could be applied to girls. What these terms really describe are boys who show their emotions openly and do not match the 'macho' man stereotype.

Acknowledging feelings does not create passive, dependent and unassertive men; on the contrary it creates men with beliefs that feelings, both their own and others', are important and something that can be expressed, rather than hidden.

- **Acknowledge his feelings**

   For boys to know their feelings are acknowledged they need their mother's full concentration and involvement. This can be tricky if you are halfway through the dishes, rushing off to work, or exhausted after a long day. It may be helpful to make some choices about giving time for those particular events where it is particularly helpful for your son's experience of having his feelings validated, such as when he is hurt or having difficulty at school.

   Acknowledging feelings means being able to listen, stop what you are doing, perhaps bend down to his level, and respond verbally: 'I see …', 'That sounds upsetting…', or even 'Mmmm'.

   When your son expresses his feelings you can reflect them back to him: 'You felt proud because the teacher really appreciated how much work you put into your project', or 'It was lonely for you because you were the only one without a partner'. He may not directly express a feeling, but you can help him identify the feeling contained in his language. So if he says, 'Tom said I couldn't play with him because I'm too little', you could reply 'It sounds like you felt sad and left out because Tom said you couldn't play.'

   Often helping your son to identify his feelings in this way can actually assist him to find a solution for his problems or gain a sense of containment about an issue he is experiencing. He may reply to your acknowledgement of his feelings by saying, 'So I went to play with Max instead' or 'I'm going to tell him that makes me feel sad'.

   It is also important that your son sees you express your feelings. This doesn't mean you should share all your adult feelings with him (you wouldn't tell him that you feel lustful towards the next-door neighbour!), but tell him what you feel about your life experiences and events. It may be better to keep your feelings about your separation to a minimum — if your son thinks his mother is not coping or is too overwhelmed with her feelings, he may feel scared and insecure.

Often mothers wonder how much to express their negative feelings about their son's father. It can be detrimental to constantly express critical feelings about his father, particularly if your son feels they somehow reflect on him or that you want him to take sides. It is reasonable to express some negative feelings such as 'I feel really angry when your father doesn't keep to the arrangement we make'. Often expressing a feeling quickly and succinctly is enough — there's no point in going into tirades of criticism about his father, you may end up alienating your son and stopping any sharing of his own feelings about his dad to you.

- **Involvement in rituals and celebrations**

If your son is expected to respond to emotional events such as illness or death, then he will be more likely to incorporate empathy and other emotional responses into his development.

Rather than being excluded from illness or death, he can be helped to understand it and to be part of the process of grieving. It is helpful for children to see adults cry and grieve. If there are males present who are also able to grieve and express their feelings openly, he will be given additional assurance that this is okay for boys. From a young age he can help make a cross for the pet rabbit who died or he can help pick flowers for its grave. Talk about what it means to him that his beloved pet has died.

He can be part of the process of rituals and celebrations by making and sending a card to someone for a special occasion and writing thankyou notes for presents he has received. Your son should learn that this isn't something that just girls do, but is equally important for him.

Melanie writes about the experience of her fortieth birthday:

> My fortieth birthday was really special. It started two weeks before my birthday when I took the boys on holiday to Rotorua with my mother.

The boys had their savings with them. We had a look in a tourist shop at the rulers and pencils and other inexpensive souvenirs. My ten-year-old went off to buy something.

Later in the day I realised he had no money left and I realised he had spent it all at the shop. I was stern with him — what on earth did he buy? He looked up at me and said that it was a surprise for my birthday. Inside I felt disappointed that he had spent all his hard-earned money on me, but he was so proud when he gave the gift to me. His little face lit up. He presented me with a jewellery box, and on opening it, I found inside it a beautiful paua shell necklace. I felt so honoured, he so loved and proud — it was really romantic, and I felt that he was practising for the future to appreciate and treat his girlfriends as special. I wear it always, and he asks to look at it and admires the pretty colours.

My eight-year-old took the money that he'd saved up and went across the road to the dairy on the day, and came back with his hands behind his back. He shouted 'Happy birthday', and presented me with a beautiful bunch of flowers.

So you see, each in his own way placed a great importance, showed a lot of love and care, and expressed where they were at emotionally through their gift buying.

For years I have encouraged them to make me their cards, and the best present is if they bring me breakfast in bed (often burnt/cold/soggy) — a cup of tea made with cold water, or a birthday cake cooked on top of the stove. One year each of them made me breakfast — I must have eaten a loaf of bread between them and my cholesterol level would have been way up after six eggs!

The boys and I had a wonderful night that night. We ate takeaways, lit candles, turned the music up, and danced together in the lounge. I will remember that night forever, and so will they.

Your son can also be encouraged to decorate the Christmas tree, prepare for a religious ceremony, and express care for those who have experienced the death of a loved one. Empathy is an emotion that can be developed by children seeing it modelled in others, and seeing that caring is valued and that the emotions and feelings of others matter.

Boys feel life passionately. Their energy and vitality is there as much in their emotions as in their physicality. You are in an excellent position to assist your son to locate and acknowledge his emotions without fear of reprisal and with self-confidence and openness.

Chapter 5

Setting Limits and Boundaries

Ideas about how to set limits and boundaries with children change across the generations. They have shifted from ideas of tough parental control (in the 1940s and 50s) to permissiveness (in the 1960s and 70s). They were preceded by ideas that a child should have the utmost respect for authority, and that conformity, rather than individuality, was valued. The more permissive parenting techniques which followed aimed at encouraging self-expression and individuality and fitted with the radicalism of the 1960s that challenged authority and encouraged self-exploration.

It is useful to think about why you as a mother set limits. Is it because you want your son to follow a certain path in life? Is it because you want to equip him with what you see as the necessary skills for adult life? Is it to protect him from harm? Is it to control him?

If you can be clear about why you are setting limits and boundaries, you can be clearer about what is important for you to enforce, and what you can be more flexible and relaxed about.

Current parenting approaches can be influenced by a number of factors:
- parental guilt for not being able to provide an 'intact' family, for not being so readily available, and for feeling inadequate as a parent
- conflict over wanting to encourage non-material values but at the same time wanting to provide for all a child's material needs
- a desire to foster healthy self-esteem and emotional connection
- a belief that children develop 'naturally' and will learn many of their life skills outside the family structure

Many sole mothers today are stretched to the limit, and battle to provide an income and reasonable access to material resources for their son, as well as to provide effective parenting that will help guard him against delinquent, 'at risk' and destructive behaviours as he matures.

They may feel confused, and struggle with ideas about what is reasonable behaviour to expect in boys. They hear that boys are 'in trouble', that boys need men to parent them, and that anger and violence are endemic in boy culture. Their confusion is understandable, particularly as a response to the media's emphasis on the vast differences between men and women. The rise in emphasis on strong biological differences between males and females may lead many mothers to believe that their sons' behaviour is biologically, rather than socially, determined and influenced. The perceived importance of testosterone appears to have undermined mothers' beliefs that they too can influence their sons' development. Some women say that they can be assertive and strong with their daughter but are not sure what aspects of their sons' behaviour is 'normal' maleness, and hence has to be accepted, and what is unacceptable and more a product of parenting, family background or life experience.

Mothers who have experienced violence and abuse may find themselves in a difficult position — even though they may have left the relationship, they find themselves with sons who have followed in their fathers' footsteps and learnt disrespectful, negating and abusive ways of relating to women. In addition, as mothers, they may feel worn down, disempowered and self-doubting of their parenting abilities.

Some mothers speak of the guilt they have because they have ended a relationship, and feel that this means they have deprived their son of a father. Guilt is more likely to be strongly present in mothers who have been led to believe that sons cannot progress without a male role model. These ideas can be very powerful, and can be strongly supported by some common myths that abound in our society. For example, what message does our society give us about boys needing a man to grow up into an adult male? Where do these ideas come from? What purpose do they serve? Guilt can talk a mother into thinking she needs to compensate her son for not having a father or a 'normal' family. Mothers say guilt encourages them to view disrespectful behaviour as a normal grief reaction or to let their sons 'get away' with bad behaviour because 'after all he has been through enough already'. Guilt encourages them to think that taking a firm and assertive hand in parenting would be damaging, rather than helpful, to their son.

Certainly separation and divorce can leave children feeling grief and loss. But mothers do not leave relationships lightly. On the contrary, it takes many months of thought, deliberation, and usually a great deal of angst, to come to that decision. In fact, many mothers leave relationships believing their children will be better off — not necessarily because they will not see their father as much, but because it will put an end to the conflict and emotional deadlock that can be so undermining to a family's happiness.

Children who experience grief and loss recover by having stability and firm boundaries. They need to be able to express their grief and unhappiness, but in appropriate and non-destructive ways. They need to be able to do this safely and to know that there are boundaries around their behaviour.

The term 'boundaries' is an unusual word. In a sense it is nebulous and arbitrary: Who sets such boundaries? Are they mutually agreed upon? Who defines what they are? Most mothers know what is meant by the word, yet it is not clearly defined in any parenting literature. Boundaries are generally the guidelines that a parent imposes so as to give a child a knowledge about what is, and what is not, acceptable behaviour, and what the consequences are when such behaviour is not adhered to. Boundaries are essential for children, as they provide a clear expectation for the children's emotional, psychological and social development. They make them feel safe and cared for. Without boundaries children may be physically unsafe, and unsure of how to take responsibility and respond appropriately to others in our society. A teenager who has grown up without necessary boundaries may be aimless and more vulnerable to sadness, depression, destructive behaviour and 'risk taking'. Of course, boundaries are socially and culturally constructed, and what is acceptable to one culture may be entirely inappropriate to another. In addition, ideas about boundaries may vary across socio-economic class and time.

The more that mothers adhere to ideas that emphasise the differences between men and women, the harder they say it is for them to raise sons on their own. If you believe, for example, that boys can only be disciplined by a male authority figure, that women just haven't got what it takes to discipline a boy, then you may find it very difficult trying to parent and set limits and boundaries on your own.

Laurel speaks about her experience:

> I haven't had much trouble with discipline. My son has a good temperament; he's calm and easygoing. We are well attached, and our anger at each other doesn't last. I had a reasonable amount of authority with him as a child. I didn't smack him or make him afraid of me. I think it's so important for sole mothers

to develop personal authority more than a set of techniques: for example, to say 'No' and mean 'No'. You also need to have enough in your own life so you can be happy and not just focus everything on your child.

Disciplining adolescents is different. We've had more fights as I've tried to set limits. It's more complex: you have to negotiate and supply good reasons for your decisions, you have to give up the idea that you are totally in charge. It's a delicate process that involves a balance of him becoming an adult and us having an adult relationship where I don't control everything. Now he can argue and be angry, although he's never abusive.

I would tell sole mothers that you need to tell your kids 'No' sometimes. They actually want you to set the boundaries that their peers won't and respect you more when you do.

I used to be strict about him not smoking dope but I've gradually relaxed my stance, although it's hard. I used to say, 'If you are going to smoke, you can't do it in the house, but then he was always away. Then I told him it was okay in the garage, but that meant he was always outside, and the garage is not a convivial environment. Now I let him smoke in his room, because at least I know he's home and he's safe. He is sensible, and I have to trust that he knows what he is doing and is responsible.

We talk about the drugs that he's used and he's very anti-heroin. I've talked to him about smoking dope and psychosis, of what the early warning signs might be. It's really that I've made dope smoking a health rather than a moral issue. I do mention that dope could account for his recent drop in motivation and his grumpiness. In a way I think he wants me to disapprove of his smoking.

Some women say that they find it hard to set boundaries because boys 'want to be the boss'. They may also believe that boys should be encouraged to be 'the boss', that it is part of the 'natural order' of things. Such mothers may also believe they should let their sons get away with more, or that they may emasculate their son if they try to discipline him too much.

Thinking about your style of parenting

A good starting point in thinking about how you parent now and what ideas influence your parenting is to recall the kind of upbringing you had as a child.

> ### Ask yourself:
> - What ideas about the world and society influenced my parents' ideas of parenting?
> - What ideas did my parents have about how boys and girls should be parented?
> - Were my mother's ideas the same as my father's?
> - Did they share the same ideas about parenting different-gendered children?
> - How did they express their disapproval of things I did?
> - Did their setting of limits and boundaries involve hearing what I had to say and negotiation, or was it imposed on me?
> - Did they parent in a way that encouraged my responsibility, independence and self-confidence?
> - What did I like about my parents' way of parenting?
> - What would I most want to repeat about my parents' way of parenting?

These questions are worth exploring because undoubtedly your childhood experience will impact on the way you parent your child. Sometimes as a parent you want to parent in the same loving way that your parents did — you remember how this helped you in the development of your own identity and to grow into a loving nurturing parent yourself. Some will challenge the way your parents parented — you may look back and see how constricting or controlling they were as parents. You may decide that you do not wish to use fear or intimidation as a parenting technique, and remember how destructive this technique may have been for you. Often mothers who consciously want to challenge and change the way they were parented find it difficult to learn new ways and to avoid falling into similar patterns that may have continued across many generations.

Sandra writes:

> It's taken me years to get over the way my father and mother brought me up. My father was very critical; nothing was ever good enough. And there wasn't any fun in the house. My mother just went along with what my father said, and never challenged him. I wasn't allowed to express an opinion or argue back. His word was the last word. He was never violent or said nasty things, but he didn't have to. My sister and I were scared of him.
>
> So I grew up finding it hard to make a decision, or needing to always ask other people's advice. It took me years and years and a lot of therapy to find out who I was as a person.
>
> Now I am a parent I certainly don't want to be like that, but it's hard not to fall into that trap and either be authoritarian or totally back down to Steven (aged 11) like my mother would to my father.

Sometimes the guilt that mothers feel from deciding to leave the relationship, or from the process of separating can get in the way of setting limits and boundaries. If you are under the influence of guilt you may give in to your son because you believe that setting boundaries will make your child unhappy or angry. Children certainly have a way of giving this impression — they can protest magnificently when they don't get their own way, but this does not mean they will be happier if their mothers give in.

Naomi, mother of eight-year-old Callum, recalls:

> Because he had to move schools twice I felt so bad I let him get away with things like not helping out, or even on occasions being disrespectful to me. I thought he was just expressing his sadness, and I felt bad that it was due to my decision to leave Jack. But it escalated, and got to the point where Callum was

being downright abusive to me and refused to carry any responsibility at home.

So I then had to get really tough to get things in line. Now it's much better, and I actually think Callum feels safer and has more security now that he knows what he can and can't do.

Traditional parenting models were based on threats, rewards, bribery or control. While these may have kept children 'seen and not heard', and dutiful and obedient, it did not actively contribute to children having a high self-worth, internal restraint and discipline, and a sense of responsibility.

Parents who use bribery often find that the bribes need to keep on getting bigger as the child gets older and demands more. What started off as a chocolate bar becomes a Porsche once the boy reaches his teens.

Threatening children is really tantamount to bullying, and these children often become discouraged, lack confidence and lose respect for their parents. They, in turn, may also become bullies.

Children today know they have rights. The old ways of parenting were not always helpful in raising independent, happy and co-operative children, and they just won't work now anyway. Children have wised up. The approaches that work with boys must be strong, but must focus on the mutual mother/son relationship, and on respect and co-operation rather than power.

Setting limits with boys

Many sole mothers speak about the difficulty they have in setting limits with boys. They cite a number of reasons why this is so. These include:

- Boys want to take on a dominant male role, particularly in the absence of their father.
- Society supports the idea that boys can get away with being rude, disrespectful or difficult to handle.

- Mothers can feel tested by the physical presence of their sons and their stronger voices.
- Boys can put up a good argument, and win.
- There's an idea that a woman needs an adult male to back her up or enforce her decisions.
- Guilt gets in the way of setting limits and sticking to enforcing them.

Some mothers are concerned about being domineering, emasculating or overbearing, and hold back on being assertive in the setting of limits and boundaries with their sons. They may also be concerned that if they are too 'superior' to their sons, their sons will not develop appropriately into strong men.

It is interesting how often mothers wonder if they 'need to be like men' in order to parent successfully. It is important to remember that parenting is a gendered activity — there is 'fathering' and 'mothering'. Mothers often wonder about what happens to the fathering when there is no male role model present. The focus on mothering and fathering often neglects to acknowledge that these are socially constructed roles, which closely follow stereotypically gendered roles. Fathering typically relies on a man being a breadwinner and disciplinarian, and mothering relates to the nurturing and caring of the other family members. Many men are starting to question the notion of fathering and are wanting to expand these historically- and gender-prescribed roles, and instead do more 'mothering' of their children.

Sole mothers need to keep up with the mothering but also take on what has traditionally been a fathering role.

Three approaches are necessary for successful parenting of a boy by a sole mother.

1 Stay emotionally attached to your son

Never fear that you are being too loving or caring. Always try and communicate with your son, encourage him to attend family events, include him in special moments of your life, and talk to him about how you both feel. Do not let the fact that he is a boy get in the way of your expectations of what he can or can't do. Expect that he can iron his shirts, will set the table, will buy or make you a birthday present, and expect that his contribution to the household and family will increase as he gets older.

Never use the threat of emotional withdrawal as a means to discipline him.

2 Have clear and consistent expectations

Do not minimise your expectations of your child because he is a boy. Expect the best of him — that he will try as hard as he can, that he will be responsible, that he will be open and loving, that he will respect you as his mother, that he will face the consequences of his actions.

Expectations should be set from a very young age, and should be communicated clearly to him. A boy raised by a sole mother most likely needs a higher degree of expectations than a boy raised in a two-parent family. You should expect him to take on more responsibility, but without him being overburdened with it.

He should participate in household chores, and take responsibility from a very young age. In addition, he should know what your expectations of him towards you are — that you will be treated with respect, that verbal abuse is not permissible, that violence in any form is not tolerable.

3 Act with strength and self-assurance

Women, and particularly mothers, in our society are not held in or imbued with great authority. The majority of authority figures are still male. Many mothers, both sole or partnered, still adhere to the myth that only a father, because he is male, will have enough authority to control and discipline a boy. Women in our society are taught to defer to men's supposed greater knowledge, intelligence and wisdom. This is where it appears sole mothers face problems; they feel they do not have the right or ability to take an authoritative stand in the parenting of their sons.

Your son may pick up on this from an early age. He sees how men and women relate, how women often defer to men, how men are the powerful and decisive adults. This means that you may have to put in extra effort to maintain respect and compliance from your son. In a sense you need to 'father'. It is most important that you take on this part of parenting, and feel strong and confident in doing this. Mothers who have felt confident in being strong, setting and sticking to limits have found that their sons are more respectful and less inclined to argue or go off track.

This does not mean being totally authoritarian, unreasonable or a 'control freak', but it does mean being authoritative and in control. Insist on respect — you are entitled to it. If a boy grows up with a mother who is clearly in control and does not doubt her decisions, he will grow up with a respect for her and the decisions she makes, as he would have done with a father in this position.

The success of parenting is not about the gender of the parent but the complementarity of the parenting, having aspects of authority and nurturing, strength and love.

A guide to setting limits and boundaries

Some basic points in setting limits and boundaries:
- Have age-appropriate expectations: for example, don't expect a three-year-old to pour his own glass of milk.
- Encourage responsibility through choice and consequences, rather than through the use of parental power.
- Set reasonable limits.
- Be consistent in setting limits.
- Offer choices, but only when you are prepared to accept your son's decision. Limit the choices: for example, 'Would you like to come home at 4 p.m. or 4:30 p.m.?'
- Change the environment in order to avoid misbehaviour, rather than trying to change the child: for example, move precious glassware out of your son's reach instead of telling him not to touch it. Where possible, prevent misbehaviour before it happens.
- Guide your son with actions and words, demonstrating if necessary.
- Encourage respectful communication by giving a brief explanation when you set limits. It should be stated in a positive way that emphasises that you believe your son is capable of fulfilling this expectation. So you might say, 'When we clean our teeth we always put the lid back on the toothpaste. You show me how you can do that', or 'It's

time to put your toys away — just like you did yesterday.'
- Praise your son for good intentions, even if his intentions were not carried out successfully.
- When your son co-operates, thank him, but there's no need to go overboard in a way that implies that by helping or co-operating he has done something earth-shattering. Respond as if this is a normal and reasonable expectation that you are pleased he has fulfilled (which, of course, it is!).
- Tell your son what to do, not just what *not* to do: use 'do' instead of 'don't'.
- Praise your son for desirable behaviour: avoid letting undesirable behaviour be the best way of getting attention.
- Encourage a positive self-image: avoid making your son feel frightened, ashamed, embarrassed, insecure or bad about himself.
- Be a positive role model: your son will follow the example in the way you live your life!

In setting limits and boundaries it is important to think what ideas and attitudes will shape the way you address this issue with your son.

Ask yourself:

- How might my beliefs about males and authority make it hard to discipline my son?
- How might my fears about being an overbearing mother get in the way of disciplining my son?
- How might my ideas about wanting to have a close relationship with my son get in the way of setting appropriate limits?
- How might my wanting him to be a happy, carefree boy get in the way of setting appropriate limits and boundaries?

> ◆ How might my upbringing and my own experience with my father and mother impact on the way I set limits and boundaries with my son?
>
> ◆ How does guilt get in the way of setting limits and boundaries with my son?

Children need to know what their limits are, and what the consequences of breaking them involve. Clear and firm limits mean that children are clear about their parent's expectations, they feel safe and contained, knowing what they can and can't do. Boys who have clear limits are reassured that their mother cares about them, and they are clear about the responsibility both they and their mother will take in the family. Boys often protest and complain about limit setting, saying things like:

'But Hamid's mother lets him do that.'

'But everyone else in class is going.'

'You're so mean!'

'I know you don't love me now.'

'You would have let me do this if we were still with Dad.'

'Dad said I could do it — *he* trusts me.'

'I always do that at Dad's.'

'Don't you care if I have homework to do? Okay, then I'll do the dishes, and fail at school, if that's what you want!'

'How come I have to do all the work round here?'

'Jack's Mum pays him to do that.'

Be clear in your own mind about what you think is fair and reasonable, and stick with it! Have these ideas and expectations written down if it helps you to stay firm in spite of such performances.

When your son is young, you will set limits. This is vitally important for his safety, for example, you will need to set limits that your son cannot play on the road. As he grows older and can take more responsibility, limits and boundaries can be negotiated, as can the consequences for breaking them.

When you change or adapt your old ways of parenting to newer ideas you may experience some resistance from your son. Initially this may make it seem easier to go back to the old ways of being inconsistent or yelling or threatening. The two keys to getting your son to observe limits are to be consistent and clear. Do not negotiate, back down or change the limit or request you have originally set. If you have a particular limit, for example, that your son cannot watch TV until he has put away his toys, then you must ensure this happens every night (with perhaps an occasional exception) for him to respect and honour the limit without an ensuing battle.

The benefits of limit-setting far outweigh the initial struggle you may have in putting them in place. They also set the groundwork for a respectful relationship to carry your son into his teen years.

Pocket money

Giving your son pocket money can be a way of teaching him to value finances, to learn responsibility and to be rewarded for his contribution to the household. Pocket money should not be seen as an expectation from your son, without contributing. You could draw up a list of your expectations of him that he will need to fulfil in order to receive pocket money. These may include age-dependent chores such as making his bed every day, washing up twice a week, and feeding the pets. If your son does not meet these expectations, don't deny him all his pocket money, but perhaps take a dollar or two off his usual amount.

As he gets older the losing of pocket money may be a useful consequence for destructive or careless behaviour; for example, if he breaks your vase because he is running around madly inside the house, you could expect that he will use his pocket money to buy you a new one.

Some children receive a huge amount of pocket money.

Generally speaking a primary school child could receive about $2–$10 a week. He should also know that this money is for treats such as lollies, or to save to buy himself something special he wants. It is a good idea to also encourage him to save money in a bank account.

Fighting

Most siblings fight. The difference seems to be in the frequency and the intensity of the fighting. If your children seem to be fighting constantly over every little thing, or if one child seems to be bullying the other and one is getting hurt, then the fighting is serious and should be professionally addressed. Fighting can occur for a number of reasons, and if you have separated from your partner you may find that fighting increases or begins after the separation. It may be a way of your son airing his emotions and frustrations, it may be a means of gaining attention.

It can occur for seemingly no reason whatsoever, or because certain family dynamics precipitate one child into feeling left out or unfairly treated. It may be because one child wins all the accolades at school, or because one is obviously favoured by a family relative, or because one child is the oldest and now has to share his mother with another child or family. Sometimes siblings genuinely dislike each other, and this attitude can persist through their lives, but usually it is a childhood phase that eases over time.

Whatever the reason, the bottom line must be that no family member is allowed to be physically hurt or emotionally abused.

Many mothers attempt to be fair and equal in their parenting. This is a fine ideal, but if you try to be fair by treating children as equals you may be surprised at the outcome! Children are different from each other in a myriad of ways; some need more attention, other more responsibility; some respond well to a particular way of parenting, some to others; some love routine, others hate it. It is impossible to treat siblings equally, and, in fact, this can exacerbate fights. The basic differences in gender and age also mean a different way of parenting each child may be important.

Helpful suggestions

- **Encourage siblings to support each other from a young age**

  If you presume that boys and girls don't get on, then the chances are that you will have a self-fulfilling prophecy. If you encourage siblings to enjoy each other's company, celebrate each other's achievements and care for each other, the risk of fighting will be much reduced.

  It is important to ensure that siblings attend each other's school, sports or arts performances, even as they get older. This will maintain a family connection, and emphasise family responsibility from one child to another.

- **Be careful not to blame**

  Some children are particularly good at surreptitiously annoying their siblings but declaring absolute innocence. They could win Academy Awards for these role plays of 'Who, me?' Trying to sort out who was right or wrong can only bring disaster.

  It is better to have generic household rules about fighting than to risk escalation by trying to sort out whose fault it was. You may decide that if they wish to argue they can go outside, or have a rule that each child's bedroom is private and the other child can only go in there with permission. If they share a room, you might insist that each have his or her own chest of drawers as a private place to keep things.

  Similarly, don't buy into hearing stories about what happened. Encourage responsibility, but not blame or judgement.

- **Acknowledge that it is impossible to stop squabbling and arguing**

  Instead, have a family meeting and write up some rules for fair fighting. These may include agreeing they can argue

outside, no swearing, no put-downs, no one to be hurt. Some families have experimented by agreeing to allow certain times to fight, such as from 5–7 p.m. at night: predictably there was no fighting during this time — in fact, the overall fighting diminished markedly once the children were given permission to fight. Sometimes sending children outside to fight may mean they end up having a great time playing instead.

- **Fighting children thrive on attention**

If your children are old enough, you may decide to go for a walk as soon as they start fighting (providing it is safe to leave them alone). Or you can grit your teeth, and go on with what you were doing, trying to be oblivious to the noise. You can tell them, 'I'll be ready to talk to you when you've finished fighting.'

- **Don't get into debating or arguing different rules**

Because children are different and experience different rates of growth and maturity, they may need different sets of rules. One child may be allowed to ride a bike to school, while another is not. You may feel comfortable in allowing your son to walk to the shops alone, but not your daughter. It is important to explain why rules may differ, and not to back down when these differences cause fighting. However much you want to be fair and equal, sometimes it is neither practicable nor reasonable to be so. Your children may think 'It's not fair', but sometimes they just need to accept your decision.

- **Fighting seems more likely to occur when limits are more relaxed**

Sometimes you will need to be very organised to preempt fighting and set strong, but flexible, boundaries. For example, you may agree that one child travels in the front car seat on the way to school and the other on the way home, or that the television cannot go on until both children have decided where they will sit, or that each child can choose a television program on alternate days. Many fighting families find they make lists, rosters and schedules for almost everything — but it works. It is important that your children are involved in setting out the rules and consequences.

Another limit could be that you won't be able to leave home for a social event until they agree not to fight in the car; or perhaps it may mean that if you are out socially, and they start fighting, you will take them home until they work out what is socially appropriate behaviour.

- **Encourage and comment on co-operation**

When children fight, it is easy to be continually critical of their inability to get on. But when they do co-operate, make sure you comment on this with 'Oh, I like the way you two organised that together' or 'You really helped out your younger sister then' or 'I loved the way you were so caring to Justin.' Children much prefer praise and encouragement to criticism, and respond well to this as a mean of directing their behaviour.

- **Encourage a family life where you do things together**

Ensure from an early age that siblings attend each other's sports or school presentations. Display their certificates and artwork around the house, and comment on it to all your children.

Make sure you find things that you appreciate in all your children, and they all know this. For example, you may comment on your daughter getting into a school competition and your son on cooking a meal. Try encouragement, rather than competition and comparing.

What if someone gets hurt?

Sometimes one child is becoming a bully, and the others are being hurt or verbally abused. It is important to distinguish between normal fighting and bullying, abuse and harassment. The latter is not 'normal' boy behaviour, and is not acceptable.

Derogatory put-downs, inflicting pain, sexual harassment, and continual nastiness are not acceptable, and can have severe negative effects on the person who is the recipient of such behaviours. It can also get in the way of your son establishing intimacy and good social relationships. If this behaviour is happening, it is most important to nip it in the bud immediately. This may require you to seek professional help.

Smacking

In general boys get smacked harder and more often than girls. A study in the UK in 1985[1] showed that two-thirds of a large sample of British mothers were already smacking their baby before the age of one. The same researchers had found that almost a quarter of seven-year-olds had already been hit by a belt or implement.[2] Perhaps this says something about the way we view children and how we think they should be parented. Whatever, it is a sad indictment of our society. Some mothers rely on smacking as a means of controlling their son, and will say that it is the only means of control that works. Indeed, smacking as a mechanism for control can be effective, but it has a time-limited basis. While it may work for a four-year-old, it will not only be ineffective but will backfire badly with a twelve-year-old. Apart from any physical or emotional harm smacking may cause a child, it has grave ramification for mothers because boys who are smacked as younger children may turn around and smack their mothers when the boys are in their teens.

Smacking boys emphasises the use of fear and pain to control. It is also a way of parenting that relies on external means of control, that is, rather than your son learning self-control in himself, he learns that it is up to others to impose it on him. This does not help engender responsibility in him.

Mothers who use smacking find that boys generally ignore the smacking anyway after a time. The smacks need to get harder and harder to be effective. A boy who is smacked is more likely to smack other children (and get himself into trouble at creche, preschool or school), and see violence as a means of getting his own way. In addition, if you smack, you may be more at risk of physically harming your child if you lose control and go one step too far in your disciplining.

It can be difficult when you decide to forgo smacking for other means of parenting. It means that both you and your son are going to have to try extra hard in this new way of parenting. For a time your son may rebel, and it may seem that a return to smacking is the only answer. But if you persist, then you will be rewarded by more co-operative and responsible behaviour in your son.

Jenny says:

> We negotiate a lot. I don't smack him. We talk, and I've been lucky because I've always felt extremely close to him and so lucky to have him. We have arguments, but we always end up hugging each other. Lately if we argue he says, 'I think this argument is stupid — let's stop it.' And we do, with a big hug.

If you want to stop smacking, you must think clearly about what behaviour you will and won't tolerate, and what limits are important to you. You must reframe your parenting from one where you will take responsibility for your son's behaviour to one where he starts to take responsibility for his own behaviour.

> Sue has a three-year-old son, Michael, who is always opening the fridge and helping himself to food. Sometimes he would try to pour his own juice or milk and it would spill all over the floor, which led to him being smacked. Sometimes if Sue is on the phone or has visitors she lets him do it, because at least she gets some peace.
>
> When Sue decided to stop smacking, she needed to realise that, in fact, she did not want Michael to go to the fridge at all. She told him that he had to ask her if he wanted something, and that sometimes he would need to wait: for example, if she was on the phone. When she saw him going to the fridge on his own, she reminded him of this new limit. When he still persisted, she told him he had to go to his room for a few minutes because he was not allowed to go to the fridge on his own. Of course, he vigorously protested, but Sue carried out her plan.
>
> It took three weeks for the message to sink in, but now Sue

is happier that Michael's eating habits are more regulated, there are no spills on the kitchen floor, and that she doesn't feel guilty about any smacking.

Consequences

The term 'consequences' refers to a mutually agreed upon setting of the action that will be taken when behaviour limits are not observed. Consequences place more emphasis on creating a 'working' agreement between you and your son, based on respect and mutuality. The main considerations of consequences are:

1 **Your expectations should be clear and well communicated**

You may say, for example, 'I'll be doing the washing on Friday night. Put your clothes in the laundry if you want them done'.

2 **Both you and your son must set the consequence**

Your son must also be involved in setting the rules, and these must be mutually agreed upon; for example, you could say to him, 'We need to work out some rules about how often and for how long you use the computer, and how you are going to fit in your homework and reading too'.

You and your son may decide to write a contract to be stuck up on the fridge. The contract may include the consequences if this agreement is broken; for example, no computer play on Saturday if his homework is not completed.

3 **Consequences must be kept simple and brief, so they can be enforced and easily maintained**

It will not work to just have lists of rules and what will happen if they are broken. Concentrate on the essential and meaningful things like homework, basic tidiness, respectfulness, and responsibilities like feeding the dog. Increase the responsibilities as your son gets older, and the severity of the consequences with the severity of the transgressions.

Chapter 6

Attention Deficit Disorder and Attention Deficit Hyperactivity Disorder

ADD (Attention Deficit Disorder) and ADHD (Attention Deficit Hyperactivity Disorder) are two conditions defined by the behaviours that accompany them. Boys make up 90 per cent of the diagnosed cases of ADD, and there has been much speculation about why this is so.

The causes of ADD/ADHD are uncertain. Some specialists argue that it is due to a minor neurological dysfunction in the brain, others that it is a result of family dynamics and parenting. Whether this is genetically transmitted or a social/environmental influence, or a combination of both, are hotly debated. It refers to a cluster of behaviours, including:
- inability to concentrate
- hyperactivity
- being easily distracted
- disorganisation
- impulsivity
- inappropriate responses, e.g. yelling out in class
- forgetfulness
- interruptions to others
- constant movement, such as fidgeting

Laziness, poor diet or bad parenting do not cause ADD/ADHD. It does not mean a child with ADD/ADHD is not intelligent, nor that he does not have the ability to lead a 'normal' life.

Over half the children who experience ADD/ADHD are also troubled by specific learning disabilities such as dyslexia, language disorder or weakness with maths.[1] It is often when children begin preschool or primary school that parents begin wondering about their child's hyperactive behaviour, and teachers recognise such children as being easily distracted and disruptive in class.

Diagnosis

There are many forms of diagnosis, but if you are querying whether your son has ADD/ADHD, or whether the diagnosis is correct, you should consider a thorough diagnosis by a paediatrician or child psychologist. This will include a family interview to explore parenting dynamics, the couple relationship (even when the parents are separated), your son's relationship with his siblings, family background, and any issues such as drug and alcohol abuse, domestic violence and other family stressors. The diagnosis should also include reports from the teachers at his preschool or school, from a child psychologist and/or paediatrician, plus a specific and detailed history of your son, and an exclusion of any related diagnoses that could be described as, but are not, ADD/ADHD. Your son should be viewed in his 'natural' surroundings, such as school or with his family, to see how he interacts with others.

The history should investigate how long he has been behaving in a 'problematic' way, and whether this is, in fact, a reaction to home stressors such as family conflict, separation or domestic violence. If a set of behaviours has only recently emerged, it may be a grave error to describe them as ADD/ADHD.

Most diagnoses would rely on locating a set of behaviours that fit with the diagnosis, rather than one or two specific behaviours and, in particular, would focus on identifying behaviours that impair his academic performance.

Many counsellors and educators are asking why there is an increase in this diagnoses. Some health professionals state that there is a greater likelihood of ADD/ADHD occurring in families where there is already a (usually male) relative with ADD/ADHD.[2] This may not mean that there is a biological connection, but may relate to patterns of behaviours and parenting that exacerbate ADD-like symptoms. This does not mean that ADD/ADHD is related to poor parenting. Children with ADD/ADHD come from a wide variety of cultural and socioeconomic backgrounds, and their parents vary tremendously in their style of parenting.

It is interesting that children who have experienced trauma of one kind or another, particularly physical or sexual abuse, war trauma or witnessing domestic violence may exhibit a range of symptoms similar to those of ADD/ADHD, and in fact may be wrongly diagnosed with ADD/ADHD or other behavioural problems. The symptoms of ADD/ADHD are very similar to those of post-traumatic stress disorder, a reaction to growing up in conditions of extreme stress or conflict. However, no scientific link has been determined between trauma and ADD, and certainly not every child with ADD/ADHD has experienced trauma or abuse. It will take further research to conclude the 'causes' of ADD/ADHD and why this diagnosis is increasing in our society.

It is important to distinguish behaviours similar to those of ADD/ADHD that may originate from learning difficulties that have not been picked up and addressed. Such difficulties may be exacerbated by erratic and inconsistent parenting practices that make it difficult for a child to settle and concentrate at home or school.

William Pollack raises the question of whether boys may

be being misdiagnosed with ADD/ADHD, 'One cannot help being concerned by the sheer number of diagnosed cases, the frequency of diagnoses initiated by overwhelmed classroom teachers and child guidance counsellors, and the possibility that many mild to moderate cases of ADD are a normal variant of boys' temperament that could be corrected by a properly trained, attentive adult.'[3]

It is important to obtain an accurate diagnosis from a paediatrician. If your son is exhibiting these symptoms it is better that he be diagnosed and receive treatment and intervention as soon as possible, so that he doesn't miss out on his schooling and peer interaction. You may also then wish to get a second opinion. Although medications such as Ritalin can be helpful in settling your child's behaviour, they may work better for some children than for others and shouldn't be seen as the answer to his problems.

Pollack argues that we need to consider the school and classroom environment in which boys are educated, as well as parenting strategies and medications when dealing with ADD/ADHD.

Reactions to the diagnosis

You may experience a range of emotional responses on being informed your son has, or may have, ADD/ADHD. This can range from anger to guilt, from grief to relief. You may feel angry that this is yet another stress with which you have to deal. You may feel unsupported and cheated of your 'right' to have a 'normal' son. You may feel angry that your son is seen as having behavioural problems when, in fact, you believe his behaviour is within normal limits. You may feel angry that as a sole mother, you have been left to deal with what you view as the result of your partner's violence or a conflict-laden relationship.

Women are socialised to take responsibility for others, and when your son has behavioural and developmental

issues you may feel that you are somehow to blame. You may worry that you were not strict enough, were too permissive, were too demanding, or didn't give enough attention to your son, and may feel guilty. Unfortunately the 'helping' system may encourage such guilt by the questions and advice that is given to you. Many of the interventions can seem judgemental and value-laden, particularly where sole mothers are bringing up boys. Feeling guilty will not help your son, nor will it assist you to respond appropriately to his needs. Accept that you did, and will do, the best you can.

Dealing with ADD/ADHD

The most common medications used are methylphenidate (Ritalin) and dexamphetamine. Other medications are also prescribed, particularly if your son fails to respond to either of the above. Medications used to treat ADD/ADHD are actually stimulants: they act by fine-tuning a child's responses and abilities so that he is then able to shut out what has been causing distraction and lack of focus. However, medications do not cure ADD/ADHD, and once a child has commenced medication it is likely that he will need to maintain the medication to ensure his abilities and behaviour are stabilised. Although this form of medication has been available since the 1940s, it has only been within the last ten to fifteen years that Ritalin has started to be prescribed so frequently. We do not know the long-term effects of such usage.

If your child is exhibiting symptoms of ADD/ADHD, look at adjusting some of your parenting strategies to see if this makes any difference to his behaviour. This approach may be particularly useful if he has experienced domestic violence, sexual abuse, or a particularly conflictual relationship break-up. If he has been diagnosed with ADD/ADHD, it is important to reassess parenting strategies that are better suited to children with ADD/ADHD. These strategies can be used in conjunction with medication.

These strategies are very similar to those advocated for parenting in general. All children need boundaries, but perhaps those with ADD/ADHD need to have them more clearly spelt out and adhered to. Children with ADD/ADHD need a clear routine so that their day is well organised, with a high degree of routine. They may have difficulty ordering their day's events, so it is important for a set sequence to commence at the start of each day. This is also important when children attend preschool and school.

It is important that parents and educators communicate in simple, clear and calm instructions. Children should be praised and encouraged when they are co-operative, and given 'time out' when they are disruptive. Often including them in energy-demanding activities, such as athletics or other sports, can help them to focus and give their energy a positive direction.

Having a son with ADD/ADHD can be stressful, exhausting and demanding. But it does not mean that you cannot experience the joys of parenting and that your son will not grow into an achieving and happy adult. ADD/ADHD is a behavioural disorder, not a life sentence!

The most important thing is for you, your son and other family members to get support, and not to feel isolated in dealing with this condition. Contact community health services, family centres, child psychologists, parenting groups and ADD/ADHD support groups to access support and advice in relation to parenting.

Chapter 7

Helping Your Son with School Life

The issue of boys and schooling has made many headlines over the past decade. Most of these headlines have focused on how poorly boys are performing at school. In Australian schools it is acknowledged that boys perform less well than girls on literacy tests, have lower scores on entrance exams for higher education, and leave school earlier than girls.[1]

A recent study from the Australian National University showed that the risk of dropping out of high school was 59 per cent higher for a child from a divorced family than for that of a child from a nuclear family.[2] However the research available does not definitely mean that girls do not have issues in the education system. Nor should it imply that we should be complacent about girls' education.

It certainly does seem that in many academic fields girls are surpassing boys. However, this does not mean that boys are missing out completely; it reflects that girls achieve the highest results in the fields of mathematics and literature. It is of concern when boys do not finish their schooling, particularly those who have ability and when access to trades or arts-oriented options, such as that provided by technical schools and apprenticeships, are not now so readily available. In addition, unskilled jobs are no longer as abundant as they once were.

School marks a great leap for any child. It often marks the beginning of independence and the exploration of the world of learning. It brings with it the acquisition of new developmental tasks, and the associated social, mental and emotional challenges.

There are a number of influences that may impact on boys' poor academic achievement. These include:

- the stigmatisation of sole-parent sons — a self-fulfilling prophecy
- disruption of schooling following separation
- the effects of family breakup and separation that impact on schoolwork
- a school curriculum that no longer matches the changed needs of boys
- a school curriculum that does not cater for individual children
- the lack of family income to support the appropriate technology and study guides to succeed academically
- lack of availability of support, counselling and education within the school community
- the lack of parental involvement in the school and broader community
- marginalisation of sole mothers in the school community
- difficulty for sole mothers assisting their children with their education
- the stereotyping of boys who are achievers as 'wimps' or 'mummy's boys'

Marginalisation occurs for many reasons, and children who feel marginalised are more likely to withdraw from full participation in school life and feel less confident and sure of their own ability. Mothers who feel marginalised are also less likely to be involved in school functions and in ways that would encourage their son towards academic achievement. For example, many sole mothers dread Father's Day. They worry about dealing with their son's disappointment at not having a dad for whom to buy a gift, but they also know their son is aware of feeling marginalised because of this. Some mothers have suggested that a Parent's Day may be a better alternative.

Sole mothers frequently end up being financially worse off after separation, and this can impact on their children's education as even public education becomes more and more expensive. The move towards computer technology being synonymous with achievement may mean that financially disadvantaged families lose out on opportunities.

A study called *Growing Up with a Single Parent*[3] shows that about half the lower performance of children in sole-parent families is due to the family's loss of income. The single parents most likely to suffer were non-employed ex-wives of more affluent men, probably because of the huge income differential experienced by their family following divorce.

Many studies on boys' lowered performance in school have indicated that it is lack of self-worth that gets in the way of scholastic success. They state that, if boys do not have good self-worth, they may be reticent to ask for help, and instead falsify their understanding of subjects. They may turn to 'acting out' in class as a way of being noticed or to distract from their academic performance.

Schools that are 'gender blind' fail to address boys' unique social and emotional needs, and do not provide the kinds of classroom activities and approaches that will help most boys to thrive. It may be easier to label active boys as ADD/ADHD. Once boys are so diagnosed, they can be more easily overlooked while teachers concentrate on children who show greater interest in learning.

Starting school — how to help

Most Australian children start school when they are about four or five. This differs from some European countries, where the children are usually six or seven. Some child 'experts' have argued that boys who start school at an older age are more advantaged than those who commence when younger. They argue that girls develop academically ahead of boys and that this also contributes to boys feeling that they are lagging behind. Boys appear to develop their fine motor co-ordination more slowly than girls, and may also be slower in the development of verbal and communication abilities.

It does seem that, if there is a choice and your son falls into the younger age cut-off point, it may be more helpful and advantageous for him to start school at the older end of the spectrum. This, of course, can be problematic if you are a mother in paid employment, especially if you are paying expensive creche or childcare fees, or you are waiting for that precious time to yourself while he is at school. You must weigh up the benefits to yourself, other family members and your son.

If your son's first year at school is a difficult one for him, either academically, socially or emotionally, speak with his teacher about the possibility of him repeating the year. There is rarely any stigma or disadvantage when a year is repeated at a young age, and it can be a means of early intervention for children who are not quite grasping learning or the school environment.

The first few years of school experience can really set the scene for your son's future attitudes and approach to school. Your attitude towards school will also make a big difference to how he feels. You may feel concerned for your son's wellbeing, and rightly so, as school life is such a dramatic change for him.

Although most boys go happily to school, there are some who may find it more difficult to deal with being separated from their mother. It is really important to be with your son and support him if he is feeling scared, just as you would if you had a daughter. It is not 'wussy' for a five-year-old to be frightened of something new — remember he is still a little boy, and he may need you to spend time in his classroom (with the teacher's agreement) for the first week or so while he gains his own confidence and a sense of the school environment.

If you or your son's preschool or creche have noticed issues that may evolve into problems, it is worthwhile linking your son into school support services when he starts school. He may have a speech problem, lack of fine motor skill co-ordination, or early learning difficulties. If you wait for these issues to exacerbate, they may need more intensive therapy.

If you have a choice in the school your son attends, check if the school is sole-parent friendly. This does not mean sending your son to a school where there is a high proportion of sole-parent families, but it does mean questioning the principal about any programs or policies the school may have to assist sole parents. These may include encouraging sole parents to attend school social events, a before-and-after-school program, openly acknowledging and addressing differences in families, and pastoral care programs. Some insightful schools have anti-bullying programs, buddy systems and peer mediation programs that ensure that children are not marginalised; there may be male teachers who take a special interest in boys and sports or recreation events that boys are encouraged to attend; it may have a curriculum that offers boys the opportunities to explore a wide range of interests, and to delve into feelings, emotions and communication, as well as the more traditional subjects.

Talk to the school about your concerns with boys' education to see if the school acknowledges this and has any strategies to encourage gender equality in schooling.

When your son starts school he will still need his mother as much as ever, but the communication and relationship with you may change. Little boys are keen to show their mothers what they have made at school, who does what, and what they learned that day. At the end of the day he will still need a hug, and to know his mother takes a special interest in him. It is unfortunate that some mothers are encouraged to draw away from their sons once they start school — they may believe that their son will be embarrassed if they kiss him, or that they should withdraw their physical contact and verbal affection now their son is a 'little man'. Nothing is further from the truth.

Let your son still enjoy dressing up, sitting on your lap, dancing, and having a teddy bear. If you feel proud and strong that this is what he wants, then other mothers will also feel less pressure to push their sons to conformist ideas of masculinity that will hinder rather than help them through their school years. Encourage your son to stand up for what he believes in and to feel okay about being an individual.

It is sad that some mothers are so concerned about sole-mother prejudice that they do not inform the teacher about their marital status. On one hand, this is no one's business and what does it matter, but, on the other, it may be helpful for the school to be aware so that teachers can be sensitive to your son; for example, on Father's Day, or if he doesn't draw a father in his family pictures. If you are a sole mother but your son has contact with his father, it may help the school to make sure they send out two separate invitations to events such as the school concert or give your son scope to talk about his separate relationship with his father, even though they may not spend the majority of their time together or your son is mainly in your care.

In addition, it may be helpful for your son to feel you are not embarrassed or shameful about being a sole mother, but are in fact proud and believe that your mothering is as good as any others, and that he has the same ability and rights as other children in the school.

Bullying

Bullying is endemic in Australian schools, and indeed in broader society too. It affects both boys and girls. Sadly, many schools and many parents believe that bullying is part of schoolground behaviour. There can be a 'blame the victim' approach, where the child who is bullied is seen as being deficient, perhaps not manly enough or lacking in social skills. The emphasis may be on the bullied boy to learn new ways of handling conflict and becoming more assertive. Often the advice given by parents reflects this: 'If someone hits you, just turn round and hit them back'. Children who are bullied are also viewed as individuals with problems; schools may not focus on how their school culture may inadvertently encourage bullying to thrive.

Bullying is more prevalent when schools view this as 'normal' boy behaviour, and take a laissez-faire view that they will work it out themselves. Schools that stress conformity, rather than the appreciation of difference, may also experience a greater degree of bullying. Some teachers may themselves use bullying tactics in their teaching — they may belittle students by using sarcasm or by making fun of them.

A child who is bullied can suffer dreadfully, and the experience can have lifelong ramifications. Boys may sometimes be reticent to talk about being bullied because they think there is something wrong with them, and feel ashamed and weak for 'allowing' it to happen. They may fear they will get into more trouble if they tell anyone, and indeed may have been threatened that things will become worse if they do tell. No one deserves to be bullied, and all children need to feel safe to attend school and do their best.

If your son tells you he has been bullied, validate his experience by listening carefully to his story and by reflecting back how he felt: 'It sounds like you felt really scared' or 'No one should be embarrassed in that way — that's not okay.' Bullying not only includes physical intimidation but also verbal abuse, including threats, put-downs and intimidation. It is important that you keep a note of what occurred, as most bullying continues if unchecked, and you may need evidence for your school that the situation has not improved.

Sometimes it is not appropriate to contact the school if your son is bullied — it depends on the extent and severity of the bullying. If, say, your son is upset that someone ran past and hit him or called him a name, you may see it as a one-off episode and help him to find ways of dealing with this; for example, by saying 'Go away' or telling his teacher. It is important to assure your son that you value him telling you about this incident, and would like to know if anything like this happens again.

If the behaviour is repeated and it seems like your son is being targeted, contact his teacher and work out a strategy of how to address this, be it by the teacher talking with the offending child or planning to talk with the whole grade about bullying and treating people respectfully.

Boys who experience domestic violence from their father may themselves become bullies. This is partly a role modelling of their father's behaviour and partly because what conflict resolution skills they have learnt have been based on 'might is right', rather than co-operation. Boys who have witnessed domestic violence may be particularly disrespectful and bullying towards girls.

If you are notified or aware of your son's bullying, try to understand why he is behaving this way. This does not mean you must accept it, but it can be useful to see if there is a set of circumstances behind his behaviour. Notify his teacher if your son has experienced any emotional trauma. It is also important that you and his teacher emphasise that bullying and violence are not acceptable, and that he is responsible for his own behaviour. While you may be aware of emotional trauma he has experienced, this should not be an excuse for bullying nor condoning such behaviour. There are programs available for children who have experienced domestic violence, and he may find one of these beneficial. Review your parenting, and deal with any behaviour that is disrespectful or abusive.

It is also important that a child who bullies is given love, nurturing and encouragement — it may seem like a fine line between being caring and being firm on what behaviours are unacceptable, but a boy who has a greater sense of identity and self-worth may be less likely to bully.

Bullying is dealt with most effectively when the school takes responsibility for ensuring all students are safe. This means that schools need to put bullying on their agenda by having policies that recognise differences in the schools community — whether it be gender, sexuality, ability/disability, race, religion, socioeconomic status — and put in place a number of strategies, both to circumvent bullying and to deal with it when it occurs.

Programs that have been successfully introduced into schools to lessen bullying are:
- peer-mediation programs
- self-esteem programs
- gender-awareness programs
- conflict-resolution programs
- buddy systems
- bully-reporting system

Although most school communities are aware of bullying and its effects, and are vigilant about both preventing and dealing with bullying, some parents and teachers may not be supportive if your son is bullied. Some mothers have reported being given a Darwinian type of explanation for bullying: 'It's survival of the fittest in the schoolground'. Others have been told that it is natural, others that it is a fault of their son or their mothering (a blame-the-victim approach), and others appear to pretend it isn't happening and that you, as the mother, have a heightened imagination or a tendency to neuroticism.

It is unfortunate that some schools may encourage bullying in their attitudes to boys — such as encouraging extreme competitiveness, comparing practices, strict gender stereotyping and macho school culture. Within this environment are the parents of children who are interested only in their sons being 'winners', and spare nothing to ensure their sons' material success to the detriment of learning social skills and nurturing of others.

In these situations it can be very difficult for you to see your son suffering and yet feel powerless to do anything about it. Your son may even feel ashamed, and that he is at fault for not being manly enough, and may ask you not to tell. As with any abuse, it is important for you to tell someone in authority and to do whatever is necessary to stop this abuse.

Often the only recourse is to take the matter to a higher level — from his teacher to the principal, to the school committee, to the regional education sector. It may also be helpful to find some allies, perhaps by approaching an adolescent service or social worker who will validate your concerns for your son, and be both a support or advocate to your persistence in addressing this issue.

If you feel that you have unsuccessfully tried everything to help your child, investigate other schools and their attitudes to pastoral care, nurturing and conflict, and it may be worthwhile changing schools. Sometimes children who seem to be poor achievers or loners can flourish when moved to a different school environment and away from being branded in a certain way.

Changing the system

Many educationists argue that gender stereotyping is having a detrimental effect on boys' schooling. They argue that boys need to be able to show a fuller side of themselves, a side that challenges stereotypical gender images of boys as macho, tough, active, argumentative and insensitive. In the same way that traditional girls' subjects were expanded to include those undertaken by boys, so should those traditional subjects expected of boys be expanded to include a focus on life skills that will assist them to thrive in today's world.

A school's curriculum should encourage boys to talk about their feelings, to have fun and enjoy being creative and artistic, and to interact with girls without being labelled 'wusses' or having teasing remarks made about the relationships ('She's your girlfriend'). Traditional masculinist and patriarchal frameworks for guiding boys into manhood are no longer appropriate, and parents and schools should energetically challenge these and begin to replace them with frameworks more relevant to today's culture.

It seems that when the pressure is less for boys to be macho and non-feeling, a space is opened up for them to expand their horizons and recognise a variety of skills in themselves. The film *Billy Elliot* demonstrates this beautifully. One school, the James Cook Boys' Technology High School, Kogarah, NSW, has introduced dance, singing and musical instruments as a core educational focus for its boys, and found a corresponding decline in truancy, less aggression in the playground and less limitations to enact stereotypical behaviour.

Although school curriculum is set, there is a high degree of flexibility in how it is taught and what additional options are provided for children. Making use of the outdoors, learning by doing, and the introduction of programs to assist all children to learn communication, assertiveness, good self-worth and confidence, and conflict resolution is important.

It can also be helpful for even young children to explore gendered ideas: Who says how boys and girls should behave? What does this mean? Why don't boys and girls play together? Even young children are able to dissect these myths, and teachers and parents can encourage co-operation between boys and girls so they can learn from each other.

Challenging gender stereotyping allows both girls and boys to participate in activities, regardless of their gender. This means that even before- and-after-school programs will insist boys as well as girls clean up, or that boys can help cook too, or that girls play football. When schools have working bees it may be the dads who provide the drinks and weed the garden or clean the blackboards, and the mothers who mow the lawn. Sole mothers are in an excellent position to challenge existing school hierarchies, which are often hotbeds of patriarchy.

Although most teachers in primary schools are women,

the school principal or school council president is often a male, and the mothers (at least the term Mothers' Club has been changed to Parents' Association) do the cooking and fundraising. This is partially because more mothers are at home but also because there is an expectation that this is what women do. Many fathers are also wanting to play a significant role in their child's school, and schools can start to encourage fathers to take on more hitherto traditionally women's tasks, such as hearing reading, or tuckshop duty. Perhaps sole mothers could start a sole-mothers' support group or invite guest speakers to forums to educate teachers and other parents about sole-parenting issues.

Chapter 8

Dealing with Your Son's Anger, Understanding His Grief

Parents of both boys and girls report consistently that the issue they find most difficult to deal with is their child's anger. Boys and girls are exhibiting greater displays of anger than ever before. Whether it is shown in verbally abusing their mothers, destroying family possessions, swearing at teachers or slamming doors, anger and inability to delay gratification has emerged as the key issue at the beginning of this century.

Anger is the one emotion that stands out as being difficult for sole mothers to deal with. They speak about feeling certain they experience it from their sons, but are unclear about its validity and how to deal with it. On one hand, they feel anger is unacceptable if expressed in destructive ways; on the other, they want their sons to express a range of emotions.

Anger may also be a problematic emotion for women, because women are socialised not to be angry and that anger is very 'unbecoming' for a woman, unladylike and 'bitchy'. Women are socialised to be nurturing, loving and more considerate for others' emotions than their own. A key theory about the greater incidence of depression in women is that depression is actually anger turned inward — anger that is totally unacceptable to express. It may be that women who experience depression have suppressed their anger so much that they are not even aware that they feel it, let alone have the right to feel it. Some women who have been abused and violated as children or adults may never have been able to safely express their anger.

The way that women view anger may have a direct bearing on how they deal with their son's anger. If a woman was brought up in a family where anger was considered 'bad', she may find it difficult to tolerate her son's expression of it. If she had been exposed to violence she may either fear any expression of anger, because she thinks it will lead to violence, or see it as 'normal' boy behaviour.

Mothers may feel angry with their children, their ex-partners, the courts or their financial situation. It may be difficult for mothers to separate out how they can deal with their own anger and how they can help their son deal with his anger.

Ask yourself:

- How did my parents react when I expressed anger?
- What sorts of things did I feel angry about when I was a child?
- Did my parents treat my expressions of anger differently from those of my brother?
- Did I misconstrue any childhood experiences of anger as violence? (Did you think your father was angry, when in fact he was violent?)
- How are women labelled in this society when they are angry?
- How does distinguishing anger from violence alter the ways I might raise my son?

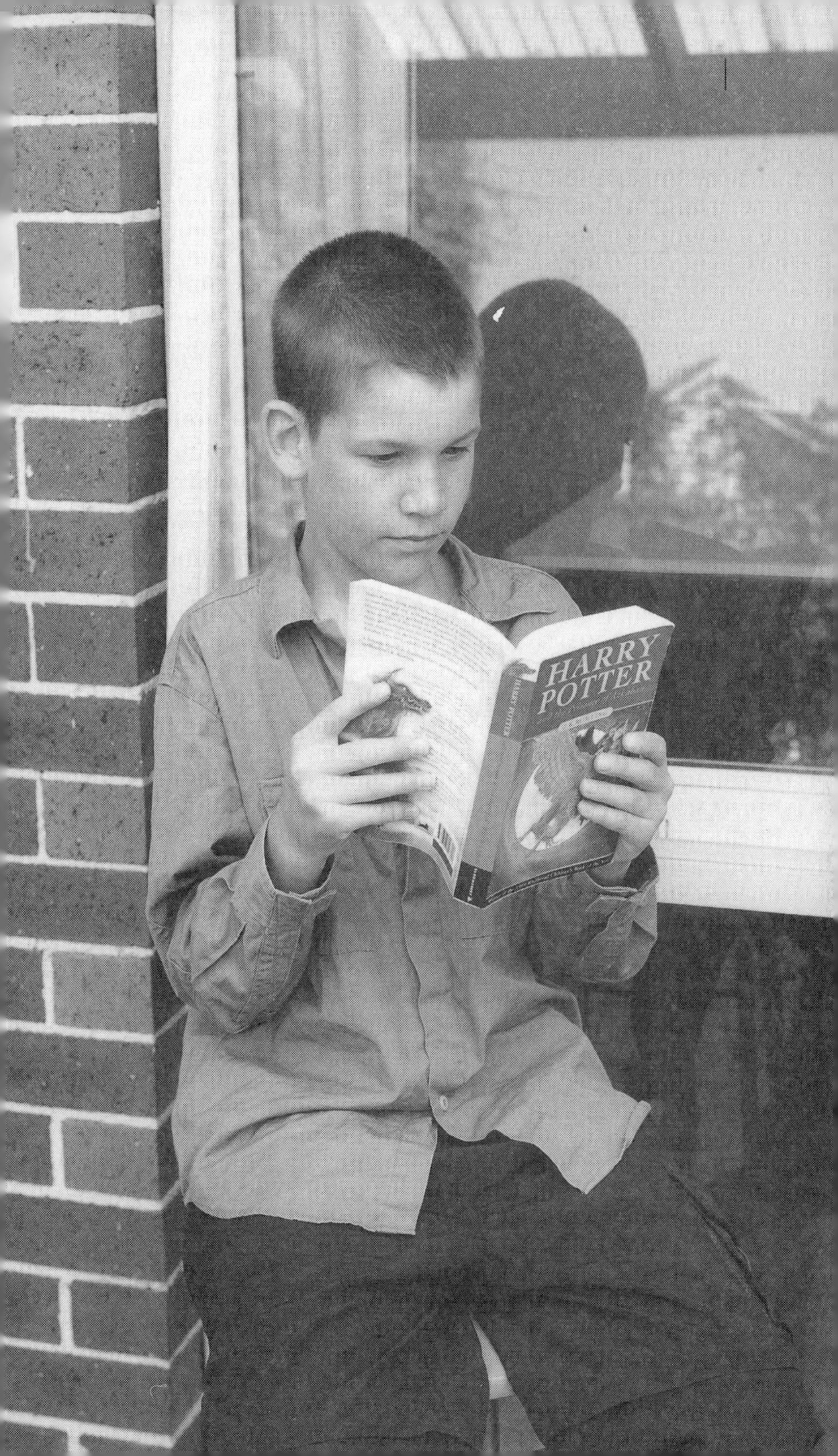
HARRY
POTTER

Sons can feel angry for lots of reasons: because they have no father; because Mum left Dad; because they feel their family is different; because they feel responsible for the breakup; because their Dad rarely sees them; because there is never enough money; or because Mum and Dad still argue. Anger is a valid and justified emotion like any other. Anger is a natural and normal process of grieving and loss. You and/or your son may experience anger as a response to loss, even though the actual loss happened some time ago. Anger may surface years after a distressing event.

The rise in children's anger may also be linked to parenting styles. Many mothers feel that they want to parent in a different way from the way they were parented. In addition, they may want to compensate for the hardship that their son has experienced in the marital breakdown. Mostly they want to parent the *right* way, and are hesitant in case they are, in fact, being too harsh or oppressive to their child. This may mean that they accept behaviour in their son that is, in fact, unacceptable.

What is anger?

Anger is an emotion like any other emotion. One psychological view is that emotions result from thoughts; that is, they are constructed rather than appearing out of nowhere. This can be illustrated by the following example:

> A woman sees a child being smacked. If she believes that smacking children is a mark of good parenting and is necessary to bringing up a child to be respectful, she might think to herself, 'Now there's a good mother'. As a consequence of this thought she may feel validated, because it mirrors her parenting.
>
> Another woman may see the same incident, and believe that smacking is abusive. She may think to herself, 'That is appalling — that poor child' As a consequence of this, she may feel angry because this woman's behaviour was so different to the way she parents.

Anger is often a response to not feeling good — to feeling being taken advantage of, misrepresented, misunderstood and treated unfairly. Mothers can encourage these thoughts in their child by their own ideas and attitudes about the world; for example, a mother who believes her son should not clean up may side with his feelings of anger when he is required to help at school camp.

A mother who encourages self-reliance and responsibility in her son will lessen the chance for anger to develop.

Anger can result from a range of emotions such as bewilderment, fear, loneliness, abandonment, a sense of unfairness, and anxiety. Boys may express anger as a way to get help or indirectly to ask for attention. Anger is often broken down into two types: 'instrumental' or 'expressive'. Instrumental anger aims to control or dominate, to make people do something; for example, a son who has temper tantrums when he isn't allowed to spend the night at a friend's house may be demonstrating instrumental anger in an attempt to control his mother's decision. Expressive anger is usually a combination of other underlying emotions, such as frustration or powerlessness. It does not have an aim in particular, but is an expression of pent-up emotions that are let loose.

It is important to separate the difference between anger and violence. Anger is an emotion, but violence is a set of behaviours and attitudes. Anger is not a problem; what it signals is that something is wrong. Anger can be helpful in encouraging a person to stand up to injustice or wrongdoing. It actually protects a person's sense of self-worth by encouraging action related to self-protection and self-validation. If we didn't feel angry, people might take advantage of us. Violence is not an emotion, but sets of behaviours aimed at controlling and intimidating. Women who have experienced domestic violence may see their son's anger as a precursor to violence, and remember how powerless they were to change their partner's behaviour. This may result in them feeling a similar sense of powerlessness to challenge their son's anger.

Some mothers who believe in the 'testosterone myth' may see actions such as kicking walls and breaking things as 'normal boy behaviour' and linked with 'surging testosterone'. There is no evidence to indicate that testosterone is linked with violent behaviour, and certainly testosterone, although it may abound in puberty, is often highly exaggerated in relation to its influence on boys' behaviour. It may have an influence on how boys express aggression, but so do other influences, such as family styles in dealing with conflict, communication, and the ability to show positive emotions.

There are many myths about how men and women should express their anger, and these can be unhelpful in assisting mothers sort out whether, in fact, their son's anger is violence, and how to deal with anger. If you grew up in a home where there was domestic violence and/or you were not allowed to express any feeling of anger, then you may have difficulty in being assertive or coping with anger directed at you. Anger can seem a scary thing, or may be inextricably linked with violence in your own mind.

While a mother may be thinking the anger is about her 'bad' parenting, particularly if her son is influenced by mother-blaming ideas, he may be convinced that, if only his mother did whatever he wanted, all would be well. He may believe that she is being totally unfair in not giving in to his demands.

So, in a way both of you feel powerless — you because of your son's behaviour, and he because of tantrums and your not wanting to give in to him. The way forward has to be for you both to challenge this feeling and move towards taking responsibility — you for parenting assertively, and your son for having a greater influence over his temper tantrums.

There is a prevailing myth that if boys don't express their

anger aggressively it can lead to problems later in life. This is not true. Boys need to be able to express a full range of emotions, and it is healthier for boys if many of the emotions underlying anger can be expressed and shared with a caring adult. What makes a difference in boys' development is being able to express emotions safely and openly.

Carla talks about her experience of Ben's anger:

> My son Ben was only four, but he seemed to get angry very easily. He would throw things on the ground or break things. He would throw tantrums if he didn't get what he wanted straight away. It meant I had to drop whatever I was doing to get what he wanted or help him. He was growing up into a real tyrant, but I couldn't bear his behaviour if I tried to make a stand. He would scream so loudly and break things and throw himself on the floor. The longer I ignored him the worse it would get, until I couldn't stand it any longer and I would go to him.
>
> I realised that because I felt guilty about breaking up with his father I would give him what he wanted straight away. I would run after him, even let him make a big mess because I wanted to make up to him and show him he was loved. If I asked him to do something and he didn't want to, he would have a huge tantrum until I gave in. It was getting really stressful.
>
> I realised it would be to his disadvantage to let this continue, so I stopped being at his beck and call and started to impose some limits. It took an awful lot of strength to do this, because in the beginning he went absolutely bananas. Sometimes I would think he was going to die because he would choke and hit his head on the floor. He was so mad!
>
> For a while his anger got worse, but now there is much more respect between us, and I feel like it is far more helpful for him to feel safe in the limits I have imposed. I'm still helping him to learn to express his anger constructively, but now it also seems that he actually doesn't get angry much at all.

> ### *Ask yourself:*
>
> - If I have been in a relationship where I have been abused, how might I view my son's expressions of anger?
> - What ideas have I heard or taken on board about how women should or shouldn't express their anger?
> - How might these influence how I deal with my son's anger?
> - How might my experience in the relationship with his father influence how I see and deal with my son's anger?
> - How might the way I was parented influence the way I deal with his anger?

Preventing anger

It may seem a contradiction to speak about preventing anger. But often anger in men comes from a range of attitudes and ideas about their place in the world. Some of the following thoughts and attitudes are ones that can lead to boys and men feeling angry:

- I have more rights than anyone else
- If I want something, I shouldn't have to wait
- If things don't work out for me, I'm entitled to get angry
- Boys/men are more important than girls/women
- My needs should be gratified
- Other people should look after me
- Other people are responsible for how I behave
- If I feel angry, it's their fault, not mine

As a mother you can challenge these attitudes by taking a stand against them. There will be a myriad of opportunities to practise taking a stand in your relationship with your son. These can include:

- making sure that you finish what you were doing before getting him what he wants
- not rushing to meet his needs

- refusing to give in to displays of anger
- occasionally asking him to wait for what he wants
- refusing to buy into his excuses for being angry
- refusing to accept the blame for his anger
- ensuring that he takes a high level of responsibility at home and helps out
- not allowing him to make derogatory or disrespectful comments about women
- making sure there are consequences for destructive anger

Ron Taffel, an eminent American family therapist, writes that it is the 'violence fostering anonymity [that] many children feel' that is the main challenge for today's parenting.[1] He cites the business of today's society, where even when families are spending time together there is more a focus on parallel activity than on joining. For example, family members may be near each other in the house, but are engaged in parallel, but remote, activities — the mother may be cooking and also getting the daughter to have her bath, the older son may be emailing his friends, and another child watching TV. They may spend three or four hours a night engaged in these parallel activities, but do not effectively join as a family, neither uniting nor communicating to each other.

He claims that what children most lack is a sense of connection and their parents' undivided attention — the consequences of this lack of attention is that children lose confidence in their own parents to guide them, and look to find something else that promises to assuage their yearnings for attention.

Taffel writes that it is often in the enactment of violent or aggressive acts that boys, in particular, make a neglected child seem instantly and uniquely recognisable. In a child's mind violence appears the perfect antidote to the anonymity of his or her life.

It would seem that one of the most successful ways of preventing anger in your son is to be with him, not just in body but in spirit also. He needs to feel that he has a sense of himself, an ability to define who he is, what he stands for, and how others see him, and your role as a mother is crucial in this.

This does not mean that you should not work or should sacrifice everything to spend every available minute with your son, but it does mean that you may need to put in an extra effort to draw your son out of isolated or non-communicative behaviour into open and connected ways of being.

Help your son deal with his anger

It can be difficult for you to respond in a helpful way, particularly if your son's anger is expressed towards you. Of course, abusive behaviour is not okay, but, rather than coming down on your son in the first instance, try to talk to him about why he is upset, and tap into the range of other feelings that may be behind his anger. Often you may have to wait until the anger has passed, say, at bedtime, or perhaps late in the day, ask him to come for a walk with you.

Ideas for dealing with anger

- **Use 'time out' from a young age**

Time out involves removing your son from the situation, and giving him a cooling-off period for a few minutes until he is willing to change his behaviour. Time out is not a strategy to stop his anger, but to deal with destructive behaviour that may be an expression of his anger.

Many mothers with sons who have indulged in tantrums for a long time say that time out just doesn't work. They say that their sons just come straight out of their rooms again, or go into their room and start to destroy it. This is alarming, and you will need much more persistence. You must convince your son that you are absolutely serious that the tantrums have to stop. You may need to remove any valuable or easily breakable items from his room.

When he has a tantrum, pick him up and tell him he is

going to his room until the tantrum stops. Put him in, and close the door. If he opens the door, put him back in again. Some mothers with escape-prone children have stood, holding the bedroom door shut, until their son has settled down. Do not bargain with your son, only let him out when he has calmed down and is ready to behave appropriately. If he comes out and starts another tantrum, you must go through the whole process again.

The first few occasions of doing this may be exhausting, and take a lot of time. But, if you are persistent, it will change his behaviour. He just needs to know you mean business.

- **Dealing with temper tantrums in younger sons**

Some mothers report that, because of their son's size and aggressive manner, conventional temper tantrum techniques, such as 'time out', are not useful. It can be extremely challenging to deal with a boy who is strong, used to throwing his weight around, and wants his own way!

It is vitally important for you to address temper tantrums while your son is young and before he gets too strong or worldwise to ignore you. It does require a lot of persistence and strength to change your son's behaviour, but the payoff is huge. Do not believe that your son is so set in his ways that he won't or can't change. He can and will, given that you stand firm. It may take a few weeks for his behaviour to change, but it will.

Once you've started the process you need to continue. So choose your timing well! Perhaps wait until the school holidays, or start during the weekend when the pressure is off to be at a certain place at a certain time.

If possible, act early when you start to see your son getting angry or beginning a temper tantrum. Try some early intervention — distracting him by pointing something out or making a funny face. Humour can work wonders in dealing with anger.

Sometimes ignoring anger when it seems like an attention-seeking behaviour can be helpful too, but it is still advisable to talk to your son later to see what is happening for him.

Parents usually give more attention to the negative behaviours exhibited by their sons, but it is important to praise and encourage positive behaviour — like the times your son could have shown his anger in a destructive way but chose not to. It is helpful to emphasise choice, to tell him that anger is okay, but how it is expressed can raise difficulties.

- **Teach children problem solving**

Teaching your son how to work through a threat, problem or disagreement is more helpful than yelling at him to stop. Sit down with your son and ask what might have been helpful in solving the dilemma and how he might approach this next time; for example, if a young boy is building something with Lego and it collapses, he may smash the whole construction in anger and frustration. Take time to inquire what he might have done differently, and also explore the range of his feelings. You could say, for example, 'You feel really frustrated because you spent so much time making that tower, and now it's collapsed. What else could you have done rather than wrecking the whole game?'

A useful strategy is to remove items as a consequence of your son's angry behaviour; for example, if he refuses to pack up his toys, tell him he will not be able to play with them again until he can act 'responsibly' and agree to pack them away. If he smashes his Lego, tell him that he must put it away until he can look after such special toys.

- **Teach self-control, an ability to handle frustration, and to delay gratification**

Ours is a culture of instant gratification and intolerance for waiting, and many children grow up with a low level of frustration tolerance. Boys must learn to wait and withhold their needs. Learning to impose a sense of self-control from within, rather than relying on externally imposed control, is essential.

Melanie writes:

A family therapist taught us a wonderful technique to use for disrespectfulness between siblings, helping them to resolve their disputes and countering the negative effects of put-downs. The boys and I went to the therapist when I was concerned about the negative and down-putting way the boys were talking to each other, feeling that it was greatly damaging their self-esteem and self-image. They were calling each other 'useless', 'dumb', 'a loser', and other names.

The therapist suggested that, when the boys were disrespectful towards each other, I was to tell them I considered this disrespectful, that in this house we do not have disrespect, so they have to go outside. I was to tell them to take their brother out of the house, and not to come back until they had sorted it out. When they had figured out they could be respectful, they were to knock on the door and I'd give them a test. The test would be for them to prove that they are respectful of their brother. They had to talk between themselves to highlight something that their brothers had done that showed they respected him, something they were proud of.

The main objection the boys had in doing this was 'Why should I be sent outside when he was the one to hit me/call me names? I've done nothing wrong'. My answer was to be, 'It's hard for him to learn to respect you if you're not there to teach him'. So what I was actually doing here was teaching them how to build an alternative story for each other, as well as helping them to recognise their own strengths and qualities.

All boys get angry. But when boys spend most of their time feeling angry they are usually not happy boys. Being angry does not lead to positive outcomes in life. Helping your son to express his anger and deal with the world in a way that will not evoke anger will help him to feel safe and develop feelings of self-worth, self-respect and respect for others.

Grief and loss

Grief and loss can be experienced for different reasons. It may be the grief that follows the ending of a family relationship; it may be the grief of his father's death, it may be the grieving for the father your son has never had — both in presence and in commitment. Grief can be complex, and associated with a range of often-conflicting emotions: your son's relief that at least he will no longer have to listen to fighting adults, his feeling of loss that the family unit is no longer together, fear about how he and you will survive, jealousy if his father has a new girlfriend, and other emotions. He may also feel guilty for not feeling as sad as he thinks he should or because he experiences a sense of relief. Often the way children behave indicates what they may be feeling and thinking.

Possibly one of the most difficult things about children's grief is that the adults they are closest to are also grieving. This means that they may not be emotionally or physically available to their children. In some instances other adults are so overcome with their own grief that they do not acknowledge the experience of children, or they think that younger children do not understand.

Winnie, mother of five-year-old Joshua, talks about her own experience of grief as well as her son's:

> I am Chinese and my husband is Australian. All his girlfriends have been Asian. He is used to Asian culture and in many ways is like an Asian man because he is very old-fashioned.
>
> It was difficult when we split up. I tried so hard to keep our family together and not to split up. I worried about Joshua, although my husband was treating me so badly. I wanted him to have two parents. I couldn't tell anyone about my husband's behaviour to me: how he treated me like a slave, how he made me cut his toenails for him, how in no way did he treat and respect me like a wife. I had few friends in Australia, and I couldn't tell my family back in China because if they knew I would divorce they would lose face and have great shame. I felt so heartbroken that there was no one to help and support me, only my counsellor and two friends.
>
> I told my parents last year. They asked why, but it was so hard to explain. They thought it was because my English was not good enough. But I couldn't explain that it wasn't that, they wouldn't understand.
>
> I have noticed a big change in my son since my husband and I separated. He is moody and there is insecurity, a lot of anger, and he is a very different boy than he was before. I try to help

him by letting him know I love him. I give him lots of cuddles, and I try not to let him think about things too much. I take his mind off things by playing with him and giving him activities to do. I let him know that I won't change towards him. It's important that I don't make him sleep alone at night — I don't want him to feel insecure. I think he will grow independent in his own time.

Grief is not an event, but a process of great change. It can encompass changes in your son's environment, such as moving house, but also needing to cope with strange adults entering his life. He may have to deal with funerals, or moving away, or changing schools.

Preschool children do not understand that the loss is permanent. Even if you tell your son that his father is going to live somewhere else, they may repeatedly ask when he will be coming home. Children this age may grieve by acting out their emotions as they don't yet have the words to express them.

Primary-schoolaged children may attribute blame to themselves, and think that, if they had behaved better or helped out more, Mum and Dad would not have split. Your son may see the separation as in part his fault, or a sign of not being loved.

An older child will have a greater understanding about separation and will be familiar with other friends whose parents are not living together and with the notion of divorce. He will be able to talk about his feelings, but still may act them out too.

Towards the time of secondary school he will develop a stronger and strict sense of what is right and wrong, and may take a moral stance on the separation, particularly if it involved a third party. He will be interested in the details, and about what will happen in the future. He needs to feel that he is informed of decisions being made, and often wants to contribute to them. Boys this age are more able to show empathy towards others, as well as feel their own grief.

Children show their grief in a number of ways:
- in physical symptoms like tummy- and headaches, sore legs or arms, and feeling 'sick'
- dreams and nightmares
- eating too much or too little
- regressing into the behaviour of a younger child
- becoming aggressive and destructive
- finding it difficult to concentrate or apply themselves to schoolwork
- acting in ways that are very different to their usual selves
- withdrawing and becoming uncommunicative
- becoming dependent and clingy
- having temper tantrums
- crying or 'moping'
- refusing to talk about what happened
- making the source of grief into an idealised being

If your son is acting out such behaviours, think about what feelings he may be experiencing. For example, if he is destructive, it may be that he is angry, perhaps he thinks you have driven his father away; or it may be that he is clingier than usual, or acting in a babyish way, because he is thinking that you may not want him any more or may send him away, so he is feeling scared and frightened. Perhaps he is acting in an overhelpful and over-responsible way because he thinks that if he takes more responsibility he can compensate for his father's shortcomings. He may be feeling guilt or shame.

Many mothers report wanting to compensate for the grief they feel they have imposed on their children through the decision to divorce. They may feel shame, guilt and blame, and therefore feel they owe it to their sons to let them get away with being disrespectful, rude or irresponsible. They think such behaviour must be part of the grieving process. But it is important to separate the feelings from the behaviour. It is okay for your son to feel whatever he is feeling, but it is not okay to act in a destructive way. You can help him to find the means to communicate and express his feelings in an appropriate way.

Sometimes a boy may say he wants to die or end his life because of the separation. This is not a common reaction and should be taken seriously. If your son is saying these things to you or appears markedly depressed for a period of time you must talk to a professional counsellor.

There are numerous books that deal with grief and loss relating to family breakdown. Many of these are available through your local library; the Family Court also has some great low-cost books that will help you explain what is happening.

Chapter 9

Separation: Residence and Contact

The decision to separate may be one of the most difficult decisions a couple has to face. Although it can be traumatic, research has indicated that tension and conflict in families, particularly if it has continued for years, greatly affects children, possibly more so than the actual separation. Separation and divorce can mar children's trust in their parents, adults, and the world in general. Children do not thrive well in families where there are continual fights, silent treatment, tension and instability, and where they feel torn in their loyalties to their parents. Children may fare better in later life if separation results in an end to conflict, and is handled by adults in a way that is responsible and places the children's interests before their own. The old idea that it is better to stay together 'for the sake of the children' does not hold true, particularly in conflictual relationships, and if the conflict involves violence and abuse.

It is a myth that children from separated families cannot thrive. Many well-known and respected men and women have grown up in families with one parent. What does make a difference is the way that the separation and ensuing divorce are handled, and how a mother maintains her relationship with her son.

Separation is an ongoing rather than one-off event. The act of the family splitting and one part of it moving to other accommodation marks the beginning, not the end, of separation. Children may grieve for a long period of time, not just for the loss of a parent but for the loss of social networks, the 'normalcy' of a nuclear family, the drop in income, and the hopes they had for family life. Children are also resilient, and are able to incorporate the experience of separation and divorce into their lives in a way that acknowledges the experience, but without longlasting, damaging effects. The way a mother deals with, and relates to, her children is vital in assisting the healing process.

Separation can be difficult for children because their parents may be so full of angst, anger or sadness about their own situation that their children's needs are overlooked. Mothers can feel exhausted, overwrought and preoccupied with Family Law issues and how they are going to survive the separation emotionally and financially. Research indicates that when women separate their income drops by about 30 per cent, whereas for men their income actually increases. This is because women may still be caring for children and so they are either not working or are working part-time, and because women still earn less than men do. Because on average women have residency of their children, they are often left in a financially precarious position in having to support them. The high cost of childcare may preclude women from seeking work; in addition, women may have been absent from the workforce while they were caring for their children, and may experience difficulty re-entering the workforce. Since the Child Support Scheme was introduced the rate of payment by non-custodial parents (usually fathers) has doubled from one- to two-thirds in the divorced population with dependent children.

Different children will respond in different ways to the

news that their parents are separating. As well as differences in gender and age, there are also differences in children's ability to deal with crisis and trauma, and to express and deal with their emotions. Some boys may seem particularly sensitive to the divorce, whereas others may be resilient and adapt without any apparent impact.

Children may experience a range of emotions with the announcement that their parents are separating. At times their emotions may be conflicting; for example, they may experience relief, which is also accompanied by a great deal of grief. Children may feel overwhelmed by their emotions, which may change from day to day or hour to hour. At times children feel emotions that seem totally contradictory to what their mothers might expect. They may feel sad when their mother leaves a father who physically abused them, or they may feel guilty that the father is being left alone.

Separation is always disruptive in one way or another to children, even when they do not leave the family home. Many aspects of children's lives are affected through divorce — in some cases they may need to leave school and home, in others it means some family members will no longer see them or see them less. New people may be introduced into their lives, such as babysitters, a new partner, a new neighbourhood, teacher, lawyer, or new step-siblings.

Emotions experienced by both boys and girls following separation include:
- relief
- shock — they may have been unaware that their parents were having difficulties
- confusion — they may worry what will happen to them, and how the arrangements about their future will be made
- insecurity — 'What will happen to us?', 'What will happen to Daddy?', 'Will Mum leave us too?'
- blame — 'It's Mum's/Dad's fault.' 'It's my fault.'
- anger — 'How could they do this to me?' 'Why did Mum let Dad go?'

- over-responsibility — this may happen, particularly if there are younger children or if either or both parents seem preoccupied with the separation and are not available to meet their child's emotional needs; adolescents are particularly prone to over-responsibility
- grief and loss — children may grieve that they will seem different from other families, that they will not have as much contact with the parent who is leaving, that their lives will never be the same
- excitement and a sense of adventure

The way children respond to separation and divorce is influenced by a number of factors:

- **The child's gender**

Girls tend to internalise their feelings, and are likely to feel sadness, loss and guilt. They are more likely than boys to feel sorry for the parent who is 'left alone'. They may express these feelings by weeping quietly, being clingy or 'moping', while boys are more likely to 'act out' their feelings with temper tantrums, rudeness and physical activity. Boys may be more inclined to 'act out' in school or preschool, whereas girls, in fact, may attempt to be more pleasing and helpful. Girls are also more likely to take on additional family responsibility; for example, looking after younger siblings, especially if the mother is overburdened and distraught by the process of separation.

- **How the parents respond to each other**

If parents are able to remain civil and put their children's needs and wellbeing before their own, then their children are less likely to be traumatised. Children need to feel that both parents love them and are there for them. If family life can continue so that both parents attend school concerts or birthday parties, the effects of separation will be far less.

- **Having other adults in their lives**

Children who have other caring adults, whether friends or relatives, in their life who are able to support them, particularly at times when their parents may be grieving and not able to be emotionally available for them, may find the process of separation easier to deal with.

- **The way a mother responds to a child**

A mother who, despite her own grief, is able to show her children that she is still in control and able to cope with day-to-day routines will be reassuring to her children that they do not need to take on adult responsibilities. Children need to feel safe and secure in the knowledge that their mother is strong enough to survive the separation. If they have this reassurance, they will have less need to take on emotional or other responsibilities for their mother.

Age-related responses to separation

A boy's age makes a difference to how he may react to the separation. The following gives some clues on age-related responses.

Even small babies may react to separation, not because they understand what is happening but because they pick up on adult emotional cues, such as their mother's sadness or stress. In addition, a young child will have formed an attachment with a male adult, and will miss his presence.

Preschool children

Boys in this group are more dependent on their parents. They do not easily understand the concept of time, so they may experience distress at being separated from a parent with whom they have usually been closely connected. They may find it highly stressful to be separated overnight from a parent, and may not understand that they will see their father or mother in a week's time — to a young boy a week may seem forever. Boys of this age find short, frequent visits with the absent parent easier to adapt to than longer, infrequent contact.

Boys of this age may revert to earlier behaviour, such as wanting a bottle or dummy, or not wanting to separate from their mother. They may be clingy and not want to let their mother out of their sight. Some may regress and act as though they were a younger age. They may talk in baby language, or revert to wetting their beds.

Older preschool children are more likely to feel that they are to blame for the separation. They may personalise the separation, and think that their father left because they were naughty, or because he didn't like them. Often preschoolers may fantasise about what they don't understand, and are likely to make up their own story of what happened. They may tell a friend that 'Daddy has gone away to fight in a war', or that their 'Dad has died'. They may say that their father, in fact, hasn't left the home, but has just gone away on a work weekend. This is their way of making sense of what to them may seem chaotic or difficult to process emotionally.

Preschool children may not be able to verbalise their emotions, so will act them out, often through negative behaviours.

Primary school

Primary-schoolaged children may feel great loyalty if their mother has left their father and they see him as being alone or cut off from the family. They may even feel this loyalty if, in fact, he has left the family to be with another partner. They can take on the 'job' of trying to look after the missing parent. They often hold onto a strong desire to reunite their parents, and actively seek to do this; for example, they may tell their father that their mother was crying, or give their father a present and say it was from their mother. They may try and act on their best behaviour in the belief that their parent will return if they are 'good enough'. They may feel unloved and express their grief through moodiness, tearfulness and lack of co-operation. They are more able to show their feelings than do younger children.

Older primary-schoolaged children can be more likely to say that they don't care about the separation, but find it easier to 'act out' their feelings in anger, defiance or risk-taking behaviour rather than talking about what they are experiencing. Acting out can involve being naughty at school, having psychosomatic problems such as tummy aches or headaches, and not concentrating at school. Children at this age may say they are 'sick' in the mornings, but make a full recovery once school has started and they are at home with their parent. Often they take their anger out on the parent who remains at home. They may also start to develop a loyalty to one particular parent, particularly if there is a high degree of conflict between parents. They may be particularly vulnerable to manipulation by parents.

Secondary school

Although adolescents are able to reason about why the separation has occurred, they are still concerned about the impact it will have on their lives. Will they need to move? Will they have less money, need to take more responsibility? How will it impact on their ability to 'hang out' with friends, or complete their schooling?

Separation may impact on their own developing ideas about sexuality, relationships and gender.

Boys of this age are becoming more independent, but may feel resentful and hostile if the separation impacts on their day-to-day plans, or if one or the other parent attempts to pressure them. They may be particularly reluctant to get caught up or drawn into their parents' disputes.[1]

Long-term effects on boys

Most children do recover from the effects of separation. Research indicates that the first two years can be unsettling for children, but generally they tend to accept what has happened and get on with their lives. There is evidence that relationship conflict affects boys more than girls in both nuclear and separated families.[2]

Boys generally take more time to adjust after a separation, missing fathers more, and having more difficulty than girls do with custodial mothers. Part of this may be because boys are accustomed to having a father as the 'boss', and when he is no longer present it can be difficult for a mother to reassert the authority she needs to have as a sole parent. Of course, boys may also miss a family member of the same gender and the preciousness of a dad.

Boys may find it harder to identify and talk about what they are feeling. Often they are experiencing a huge range of conflicting emotions, and may feel it is inappropriate to talk to their already overburdened mother, or feel that the sadness they are feeling is 'wrong' and unmanly. Sometimes parents and other relatives may inadvertently reinforce this by telling boys to 'Look after Mum' or that 'You'll be the man of the house or Mum's helper now'. This only puts more pressure on boys to toughen up and grow up, and makes it very difficult for them to find an outlet for their frustrations and grief. Perhaps this is partly the reason that boys of divorced families can appear angry later in adolescence — they did not get the opportunity to grieve when the experience was actually happening.

Making the decision — who lives with whom?

In 90 per cent of separations the children end up living most of the time with their mothers. Sole-father families tend to have fewer children and to have greater proportions of older children than sole-mother families. Sole-father families are also more likely to be in paid employment than sole-mother families. This occurs despite changes to the Family Law Act that encourage both parents to have equal and shared access to their children. Only a small percentage of separations where children are involved end up in family law disputes; usually parents work out these arrangements without having to take legal action. This is certainly better for children, particularly considering that family law disputes may take years to resolve and be bitter and protracted. They are also extremely costly.

Making the decision about the children can be complicated when other issues impact on that decision. These could include:
- one parent going straight into a relationship with a new partner
- one parent has very different attitudes and values from the other regarding childrearing
- one parent seems uncommitted and irresponsible to the children
- one parent wants to move interstate or a long distance away
- one parent is abusive or violent
- one parent refuses to pay child support, or grossly underestimates her/his income

Often it is very difficult to separate what is best in the children's interests from all the emotional baggage that invariably goes with separation. Sometimes it can be helpful to speak with a counsellor to sort this out (a list of agencies that may be helpful is given at the end of the book). If there has been a history of violence and abuse, it is important to get some advice relating to the separation before you separate. You may need to consider a restraining order as part of the residence/contact agreement if you feel you or your children would be under threat by separating from the other parent. There is absolutely no excuse for children being exposed to violence or abuse, whether to them or to their sole parent. The court generally holds a critical view on domestic violence, and will take into account incidents of violence against the parent and the existence of an intervention order.

There is no real formula to help parents make a decision about residence and contact. Traditionally when parents separate the children usually spend more time with their mother. This is partly because women have been viewed as the nurturers and childrearers, and men as bonded to their careers. There are also reasons why this might be important — a baby may be being breastfed, a mother may have more time for the children because she works part-time, a father's profession may mean he works long hours.

Many parents are starting to challenge these views and the plethora of myths relating to parenting. The myth that sole mothers cannot raise 'normal' boys is one such myth; another is that men cannot parent as well as women. Parenting is learned; no one is born as a 'natural' parent, and many fathers are choosing to make it their responsibility to know how to care and provide for their children. Many fathers are now cooking, helping sons express their emotions, teaching non-violence, and taking part in preschool and school activities. It would be a grave injustice to deny sons contact with such loving fathers because of parental breakup.

If you and your partner are able to talk about what is best for your son's interests, you can weigh up all the factors relating to where he will spend his time. If he is at school, and you and his father live close by, it may be in your son's best interests to have equal time with you both, perhaps a three-day-on, four-day-off arrangement. Encouraging a loving father to have contact with his son is acting in your son's best interests.

Recognise that boys' needs change as they grow. Whereas a two-year-old might enjoy spending two afternoons a week with his father and no overnight visits, a five-year-old might spend two nights and days a week at his father's house, (perhaps separated by some days with his mother). An older primary-schoolaged boy might like to spend every second weekend and half the week. Some children would rather live at one particular home and visit another, others adjust quite well to having two homes, particularly if their parents have compatible parenting styles and values. In these situations parents may have joint residence. As your son grows older, it may be appropriate that he spend more time with his father, and this should be encouraged. Then in his teens he may start to see his father less and his peer group more, or may need extra incentive from his father in order to maintain regular contact.

How to help your son

Divorce is a traumatic situation for both men and women. It is interesting that in most research women are shown to fare better emotionally, socially and in their general health following the separation, whereas for men it is the opposite. This may be because men do not have the social skills and networks of women, nor the ability to communicate their emotional vulnerability; they can more easily become isolated, and not know where to turn. Sometimes this means they take refuge in alcohol or drugs; they may become gamblers. Sadly, for many men their partner is their only friend, so a divorce means their world is turned upside down.

Because women are shown to fare better socially does not mean that women do not have their fair share of concerns and tribulations. Mostly it is mothers who, being the primary caregivers, take on the role of dealing with the children's acting-out behaviour, particularly following contact or initially after the separation. One reason that women may fare better has been shown to be because they have the responsibility of the children, and need to 'soldier on' regardless. Mothers just can't afford to break down or give up.

If possible, it is far better for children to see their parents behaving civilly and comfortably with each other. Some parents are able to achieve a separation where they are able to work through issues and problems out of earshot of their children so that the children are not privy to those issues that may cause anxiety and fear. Such parents are still able to attend school parent/teacher nights together, go to sports events and even have dinner as a family once in a while. Their children have access to both parents by being able to write or phone whenever they feel like it, and parents encourage their children to have contact with them both, and speak respectfully and encouragingly of each other.

Of course, this is an ideal situation, and the reality of separation is more often than not fraught with high emotions and tensions, particularly in the early stages. This may happen particularly where one partner has had an affair, or forms a new relationship soon after leaving the relationship. Sometimes one partner can interpret that the other is having a far easier experience of separation and, although this may not necessarily be true, it is still painful. Tempers may flare easily, and your partner may be unco-operative, obstructive or inflammatory. Such behaviour could probably be construed as a 'normal' reaction in the early days of separation.

Many mothers have reported that their children's father seems to lose interest at separation, or perhaps never seemed committed to his children anyway. Many men have been socialised to believe that parenting is women's work, so have never nurtured a relationship with their son. Some men genuinely do not know how to parent a child. They may also 'give up' with separation, and decide that there is no point continuing to have a relationship with children who no longer live with them. These men may genuinely be at a loss at how to deal with their children's feelings, and at being sole parents themselves. Fathers may not have the understanding or skills to deal with children's needs following separation, and may reject their children because of this inability.

Some fathers may attempt to 'pay back' their partner by withdrawing from their children, and refusing to take any responsibility for their children's wellbeing following the separation. This attitude may be particularly prevalent if the mother initiated the separation. It is an attitude of irresponsibility and immaturity — the 'If you won't stay with me, I'll teach you.' Unfortunately such attitudes have far-reaching impacts on the children.

At the worst end of the spectrum are those men who are violent and controlling, and seek to use their children to continue to exert control over their partners.

Some of the above behaviours may be inevitable initially following the separation when emotions are running high, but parents' responsibility to their children should outweigh their own need for vengeance or emotional payback. There are other mechanisms for working through the gamut of emotions that adults experience with divorce or separation, and responsible adults will pursue these, rather than behave in a way that will impact negatively on their children. Counselling, both for the individual parent and for the separated couple, may be useful in exploring how best to meet children's needs.

One of the difficulties that mothers often mention after separation is the different standard in parenting and care when a boy goes to his father on visitation. A mother may have her own sets of values and attitudes to parenting. Sometimes mothers worry that their son's father is too permissive in his parenting; for example, he lets the children stay up late and eat junk food; others complain he is punitive and over-controlling. If possible, discuss this difference with the father, and try to set at least some basic ground rules on which you both agree. You may decide on a reasonable bedtime or an allocated time for homework, but disagree on what movies your son can watch, and how often he eats junk food. It may be impossible to get total agreement, although harmony is more easily achieved as time goes on and the raw edge of separation is lessened.

Try not to dwell on those aspects of his father's parenting that are not life-threatening or too damaging. As your son matures he will be able to make his own informed decisions about what is right for him. It is important, however, that you maintain your standards and ways of parenting in your own home, and that your son respects and adheres to these.

Tracy, mother of twelve-year-old Samuel, says:

> Our marriage was very even with no fights, but when we separated there was a lot of anger, and our communication broke down. So Peter doesn't feel comfortable about incorporating me into his life — there is no communication or engagement between us. He just drops Samuel off at the door, and won't come in.
>
> Samuel voices his frustration about his father's non-involvement in our lives, and I have been honest about my

feelings but never derogatory about his Dad, and I have never been blaming. It is tricky because his father and I have such different ideas about parenting.

It can be difficult if these values conflict to a point where you feel it is extremely detrimental for your son's development. Some of these issues may include where a father drinks a lot of alcohol, smokes dope, watches pornography, drives without seatbelts, uses corporal punishment and other irresponsible behaviours. There is not a lot you can do to prevent your son being exposed to these issues, other than to take your concerns to the Family Court. Exposing a child to pornography is an offence, and you should notify the child protection system or police. This can be a big step to take, given that it may alienate you further from his father and increase hostilities. If you are concerned, talk to a counsellor, either in person or anonymously through a telephone counselling service such as Parentline or Kids Help Line.

Don't underestimate your own approach to parenting and your son's appreciation of your standards and values. You can let your son know that you do not approve of his father's ways because you feel they are not helpful or healthy for young boys to be part of, but you can also emphasise why your ways are important to you. Ultimately your son will make his own decisions, and there is no reason why he will not appreciate the love and safety that you offer him.

Many mothers find it difficult to deal with their son's behaviour following a contact visit. It may be all the red cordial or being hyped up, but it may also be that your son is acting on his emotional response to the separation and to change in his life. It is important that your son heeds your rules, and although you know he may be disappointed or upset there are still certain behavioural expectations he should adhere to. At the same time you can try to talk with him to explore what it is he is finding difficult.

The most helpful thing for your son is for you to show that you are confident and capable, and that you will survive, despite not having a man's presence. Women who rely on a man's presence to keep their life on track are more likely to lose the respect of, and be undermined by, their sons. Such attitudes tell boys that they, as males, are in a stronger and more valued position than their mothers. Be there for your child, show your sadness, but send him a strong message that you can cope and are willing to take the reins to keep the family functioning and stable. This still means giving hugs and kisses, being gentle and nurturing, but it also means that you may need to show a less-often-seen side of your parenting — one that sets clear standards and values, and does not accept threats, abuse and disrespectful behaviour.

Affirm your son's pleasure at seeing his father

Boys and fathers share a different experience than do boys and mothers, or boys and any other adult for that matter. Fathers are special to boys. It can sometimes be difficult to keep separate your own feelings about his father. This can be very difficult if you have certain knowledge about his father that your son doesn't. It may be that your husband had an affair with a younger woman and you may be livid with him, yet you are expected to be encouraging and pleasant when you see your son off on a contact visit. What an effort that must take! But for your son's sake he needs you to be like that. It doesn't mean being over the top with enthusiasm, but it does mean being pleasant and encouraging. Trying to convince him of his father's lapsed morality or attempting to point out his new girlfriend's vast array of faults will not help him; firstly, because the affair did not directly impact on their father/son relationship, and, secondly, because your son will only be confused and torn if he feels you are forcing him to make premature choices. He will work out a moral stance about his father's actions in his own time as he develops the mental and emotional capacity to do so, but when he is young he needs to know he is seeing his Dad who loves him, and that some of Dad's friends might be fun too!

Contact when the father has been abusive or violent

The Family Court has long tried to grapple with the issue of granting violent men contact with their children. There has been a struggle between the rights of a child to have contact with his father, and the rights of a child to be physically and emotionally safe. A stance has been taken that children are better off not having contact with a father who is violent, and that violent fathers do not necessarily have a right to have contact with their children. No doubt these debates will continue for many years.

The court acknowledges that, even when children have not directly experienced physical violence, they have mostly witnessed (directly or indirectly) this violence to their mother, and are likely to have been verbally and emotionally abused. At times violent men have used contact visits to maintain power and control over their ex-partner, and as a means of continuing their abuse. They have also manipulated and badly treated their children in an attempt to 'get at' the mother. Some fathers have sexually abused their children. At times these attempts to pay back the mother have been taken to the extreme of kidnapping the children, and even of killing them — there have been a number of incidents where fathers have murdered their children and then taken their own lives, the ultimate act of revenge. Most of these murders have occurred within a context of ongoing family law disputes.

Many women who have experienced abuse and violence are also easily persuaded into believing the myths about fatherhood. The myths about the imperative of having a male role-model for boys may inadvertently keep mothers encouraging or tolerating a relationship that, in fact, may be harmful for their children. The idea that boys in particular need a father at all costs may make it difficult for a mother to deny or restrict visitation between a father and his son. It can be extremely traumatic for mothers who have experienced violence to be told by the Family Court that they must give the fathers visitation rights to their children. This is even worse for mothers who suspect that child sexual abuse has taken place but have not been able to definitively prove this in court.

Sometimes it can be helpful for you to make a list of what your children's father can offer your children (the advantages of contact), and what are the disadvantages or shortcomings of contact. If, for example, he has decided to seek counselling or attend a group for men to take responsibility for his violence, you may feel safer in allowing him contact, although of course attending such groups is no guarantee of change. If, despite his violence and abuse towards you, he can still consider the children's interests, discuss their needs and how best to help them through this difficult period, then visitation may work out. Many men who attend groups to deal with men's violence and abuse report a great deal of sadness that they do not have the sort of relationships built on trust and intimacy with their children that they would want. Some say, to their distress, that their relationship with their children actually mirrors that with their own fathers, despite pledging that would never be the case. The pattern of intergenerational abuse may repeat itself, and this can sadden many men. An awareness of this may mean that some fathers are prepared to work on sorting out their attitudes and ideas about women and themselves that lead to violence. Some men are able to use the separation as a means to explore a new and different relationship with their children, and you may notice some positive changes.

Keeping kids safe while on an access visit

If the court has ordered your son to have contact with his father, and you are worried about his safety, you can attempt to arrange for contact to occur at a contact centre or with supervision from a nominated person, so that at least another trusted adult is present.

Unfortunately most of these centres are privatised and charge a fee for facilitating handover, although some are subsidised. Some lawyers and children's workers argue that if contact must occur in these centres, this alone is reason enough to deny contact altogether; however, it seems the centres are being used more frequently.

If you are worried that your partner may abduct the child, make sure that a lawyer knows about your fears so that the lawyer can issue an injunction restraining the father from leaving the country by sea or air.

If you are fearful for your son's safety, it can be hard to let him go on contact visits, juggling between not wanting him to feel worried because you are and making him aware of ways he can look after himself. You want him to be able to enjoy and benefit from the contact but at the same time to be mindful of his own safety. It can be helpful to keep a journal to record times and days of contact, and details such as if the pickup was late and what you observed about your partner; for example, if you thought it looked like he was intoxicated or 'stoned', it is important to keep a record of this. Also record any differences you noticed in your son's behaviour before and after the pickup, such as bedwetting, anxiety or sexualised behaviour.

Tell your son that you want him to have a great time and that you know he enjoys seeing his Dad (if that is true). You can tell him, for example, that you're a bit worried that Dad might not use seatbelts or might drink too much, and encourage him to take responsibility for himself such as making sure he has a seatbelt on, and by making sure he has some money for a phone call to you if necessary. It is hard to feel so powerless to protect your son, but with each visit your son will be a little older, more mature, and able to be responsible for himself. You are there to reassure him of your love and support.

Your son may like to keep a diary of his own to write down what his experience with Dad was like. This can be a way for him to process his experience, and something to look back on when he needs to make decisions in the future.

Helping your child through the separation

The most helpful way of helping your son through the separation is by giving him permission to feel whatever he feels, and by being there with him. This could make a tremendous difference to the way he relates to you and feels about himself in the future.

Children often feel vulnerable and powerless when parents separate. Your son will wonder about his own future: Where will I live? How will I survive? What will happen to me when Mum goes to work? Who will mind the dog? Some of his concerns may relate to feeling responsible for other family members: Who will help Mum do the housework? Will I have to take care of my sister? Who will cook Dad's dinner? Will us kids get split up between Mum and Dad? Myriads of questions go through children's minds. Many parents ask at what age is it reasonable to ask their child who he'd prefer to live with most of the time.

Mostly decisions are made without consulting children, and as a result they may feel powerless and vulnerable. Of course, when children are younger it would not be right to consult them about adult decisions — how would a five-year-old be able to make the decision about whom he wants to live with? Most children would only be able to answer, 'Both parents'. Parents should not expect young children to take on the huge emotional responsibility of making such a decision. Parents are the adults and should take control. But older children may be able to contribute to some of the decision making so that they can start to regain a sense of control over their lives; for example, your son could be part of the decision making about when he could see his father, or what pocket money may be reasonable for him to receive.

Separation can be a disruptive experience for children and it is helpful to try and get back into a day-to-day routine in order to counteract their feelings of insecurity and 'not knowing.' This means that children need to know what the contact arrangements are; although some mothers leave the making of arrangements up to the children, it may also leave them with an overwhelming burden, not at all suitable for a young child. On the other hand, some boys are more mature, and experience no ill effects from taking a role in decisions of this kind.

As a rule of thumb, it seems better for parents to take the initiative and make the decisions relating to contact and residence, and to be flexible to adapting these as their children mature and the situation changes.

- **Do not give false hope**

Some couples decide to have 'trial separations' rather than making final decisions. Most of these trial separations do go on to become long-term separations. Sometimes mothers may attempt to protect their children's vulnerable emotions, and tell their children that the separation is only for a little while 'to see how things go'. Although well intentioned, this can actually prolong the feelings of confusion, grief and being unsettled, as children are never really sure of either their own or their parents' standing in the family unit.

If you know you are separating on a permanent basis, it is helpful for your son to know this from the start, rather than keeping him on tenterhooks. Don't hide the fact that his father has a new relationship or may be moving away. You can underestimate children's perceptions, and, even if you do try to hide what is really going on, children have big ears and pick up on the 'secret' adult business you are absolutely sure they know nothing of. Tell him that both parents love him (if this is true) and that your decision to separate was nothing to do with him, but was something that sometimes happens with adult relationships. You should be as realistic as possible about your son's connection and future visitation with his father so he knows from an early point in the separation where he stands, and at least does not have to wonder and worry about that. Be honest about what you do not know; for example, you may not know where you will move to, but tell him you will be the one to make that decision.

You must be realistic about the availability of your son's father, his responsibility and temperament. It may be tempting to paint a glossy image of his father, or to tell your son his father will change, but this is not helpful.

A first step in regaining your son's trust in the world is to be honest and upfront.

- **Do not discuss his father in negative terms**

As difficult as it may be, it is not helpful for your son to hear you refer to his father in a negative way, even if what you say seems true. You may feel resentment, bitterness, jealousy, anger, abandonment and a range of other emotions towards his father, but it is not acceptable to vent these in front of your son. Even if your partner has been highly abusive, it is not good for your son to hear this and to witness the range of emotions that accompany conversation about him. After all, he is that man's son and anything you say about his father can be construed as comments about him. This does not mean painting a glossy picture of his father. Your son will probably want to know why you separated, and want to check out his own experience and feelings towards his father.

You may wish to say something like 'Dad and I split because we got together when we were young, and we have decided that now we are too different. It's really hard for you I know, but we just couldn't live together any more', or you may need to explain 'It's really sad. I know Dad really loves you but he just wasn't ready to take the responsibility of being a father. Remember how he would stay out till late and not help? To me it wasn't okay to do that, so we decided to split up', or 'Your father was violent, you saw some of the things he did. I know that is a hard thing for a boy to face, and we can talk about it any time you like. You will need to make your own choices as you grow up about how you want to be, but I was not prepared to be hit and abused so that's why we left'. These kinds of conversations open up space for further talking. They are factual and honest, but don't incriminate the boy in his father's actions, nor are they blaming and negative.

It can be hard not to personalise the times your ex-partner may have been irresponsible or unthinking towards you or your son, but rather than saying how inconvenient it is when his father is always late it may be better to acknowledge your son's experience of disappointment; for example, rather than saying 'God, your father is always late', you could say, 'I bet you feel really let down when your Dad doesn't come to pick you up on time'.

Sometimes mothers and other women talk about men in a disparaging and often humorous way. I remember a friend giving me an *All Men Are Bastards* address book, and my son defacing it to 'All Men Are Cool'. It had not occurred to me that he would be offended (he was about eight at the time), but he was. Talking about men in disparaging and cynical ways is not helpful to your son in developing a healthy concept of masculinity. It is a good way to offload your feelings, but better to do so when your son is not present.

- **Let your son still be a kid**

At times well-meaning friends and relatives may refer to your son as being 'the little man of the house' or 'Mother's special boy', but this may be forcing him into a role he is not ready for and should not be placed in. Although you are wanting to encourage responsibility in your son, and may want him to increase his responsibilities once his father is no longer as available, he should not be consulted about adult decisions such as taking court action, arranging the conditions of visitation, talking to other adults on your behalf, and giving you emotional assistance.

It can be extremely concerning if he sees you constantly crying or telling your friends you can't cope any more. He may take on additional tasks like putting the garbage out, doing the dishes more often or mowing the lawn, but should not be expected to mind younger siblings or do all the housework. This may only cause further fear and anxiety, as he feels not only is the family breaking down but that he is the only person who is able to cope.

Taking on too much adult responsibility means taking on adult worries. This means the two of you become burdened as he struggles to shelter you from further worry. In doing this he may not feel able to lean on you to work through his own issues. Counsellors can help you deal with your issues and gain access to support services.

- **Acknowledge that he is his own person**

Some mothers find it extremely difficult to parent sons who remind them greatly of their ex-partners. Your son may look like, talk, walk, speak and, at times, act like his father, but he is his own person. If you emphasise the similarities to his father in a negative way, he is more likely to develop a negative self-image. It will not allow him the opportunity to explore his own individuality and path in life. We do not have concrete and clear empirical evidence on the relationship between genetic and environmental factors that influence a child's identity. The negative traits you may observe in your son may have developed because his father was his role model, or as a consequence of his father's parenting, rather than because he is genetically similar to his father. Foster the positive qualities in your son, whether they are similar to or different from his father's.

It is enhancing to your son's positive self-identity when you pay attention to those strengths and qualities that are similar to his father's. You may point out that his father was also a great footballer in his day, his father also loves gardening, or his father has a weird and funny sense of humour. Commenting on how his appearance is similar to his father's, or how his father also woke up early every morning, can help your son make the necessary connections about his identity.

- **Give your son the time and opportunity to talk**

Your son may tell you everything is 'just fine' or he may

act uncomfortable if you ask him directly about how he is coping with the separation. It can be helpful to set aside a particular part of the day or week when you and your son can have a quiet and close time. You could lie on his bed for a while each night and chat, or every Saturday afternoon go running together. If your son knows that you are available and that you are there for him, he will start to open up and share his deeper fears and emotions.

It can be hard for you not to want to quiz your son after a visitation: 'Who was there? Did Dad say anything about me? What did you eat? What does his new girlfriend look like?' and so on. This can be a greater temptation soon after separation. If you do feel uncomfortable about how your son fared on visitation, it is better that you take issue with his father rather than attempt to discuss his father's wrongs with your son.

Some children prefer to keep their experience with each parent completely separate, and don't wish to discuss their feelings or experience with the other parent. Accept this — the more you question the more your son will close up. You might assume that the father has required your son not to share his experience, but this may not be the case and it can be of your son's own initiative.

Children are often loyal to one parent — your son may feel sorry for his Dad, so tries to protect him or over-compensate for his shortcomings. It will take time for your son to work through his feelings, and, although you may be hurt by such loyalty, try and see it as part of the separation process and his way of working through this.

Your son may need room to talk in order to clarify his situation and make sense of all that is going on around him. Melanie writes that her eight-year-old son once asked during a therapy session, 'Daddy told the man that you were his *strange* [estranged] wife, Mum. Why did he say that?' Counselling may provide an opportunity for you to iron out some misconstrued ideas that your son may have from a child's perspective.

- **Work with his father**

It is most important for your son to feel he can love his parents equally and in the way he wants, no matter what! This can be really difficult for either parent when tensions are high or feelings still raw and vulnerable. A father can react in many ways after the separation: many become depressed and take an all-or-nothing view. Some fathers will fight tooth and nail for residence rights to their son, but then absent themselves completely from his life when it is not granted. Some of these fathers completely close off, others hang in there but give very little to their sons. Some fathers can harbour resentment and be very careful not to give their son anything that would benefit the mother of their child; he may default on child support or refuse to buy anything for his son. Other fathers remain loving, committed and responsible, perhaps even more so than they were when they were in a relationship with their son's mother. They may take to this new challenge like ducks to water, and see it as an opportunity to forge a strong and close relationship with their son.

So many aspects of the parents' relationship can be mixed up with residence and contact. It can be difficult to work with the father when you have experienced a range of negative emotions about him. It can be harder still if his behaviour is immature, irresponsible and abusive. In some situations, particularly if there has been violence or abuse to you or your child, it may not be advisable or possible to work with the father. You may need to accept that there are contact arrangements, but that any other social discourse between the two of you is not possible.

If his father is unco-operative or uncommunicative, it may be useful to keep a communication diary. This can be passed from mother to father, and back, with contact handovers. It could include any information that needs to be passed on, such as medical appointments, medication that needs to be taken, school events, homework that needs to be completed, and so on. This can ensure that, even if a boy's parents can't talk, both are still aware of issues relevant to their son's wellbeing.

Whatever your situation, it is important that your son feels he does not have to take sides. It may take some time, but if you can put your own issues behind you and facilitate your son having a positive relationship with his father, you will be helping him enormously. Your son will feel supported and loved by both parents, and this makes it easier for him to discuss his feelings.

If your son's father is generally a good, responsible and caring father, it is helpful that your son knows you approve of and support contact. This will alleviate any guilt he feels about being disloyal to you by seeing his father.

Keeping in touch with dad

- **Establish predictable and regular times for contact**

Your son needs to know when he will see his father, whether it is daily, weekly or monthly. This is especially important as he gets older and needs to negotiate around other competing interests. It also means his father may be able to be involved in your son's extracurricular activities, such as sport or music. Enabling your son to have regular contact with his father means your son is more able to deal with his emotions, fears and fantasies. Predictability also gives him a sense of safety and security.

If you are able to maintain a good working relationship with your child's father, you will be more able to set common ground rules and limits and help your son to develop skills and communication to deal with the separation.

- **Negotiate**

If your child is very young when contact starts, he may not see his father as regularly or for long periods of time. But your son's needs and ability to handle contact will change as he grows older. In his teens he may want to chop and change the times he sees his father in order to fit in with social or other activities. It may not be possible for you to be flexible all the time, but try to ensure that there is ongoing contact with his father that fits with your son's developmental and personal needs. As your son gets older he will be able to take more responsibility for seeing his father; for example, he may be able to ride to his father's home on his bike, or ring his father whenever he wants.

It is also reasonable to set some limits on father contact; for example, you may not want your son ringing New Zealand every second night for an hour. But you, your son and his father should be able to negotiate a fair and equitable arrangement to facilitate contact with his father.

- **Reassure your son**

Finally, the important thing is that your son knows, above all, that you love him. It may take time and commitment to help your son through the process of separation, but he will emerge a stronger, more open and more sensitive boy.

Answers for kids who never see their fathers

Many children have never really known their fathers, nor will they have the chance to do this. It may be that their parents were not in a secure and committed relationship when the child was conceived, perhaps his father died or moved away when he was very young, or perhaps he was conceived through artificial insemination.

It can be difficult for mothers to decide what to tell their children about their father, and when. Wendy recalls:

> I was having a bit of a fling with Maurice after my relationship broke up, and I was surprised to find, when I got pregnant, that I really wanted to have the child. When I told Maurice, he just didn't want to know about it at all; he was really angry. I told him he could be part of the baby's life without being in a relationship with me, but he wasn't interested. Dylan is now seven, and is

asking a lot of questions about his father. The weird thing is that Maurice lives so close by, near Dylan's school. Sometimes we even walk past his house, but so far I've just told Dylan that his father went away and lives in Darwin. I can't bear to tell him his father lives so close by but doesn't want to see him.

Jo adds:

Max's dad lives in France; he has never lived with us. We do see him, but rarely. I do think it's lovely when you're on holidays and you see dads playing with their children. It hurts me that Max won't have that. I'm trying to provide a good life for him, and hope that when he's older he'll be able to see us in a positive light. I do expect him to ask, 'Why isn't my Dad here?' I do expect him to be angry with me, but I hadn't thought about this issue before he was born. He has a right to be angry, and I will tell him that I am sorry about the way the way things have turned out.

I never imagined myself being the mother of a boy, I thought it would always be a daughter. My opinion of men is low, but I won't let that influence my relationship with Max. I will expect lots of him and try to encourage him to turn into the sort of man I haven't experienced in the world — that is my challenge.

I'll do this by having clear expectations of his behaviour. I feel our relationship is good, and will continue to be so. I think this closeness will be our foundation of dealing with the world. It's founded on mutual respect. I respect him as a child, his height, his weight, his being a little person. I want him to respect my position as a mother, and that I'm doing the best for him.

Kelly faces another dilemma:

My children's father was really violent. We left South Australia to escape him. At first I thought it would be important for the children to have contact with him, even though he is so irresponsible and uses drugs and nearly murdered me. I thought, 'Well, a boy needs a father'. So Terry used to write to the children, but he would send them cards, writing things that really upset them like 'Daddy is so sad without his babies' and 'You are the most gorgeous boy. Try and make Mummy love me again', things that really upset them. He had beaten them when we lived together, and done horrendous things like killing their cat. But I still wasn't sure about contact. He didn't have our address, but he would send the presents and cards to my mother for the kids.

After I had counselling I decided that I wasn't going to let the children have contact with their father. I decided to put away all the things he sent them so that one day when they are older they could read them and decide for themselves. I think they get too traumatised and mixed up getting all these emotional pleas. And I have really noticed the difference. They have accepted that I decided not to live with their Dad because of his violence, and that he is living in another state. They are much more settled now they don't hear from him at all.

Jenny is the mother of four-year-old Alex. Jenny's partner left her when she was four months pregnant and she has not seen him since. She says:

It is difficult at times when I think that Alex hasn't had a father as a reference point in his life. But at least there are no custody issues. His father cannot adversely affect him either; so he is spared being told his mother is a bad mother, he's not able to mirror the bad habits of his father.

I'm sure there will be issues in relation to not seeing his father. I experience a sense of loss about that too. When he is older he may want to seek his Dad out — but his father has vanished, I think he is out of the country. He may need to understand the environment his father came from to better make sense about what his father did. I'd also like Alex to know some good things about his father.

At times he makes statements like 'I want to see my Daddy'. I assure him he has a daddy, but that some people's daddies don't live with them. I've also assured him it's not his fault. He seems to have accepted that.

I don't think it's really had any negative effects. I think it's more peer pressure that makes it hard, ands may impact on him as he gets older.

Mothers may feel that sons who never see their fathers may be at far more of a disadvantage than those who do, but children who have never had a father do not have to deal with issues of separation or ongoing custody disputes. In some ways their situation can be easier than for other sons who may have had a father who has disappeared from their lives entirely, never to be seen again. With their mother's love and support, however, they can sort through their emotions, and grow up happy and well adjusted.

Chapter 10

Creating Connections and Negotiating New Relationships

One of the most-often-heard concerns from sole mothers is how on earth they are going to find a male role model or father figure for their son when fathers are absent from their son's life. While no one would argue that it is not beneficial for boys to have contact with men, there is no evidence indicating that the only factor determining a boy's success in life is having a specific male role model. Research that has been undertaken on boys who grow up without male role models has not taken into account other factors that may influence a boy's development, such as financial situation, access to community resources, educational opportunities, relationship between the parents and social dislocation, to name a few. Indeed, most of the women interviewed in this book cite poverty and vastly reduced socioeconomic status as the most negative influence on childrearing.

Where did these ideas arise, and what other agendas generated their development? Consider how such strong ideas may also have adverse side-effects; for example, by encouraging mothers to stay in relationships where they are abused, or by inadvertently exposing their sons to paedophiles, or by negating a mother's own input and importance at the expense of procuring that holy grail — the male role model.

There are a number of social implications from focusing on a male role model to the exclusion of other issues. It means that the lack of fathering can be blamed for problems boys face, rather than a government taking responsibility for providing affordable childcare, adequately staffed and resourced schools, community networks and financial assistance and support for sole mothers. It means that the emphasis can be put on mothers to maintain marriages rather than end them. Often the cry for a male role model comes from more conservative or right-wing elements in our society who hold views that stress individual, rather than social, responsibility, and do not account for the historical changes which have occurred in family structure.

At times such views fit with the views of the 'moral minority' who declare that sole mothers are selfish, don't work hard enough to maintain relationships, that lesbian mothers are 'bad' for their children and that mothers who go it alone should not be entitled to welfare services. Advocates of such views often argue that services that are directed to women should be targeted elsewhere — to those in our society considered more 'deserving'.

Advocates of the male role model idea may cite so-called anthropological 'evidence' that describes how men in other cultures take a leading role in the parenting of boys once they get to a certain age. They may describe traditions where boys turn away and actually scorn their mothers when they reach puberty, or spend time with their mothers until they are six, before moving into the world of men and hunting. They give examples of where older men take boys out to undergo circumcision or ritualistic rites of passage. They cite the 'male as mentor' idea, and lament that white, Anglo-Saxon, industrialised society has lost this tradition. They often advocate reinventing such ceremonies for boys in our society, and taking them to special male ceremonies with drumming and ritualistic face- and body-painting.

However, we are no longer a tribal society taking boys out to fight against the wild. Our culture has changed so rapidly that these former practices are not relevant to the society in which we now live. Now there are new things for boys to fight:

drug and alcohol abuse, suicide and depression, school dropout, unemployment, loneliness and isolation. The traditional ways of organising society and gender relationships are not relevant to the issues faced by boys in today's society. Should mothers continue to let their newborn infant sons endure the pain of circumcision because that's the way it's always been? And what about other tribal practices that are not as enticing as the romanticised idea of initiation — such as clitoredectomy or infanticide? It does not necessarily make it okay to argue that traditional practices are 'naturally' acceptable.

We must explore new ways to help our children grow and thrive. It may be beneficial, fun and challenging for boys to spend a week walking through bushland and learning the skills of survival, but why see this as a gendered experience, and why not include girls in this activity? A number of youth programs run such retreats, and have found that both boys and girls experience an increased sense of self-worth and self-appreciation after undertaking such an adventure.

The idea of the male role model arose as a way to teach boys how to be males and how to adopt qualities of masculinity. Meagan raises the issue of male role models as an opportunity to discuss with sons what behaviours they would *not* like them to adopt; other mothers have also pointed out that they so much want their sons to be different from current models of masculinity that it is more helpful to discuss what they don't like, rather than what they do:

> When I look at the male role models I think more about what my boys will pick up that they won't want to be. I think of some of my own father's ways, and think how my sons might make decisions about what negative traits they don't want to adopt from their father. They often learn by observing the negative males in their lives. It's not the ideal, but in some ways it's more mature. At least you can talk about why they don't like some characteristics in certain males — or in women as well for that matter — and how they would rather be instead. My kids and I

will talk about what they like and don't like about certain males.

It's hard to keep a kid's self-esteem up without belittling his father, but self-respect is such an important thing. They work out for themselves what they do and don't like about their father's ways.

Many mothers, in fact, find it difficult to describe male role models they would like their sons to emulate. When they think about some politicians, footballers, TV stars and men they know in the community, often it is the so-called 'winners', the scammers, the sexist and racist Australians who are projected by the media as role models — not what mothers want their sons to be!

The belief that a male role model is necessary for boys to develop appropriately has sometimes led women to go against their gut instincts. Melanie explains:

> I spent some time building a relationship with the couple next door. He showed an interest in my boys, and was keen to spend time with them, and asked if they'd come over to play dice. This happened several times, and the boys enjoyed it, apart from the neighbour using bad language sometimes. I still weighed it up and kept my own standards with the boys about respectful language, and felt that it was great that the neighbour wanted to spend time with them — great, I thought, another male role model for them, without being someone I was having a relationship with.
>
> However, there was an incident where I left the children in his care for an hour, and he kicked my eight-year-old across the room and continued to kick him several times, swore at him and continued to kick him even after my other son, John, asked him to stop. It was the sort of story I'd read about but thought would never happen to my boys.
>
> On reflection I always felt uneasy about his bad language, and should have used this as a gauge. I would not have left the boys with women who spoke like this, but I made an allowance because I wanted male contact for my boys. However, I do not see such a pressing need now to leave the boys with a male role

model — I would rather they were with a woman if it felt safer to me.

What boys need is not more skills on how to be a testosterone-charged male but skills in how to relate to a generation of women who will not tolerate men needing to assert their dominance to feel sure of their place in the world. Women of today want a man who is self-sufficient and responsible, and one they can converse with, play with, plan with, and share a relationship based on principles of equality, rather than entitlement. Isolating boys from girls and women will not be helpful in achieving this. The feminist movement has encouraged women to break out of traditional stereotypes imposed by patriarchy, and now men must also break out from traditional male ways of being and doing, and explore other options. To not do this will only marginalise and isolate them further, not just from women and children but from each other.

This is not to say that it is not helpful or desirable for boys to have males in their lives. Of course the presence of a responsible, respectful, nurturing and positive male, who will take a devoted interest in your son, is advantageous. But many women ask, 'Where will I find such a man?' They wonder if this is the only thing that stands between normalcy and delinquency.

It would be worrying to see mothers putting much energy into finding such a man at the cost of relegating their own skills, strengths and resources. It is great that boys can be linked into sports, the arts, music and other activities where they have the chance (hopefully) to witness desired male behaviour. There are organisations like Big Brother and Big Sister that provide 'buddies' for children. What seems to be a real difference is not so much that sons are linked with male role models but that they are linked to communities of caring people so that they feel a sense of connection and belonging. Such communities may be your friends, the school, your son's friends and their families, a sports association, whatever gives him this positive sense of being part of a whole.

Laurel has been a sole mother for the whole of Sam's life. Sam is sixteen. She discusses the dilemma of knowing whether to encourage or discourage father contact when his father seems an unsuitable role model:

> Sam's contact with his father has been infrequent and mostly negative. Although his father has always been unsupportive I had the philosophical view that a boy needed to have a father. At times I've really regretted facilitating contact with his father, as his father seems to have cast a negative shadow over Sam — his father is cynical, smokes dope, and has the view that the world owes him. He hasn't worked since I've had Sam, because he would then have to pay maintenance. Sam has had to struggle with this aspect of his father.
>
> But then I have thought that if Sam hadn't had this contact he may have idealised his father, so I guess that Sam has grown up to see his father realistically and clearly. His father moved to New South Wales six years ago. Sam has sought out other men with whom to spend his time. He has two lovely friends whose parents are separated, and their fathers often take the three boys scuba diving or to the bush.
>
> I don't think it's necessarily male role models that boys need in their lives. It's an enormous threat to men for them to think that maybe they're not that important. It's more the involvement of good people. They need people with whom they can have an honest and open relationship. My best friend, Beth, is a midwife, and delivered Sam. She has always seen him at least once a week, and has regularly taken him away on holidays.
>
> I'm Sam's role model. I belong to the first generation of women who've had freedom of choice and that must have extraordinary implications for our sons. We can now have bank loans, own property, work, have children outside of marriage and study. Surely this will mean our sons will grow up with a different view of women from their fathers.

New relationships

A study in 1989 found that Australian men are three times as likely as women to repartner after marriage breakdown.[1] One reason for this is that women most often find themselves 'tied down' with children, while men are freer to find another partner. In addition, men may find it harder to be alone because they are dependent on women to meet their emotional and social needs. In 1999 more women (50 per cent) than men (31 per cent) lodged applications for divorce; 19 per cent of divorce lodgements were joint applications.[2] It is also interesting that, in most couple breakups, the woman initiates the breakup. Men are more willing to stay in a relationship that isn't 'working' than go it alone. Perhaps they have fewer expectations in their relationships than women. Some women report that their partners are completely baffled when told their partners are not happy with the relationship; many men had no idea that anything was 'wrong'.

Many sole mothers laugh at the suggestion of a new relationship. 'How could I possibly manage that?' they say. 'With the children's schooling, extracurricular activities, lack of money, no babysitter and my own work, it would never be possible. Besides, who'd want to take on all that?' Some sole mothers cannot imagine that a man without children would want to take on a sole mother with one, let alone three.

But many sole mothers do have lasting and meaningful relationships, and it may be helpful to challenge ideas that block off such opportunities.

Melanie's story supports this idea.

> I have had to challenge my belief that a man without children will not want to enter into a relationship with someone who has children. My belief has been that it would be best to keep the relationships quite separate. However, you may meet someone who does not have children of their own and some men don't want the responsibility of having their own children, but this

does not mean that the relationship would not work. In fact, a woman with boys may be ideal for him. He can enjoy the fact that his partner has already fulfilled her maternal needs, he has some input with the children to the degree he is willing or able, and he can really be there to love you and support you without the complication of having his own children.

It is interesting to listen to men's (other than their fathers') views on raising boys, and to acknowledge that, no matter who you are in a relationship with, there will always be different views and conflicts around how the parenting should be done. After parenting alone for some time it is easy to become set in your ways over the raising of your boys, and much can be learnt about yourself and your children by having a third party come in and give his opinion. It is not always easy but it is useful.

Surprising as it sometimes seems, sole mothers do get to have other relationships. Sometimes these can be radical changes from the past, such as those women who choose to have relationships with other women. Loneliness seems to be part and parcel of the sole-mother experience, particularly when children are younger and it may be more difficult to get out and meet people. But you never know when you will meet someone else — at the school, at a doctor's surgery, on a train, through returning to study or work. Don't discount the possibility (if that is what you hope for) — life is full of small miracles!

Women are often concerned about how a new relationship will impact on their children. Mothers of sons often worry that their son will feel displaced and abandoned, or reject her and turn to his father. They worry that his 'masculinity' will be damaged. It is true that the introduction of a new partner can be a big adjustment for children, particularly if they are nearing or in their teenage years, and if they have lived for some time without a male presence in the house. If their father is still unattached, they may feel sorry for him and 'act out' on the mother. They may also have secret hopes of their parents reuniting, and Mum's new relationship may dash these hopes. Boys may feel intolerant of another male joining the household, usurping Dad's role, but also their own, as 'head of the household'.

Tracy says:

> I'm hesitant about having another relationship, because on one level I don't want anyone to intrude on our dynamic. I know it would alter it, that Samuel would feel silenced, and I would mourn the loss of our close communication.
>
> I have had relationships, but I'm conscious of not letting men stay the night. I'm conscious that I'm a role model to him, of how I present to him and how I present the idea of relationships.

Ask yourself:

- How might having another person involved in our lives be enriching for our family?
- How can I introduce my partner to my children in a way that lessens any negative impact this may have?
- What are the positive factors for me having a relationship at this point of time in my son's development?
- How can having a new relationship strengthen the relationship I already have with my son?
- How can having this new relationship offer my son opportunities that he would not have if I were to remain alone?
- What will he learn about communication, loving and caring if I am in a relationship?
- What else could he learn?
- How could my being in a new relationship teach him about how I'd like him to be in his relationships with women?

Children may resent their parents resuming their social lives after a separation. Melanie's experience reflected this:

> I've tried new relationships, and my boys put up resistance — they find it a threat to them and their Dad. They become quite territorial. I dated Tony for six months. I started off not introducing him to the boys. He had two boys of his own and it worked out that we both had them for the same weekends, so introduced them.
>
> There were a few teething problems, but nothing too major until Tony decided to show physical affection towards me in front of the boys. I felt uneasy about it, and told him that I didn't want him to hold and kiss me around the boys. Tony felt very strongly the other way, and convinced me that as my ex-husband and I hadn't had a loving affectionate relationship in recent years that it would be good for the boys to see us being openly affectionate.
>
> Well, Thomas wouldn't let me touch him or kiss him for quite some time after this. When I went to kiss him goodnight he would hide under the covers and say, 'No, you've got Tony breath', and 'You love *him* now and you don't love me. How can you love us both?'
>
> The next time that I introduce the boys to a potential partner I will make sure that I sit on the couch with my boys and that he sits on the chair. One of my boys didn't really have a problem with the relationship, but the one that did was really traumatised by the whole prospect of me being with another man. He took it as a rejection not only of him, but of his natural father as well. After having this unsuccessful relationship, where I introduced my new partner to the boys, I have taken to having clandestine relationships when the boys are not around.

Thinking about how you are going to introduce your new partner to your son is important. Usually, and at times in spite of themselves, boys do get to like and at times love, the new man in their mother's life. If you don't have much of a break from your children, it can be tricky when your new partner is immediately placed in a position of having to be involved with your children from the outset. It is better if possible to involve them in daytime activities where you can introduce your new man as a friend, and show a degree of affection, but don't overdo it. If at all possible, try to spend time alone with your new partner until you are sure that the relationship is going to continue. It can be confusing for children to see a succession of potential partners come and go in your life.

It is important to be open about what you are doing, and to acknowledge to your son that this may be difficult for him. Let him know that you have no expectations that this new man will replace his Dad, that his father will always be his father, but the new partner may become a friend in time. Sometimes the myth of the male role model may convince women to tell their sons that this will be their new daddy, and they may even tell their sons to call him 'Daddy'. While a small boy may adapt to this, it can be confusing if he is not aware that he does have a biological father and as he grows older he discovers that 'Dad' is, in fact, not his father. Separate out what is your longing for a family situation and what is going to help your son get on in his life. Of course, he may want to call your partner Dad in his own time, but let him work that out.

Tell him that you hope he and your new partner will get on, but don't expect that they will, at least immediately. Make sure that your son is still being given attention and not feeling left out.

Boys can be embarrassed or upset if they know their mother is sleeping with another man. They may feel this betrays their father, or feel embarrassed at having to think about their mother as a sexual person. If they are feeling distressed by a new man in the house, they may act in a negative way towards him. When sons are reaching adolescence, any displays of sexual behaviour, even behind closed doors, heightens their awareness of their own sexuality.

It is healthy for them to see adults being affectionate, but not appropriate that they see overtly sexualised behaviour. If they see their father on visitation, it may be appropriate to begin your new sexual relationship while the children are away, and gradually introduce the idea of him staying the night with you. Don't ask their permission for this; just tell them, 'Oh, Steven is staying tomorrow night.'

A boy needs to know that no one will ever replace your love for him. Tell your children that they are number one, but that you are really happy to have another adult to cuddle, to give you special attention, and to do adult things with. Your partner can be gradually introduced to family events, and you may wish to consult with your son about bringing him to special family occasions. Not that this means he will always have the final say, but initially this may be useful.

It can be difficult trying to maintain a new relationship. As a sole parent you may not have much time alone from the children at all, and may need to pay a babysitter every time you wish to go out. Finding time alone is hard, and children may make this more difficult if they are feeling under threat or jealous of the 'invader'.

Laurel speaks of her experience;

> I have had relationships. The hardest was when I lived with someone who really wanted to take on a kind of parenting relationship with Sam. Sam was nine years old at the time. This man didn't have children, and I don't think he understood nor could deal with the close relationship I had with Sam. Sam found it hard because this man wanted to take on a father role, and he also felt threatened by another man being around.
>
> I did have a relationship with a woman, which really was the easiest relationship for Sam to deal with — he didn't feel the need to compromise for another man. This woman stayed overnight a lot, and Sam was fine about it. I remember when he was twelve, and he said to me, 'So, you're going to be a lesbian, are you?' and then he asked, 'Does she love you then?'

Another day he hopped into my bed in the morning, and he had his water pistol with him. He said, 'You're under arrest. I'm the Tasmanian police.'

When your new male partner visits, or if he moves in, it is important that he takes things slowly and does not rush into the role of substitute father. Ask him to stand back for a while and let you continue to parent as you have done in the past. The best way he can get involved with your family is through playing with them, chatting, seeming interested in their activities, and helping them out rather than taking any authoritarian role at this stage. Often family issues arise because a new partner has attempted to act as a parent too soon.

If your son is unco-operative and overly rude and this continues over time so that it disrupts your relationship, you may have to forgo being reasonable, and insist that he behave politely and appropriately. Expect some resistance to your repartnering, but not to the extent that you are continually thwarted in your attempts to engage in a new relationship.

Sometimes boys who have been exposed to domestic violence, or have ideas of male entitlement over their mothers, may prove more difficult in accepting a new relationship. They need to be told firmly that this is what you are going to do, and that there will be limits set on rude and disruptive behaviour. Your son can be told he is not expected to like or love this person but is expected to respond within the boundaries of politeness and civility that you would expect him to with any one else. If he continues this unwanted behaviour, then you will need to stop this by putting in place consequences and limits. He needs to know that you have the right to pursue a new relationship, and that it is not his place to condemn or condone this. He will feel safer for having this straightened out.

Most of the family units in Australian society today consist of 'blended families'. Meagan is the mother of Alex

(16), Lewis (13) and Emily (10), and her youngest daughter Georgia (3). Georgia's father, Paul, has been in a relationship with Meagan for four years. Meagan reveals the complexities of a blended family:

> I think it's difficult. If the kids see their father, Paul can feel disempowered about his fathering role. He doesn't take a major role as a father to the three oldest children, but will tell Alex not to be rude to me at times. Basically he leaves me to sort it out, and that's what seems to work best and what I prefer.
>
> Sometimes it's horrible. You feel stuck in the middle between the children and your new partner. It's particularly hard because I'm dealing with an adolescent. Part of me thinks, 'Thank God he butted out'. But another part thinks, 'Thank God he's here.' Sometimes I get so confused about what stand to take among it all. I have to say, 'Give me half an hour to think about it', then I go for a breather to give me time to think. A lot of the time Paul is more objective about the older children, but then again he doesn't have the subjective passion that I have about them. I have that passion, and I think that's important.
>
> Paul is more of a friend to the three oldest children. Alex sees him as a nerdy adult: they are not buddies, but he does tell Paul stuff because he knows he won't get a lecture — not like his mother who would take a moral ground. Paul has a valuable contribution to make — he gives sound advice without being emotionally overloaded. He does get frustrated, but leaves me to deal with it. I don't want to be the meat in the sandwich, but I don't want Paul to overstep the mark or be in an authority position.
>
> It's funny because some of Alex's habits are the ones that mirror mine — being sarcastic and a smart arse. I can despair with Alex, whereas Paul is more tolerant. He is used to it from me, I guess! He can bite his tongue, or will say 'Alex, that is rude'. Sometimes I try and outsmart Alex, but usually I argue back or go outside. I will tell him he has gone too far and that his words are undeserving. I tell him he needs to apologise to me.

Roslyn talks about her experience:

Before I started living with Warren, Leigh's father was in England for two years, and I lived with another man, David. It was very traumatic for Leigh when David and I broke up because David had been like a father to him. He was full of grief, and angry with both of us. David just stepped out of our lives and disappeared. We never saw him again.

When Warren and I got together he was separated from his partner, and they had two children. Leigh was five at the time. So

Leigh's stepbrother and sister would visit on weekends. His stepsister was a year older than Leigh. He had a stepbrother who was four years older than him.

I'm still in a relationship with Warren, his stepfather. Both children had their own traumas to deal with, and Leigh had to adjust to this change of having a new man in his life and two new children. The children really stuck together and excluded Leigh. I was enormously protective of Leigh, who was given such a hard time by his stepsiblings, especially his stepbrother. They saw him as the outsider. I wouldn't recommend a stepfamily to anyone.

Blended families seem to be a continuing trend as marriages break down and repartnering occurs. It may be tricky negotiating this change, but it can be a positive and enriching experience for all involved. Don't deny yourself this.

Chapter 11

Combining Sole Parenting with Paid Employment

All mothers work! It is just that some are paid for the work they do and get to work outside the home. Most sole mothers work for financial security (it is extremely difficult to exist on the Sole Parent Pension), and others work because working gives them an added sense of identity and self-worth.

Roslyn has been a sole mother since her son Leigh was six months old. Now in her forties, she is working in a community health centre as a co-ordinator. She talks about the experience of being a sole mother and the difficulties of working:

> Even though Leigh wasn't aware of what was going on at the time, it was still difficult. His father left me to go and live with another woman, and he was reluctant to have access for the first six months. I also had difficulty giving him access because of the circumstances of the separation — I was totally devastated! He literally went off on a business trip and never came back. I felt deeply shocked, angry and suicidal. In a way Leigh gave me a reason to keep on living.
>
> We then lived on the outskirts of Melbourne, and he left me

with an unreliable car. We went to live at my parents' house for a few months, and then when Leigh was about seven months old I got a night duty job nursing. Mum was able to look after Leigh.

Within a few months I was in fulltime work and Leigh was in fulltime creche. It was extremely difficult juggling fulltime work and a baby, particularly when he became ill. It was very hard waking up at night for him — I would be so tired. I had a very strong work ethic and felt I should be out there working rather than being at home with Leigh.

It was difficult after I moved out from my parents' house and into shared accommodation. I moved three times in three years, and the people I lived with did not have children and gave me no support whatsoever. Also my husband went back to study, and took me to court to argue that he couldn't afford to pay maintenance. He won!

There was a part of me that had an expectation that Leigh would have to fit into my life. Although we didn't have a lot of time together, we were really close and had quality time. I'd take him everywhere with me so he got to meet lots of people and be in different situations.

I remember once being so upset at a dinner party because a woman criticised me for leaving him at creche. She told me I wasn't a good mother. That's always stayed with me, but I still believe I had no choice other than to work fulltime to provide for both of us.

Working may give a mother the opportunity to meet people and to enjoy mental stimulation, and it gives her a break from the children. But it also brings extreme tiredness, pressure and guilt.

The roles that women play in our society have changed immeasurably. Where women were once expected to stay home, at least until the children started school, they are now expected to contribute towards the finances. Going back to paid work means that a woman changes her role from 'carer' to 'provider'. Doing this may mean she may be torn in many directions, and is forced to compromise her beliefs and ideals. She may have to drop the children at school earlier than she would like or leave them unsupervised after school for a short period. One income does not allow the earning power to pay for the appropriate help that couples working could afford. When she goes back to work for the first time, often the children will complain about the extra work for them and the breakdown of normal routine.

It is helpful for a boy to see his mother working, whether in a paid or voluntary capacity. He is inculcated with a work ethic — that working is a normal, everyday routine expected of adults. He sees his mother providing for her family — rather than being dependent on male or government support — and he sees that women are competent and professional. Having a working mother is good role modelling for boys.

Despite the benefits of working, both for mothers and their sons, many mothers report feeling burdened by guilt. Guilt may lead to mothers having almost impossible expectations of themselves — that you should be able to go to work, cook for your children, read with them and help them do their homework, bathe and bed them, cook a cake for the cake stall and attend Saturday's school working bee! You expect that you should be able to do all this, and you feel you are letting your children down if you can't. You may feel guilty because you work but still cannot provide the things that your son wants. You feel guilty that the separation means a change from a life that was relatively simple to one that is hectic, exhausting and gives you far less time to be with your children, let alone your own social networks. The expectations coupled mothers may have are unrealistic if you are a sole parent. You still need to be able to have fun with your children, and feel good enough about yourself to be able to parent effectively. Just do what you can.

> ### Ask yourself:
>
> - Where do the ideas that I should be able to do all these things come from?
> - How can I increase the school supports available to sole mothers, either in paid or unpaid work?
> - What difference might it make to my son's view of me as a mother, and women in general, if he sees me financially supporting us?
> - How might my having a career influence his own attitude to school and work?

Mothers' employment does seem to protect children from some of the educational impact of divorce. The 1997 Western Australian Child Health Survey showed that children living with mothers who worked fulltime before their divorce showed less negative effect on their schooling. Boys whose mothers are working may be better able to make a link between schooling and future employment and career aspirations. The survey also found that 39 per cent of students whose lone parent was not employed showed low academic competence, compared to 22 per cent among students whose lone parent was employed.[1]

Although we may not want our boys to turn into rampant capitalists or consumers, the way that our society operates means there is a link between acquiring goods and enjoying a certain lifestyle and self-worth.

Yet there is a double bind here, particularly for sole mothers who say they are blamed for leaving their children in childcare from a young age, or alternatively blamed for relying on government assistance if they are not in paid work. In addition, even where a father or partner is present, the woman still does the majority of housework and childcare.

Melanie writes that:

> I feel historically society has needed a scapegoat. In medieval times it was witches, and now it is sole mothers. I think the whole definition of work needs to change — it's defined by paid income. The work mothers do is not counted as work, even though it may be the hardest you've ever worked in your life. When sole fathers are mentioned it's in heroic terms. I do admire them, but sole mothers aren't recognised for what they have to experience.

It is almost a luxury for sole mothers to be able to find jobs that fit with their children's needs, fit the hours they would like, are interesting and pay well.

One of the most difficult issues about being a working mother is that you are on your own. You're the one who has to deal with no food in the house, not having a babysitter for that late-night meeting, needing to take the cat to the vet, wondering what you'll do if your son's bronchitis gets worse but you have to see that client tomorrow.

Being a sole working mum can be like living on a knife-edge — there is just no room for any flexibility in the tight schedule of a working week. Many mothers are anxious about work performance. They worry that their employers will have less confidence in them because they have to meet their children's needs so they feel they must try extra hard and be extra impressive.

Mothers may find it difficult to concentrate at work if they are not assured of their son's safety, wellbeing and happiness. Tracy, mother of eleven-year-old Samuel, says,

> I work in the mental health field. It's distracting having to be there to pick up Samuel after school — my attention is elsewhere. I've made a decision not to work fulltime because I'm conscious of not wanting to be absent in Samuel's life. I'm conscious of not robbing Samuel of his childhood. Because I work I'm also conscious of incorporating close times together,

like sitting down and having a hot chocolate or preparing meals together.

I do notice in working with clients with children of my own age that I can feel burdened dealing with emotionally fraught situations like neglect. I find it difficult to separate work from my own situation.

Sole mothers may also feel a huge lack of emotional support. At times life can seem so unbearable, so exhausting, and there is no one to off-load to, to share the intricacies of your day, and to give you a little moral support.

Jane, a lawyer and mother of twin teenage boys, comments:

It's exhausting working fulltime. It used to be three days before I graduated, and I miss that period after school when I'd be there and we'd talk. Now I get home and they want dinner, and then it's homework time. But by the time dinner's done you don't have a lot of energy to listen. You finally get to bed, go to sleep, then get up, and it's the same thing again.

At least when I do get to bed it's my own time, and I don't have to worry about some man wanting sex with me.

But I think it's important that boys see women working. They develop a work ethic and see people making their place in the world. I think children need a role model who's out there achieving — if it's not in a fathered situation, it should be the mother. Children should see women contributing as part of the economy. Boys shouldn't be protective of their mothers; they should see that their mothers can look after themselves. You need to relieve them of the responsibility of looking after you; you need to show them it's not their job to provide for you economically or with friendship.

Support systems

One vital thing that can help you as a sole mother deal with work issues is to develop a strong support system. This may be easier said than done, particularly if your child's father does not assist in this way. Having a support system will not only be helpful for you but will also enable your child to feel connected with others.

Often sole mothers meet through preschool or school and become lifelong friends and part of a caring network for women and their children. Sole mothers may take turns picking up the children from school, week on, week off, or having them on a Saturday so you can get some rest. A sole mother who is not working might take care of your son in return for a day or two off herself at the weekend.

Other sole working mothers can be a great source of support. At least they know what it's like to be struggling on one income.

If you are lucky, your parents may be available to help. This can be a fantastic arrangement that benefits both grandparents, who get to spend time with their beloved grandson, and you, who will be relaxed that he is with caring, dedicated people. Grandparents may feel a little overwhelmed to have your son every day you work, and this is understandable, particularly as they get older, but even some occasional involvement is helpful.

Jan, who parented two boys and two girls while working, says:

> When I was working and the children were little, there were times I was so tired that I reached a point of exhaustion where I'd have to leave my kids with my mother in order to go away and physically rest. But I would literally have to work to make sure we could eat.
>
> I'd always make sure I was accessible to them — they'd be able to drop into work, and they had my phone number. When the kids were old enough to stay alone at home, we talked about safety rules, we joined the Safety House scheme, and always had emergency phone numbers beside the phone. I put in a number of practical strategies — smoke detectors, a neighbour on hand if I was going to be late, other friends or friends of the children where we supported each other, and at times, when I could afford it, a mobile phone.

•

And sometimes I'd just pray that my children would be safe. There'd be lots of planning about who'd be where, where and when they'd be picked up, and who they'd be with.

It was when I also chose to go back to study that my two children got into 'bad' peer groups. I was pushing it too much, and lost touch with what my children were doing. At this point my relationship also ended. There was just too much stress.

There are a number of practical suggestions, as Jan mentions, that can be helpful in ensuring your child's safety. It can be difficult for you as a sole working mother to know when it's okay to leave your son at home alone and when he should be still connected with external services such as afterschool care or a youth centre. This can be particularly perplexing at school holiday times, or when your son decides he is big enough to look after himself. There is also a risk that an unsupervised boy will get into trouble if left too much to his own devices and not adequately supervised.

If your school has an afterschool program it is probably better that he goes there, at least for the majority of the week, than to go home alone. Or perhaps he could go to a friend's home or to neighbours by arrangement. Most local councils have school holiday programs that are subsidised. It's also safer if he goes to such a program rather than spending days at home alone.

Sometimes it is too costly or difficult to enrol your son in a program. He may also decide he just is not going to go any more. You can try and negotiate with him so that maybe he goes three days a week and spends two days at home alone. It's probably easier to wean him off going to programs that he views as for 'little kids' than let him make a drastic change to totally discontinue.

One concern if boys are alone is that they can be drawn into trouble because of isolation and boredom. They may gather in groups and hang out in shopping malls, or decide to smoke or drink. Boys left alone at home with a computer may stray to sites on the internet that are unsuitable, particularly violent and sexually explicit sites.

If your son is staying at home alone you can put some strategies in place so that he is safe and still has some sense of being supervised. These may include:
- your son agreeing to ring you if he is going elsewhere
- having some type of a plan for his day — it isn't helpful for him to just stay home and watch TV or play computer games, so you could organise that he cooks dinner, does the shopping or reads a chapter of a book or does some of his school project so that his day has some structure
- your son being at home at a certain time so that you can ring him
- arranging for him to spend half the day home alone and the other half with a relative or friend
- allowing him to hang out with friends, but needing to specify when he is going with them, where, what time he'll return, and what he'll be doing — hanging out in shopping malls or parks is not safe if it encompasses the whole day, so he may hang out for two hours and then his friend could come over to play for another two hours
- installing a computer package that minimises your son accessing violent or pornographic material

Your son as support

Many working sole mothers find that their sons need to take on additional responsibility in the home. Sometimes this is necessary in order to make sure things are ready for school and everyone is fed, and sometimes mothers want to ensure their sons also contribute to the household and family unity.

You certainly shouldn't be picking up after your son when you have just come in from a long day's work. A schoolaged boy should know to put his schoolbag in his room, and the lunch box in the sink when he gets home from school. He can also help by picking up after himself, washing and drying dishes, and doing other household chores that will help you.

Older children can take far more responsibility, such as doing the washing, cooking dinner, cleaning and mowing the lawn. This responsibility will be welcomed by their future partner, and will teach him to consider others.

Supporting yourself

If you are feeling overwhelmed and exhausted, write a list of what you need to do, then prioritise those that are absolutely essential (like shopping) and those that can be done later (like mowing the lawn). You may decide that Thursday night will be your takeaway food night — at least this takes the stress off cooking for one night. Or perhaps Friday night can be 'no bath' night.

Many mothers prioritise their housework. This depends on how stressed you'll get if it's not done, but many a sole working mother I know laughingly comments on that attractive green fungus growing in the fridge or the interesting bacterial culture in the shower — it can help your son with his biology studies! Compare notes with your friends or share the chores (e.g. ironing, shopping, gardening, sewing, etc.) with a friend. If a messy house is going to save you from insanity, go for the messy house.

Mothers cannot survive without some form of respite. You need a break to be with other adults (outside of work), to relax and to wind down. Think about doing something for yourself. This can take priority over being on the school committee. Other better-resourced and supportive parents can do that work just as well as you can. If you feel strongly about a school issue or policy, you can give your opinion and influence through letter writing or phone calls.

Your weekends are also precious, and it may be that guilt tries to prevent you from using this time for yourself and your son. Remember that the housework, the school fete, the garden, will always be there, but your son will only be young for a short time. Choose him, yourself and your relationship over other commitments.

Stress

One underrated activity that helps you make a stand against stress is exercise. If you can do a quick power lap round the block before or after work, you are likely to get those endorphins going and feel a whole lot more relaxed.

You can also tackle stress by tackling those two enemies of mothers, guilt and perfectionism.

> ### Ask yourself:
>
> ◆ How is perfectionism trying to talk me into doing the impossible?
> ◆ Do perfectionism and guilt help my son to feel happy in his relationship with me, or do they undermine it?
> ◆ What would my son notice about the influence of perfectionism and guilt on my life?
> ◆ In what ways does guilt try to dictate how I parent my son?
> ◆ How is it able to gain a hold on my life?
> ◆ What strengths and knowledge do I now have that I didn't have when I was with my partner, that I can utilise now in my stand against guilt and perfectionism?
> ◆ What would be different about being a working sole mother if the influence of guilt and perfectionism was dramatically reduced?

If you are a working mother, spending time with your son, getting to know him and what he enjoys are really important. You have to make time to be with him to really get to know his good points and to be proud of him. When working fulltime, you can fall into a trap of having less energy for him so you end up spending more materially on him. What he would really benefit from is your time. One way is by reading to him, even when he is a teenager. This costs nothing, and doesn't require huge amounts of energy.

If you enjoyed work before having your son, then

continuing to work is often important for your self-esteem and socialisation. Accept that work is a part of your life and that you would grieve without it. No matter what pressures you may have from others, do not feel guilty about wanting to work. Just be creative about making it work for you and your son.

Children are extremely resilient. Not only do they recover from separation but also they adapt to changes in household routine. Not having a mother at home for their every beck and call means sons may develop a sense of self-reliance and independence they would not have otherwise.

Chapter 12

Being Open about Sexuality

Sexuality is not something that starts when children reach adolescence. It is there in a variety of forms in tiny babies. Young boys may enjoy holding their penis — both for comfort and because it feels good (or if you are a Freudian, because they are worried it will be cut off!). Little girls also touch their vagina. Children enjoy the touch of skins, the smell of their mother, and being cuddled and kissed.

Many mothers of sons report feeling perplexed and overwhelmed when faced with talking to their son about sex, dealing with specific male issues such as toilet training, and finding the means to communicate about sex. They may feel confused about the obvious physical difference between boys and women, and how to address this in ways that encourage mother/son intimacy but maintain respectful and healthy 'boundaries' in their relationships.

Many of the questions mothers ask about sexuality relate to the timing of information. Some of the questions they raise about sexuality and their sons include:

- How do you look after a penis?
- Should I get my son circumcised?

- How and when should I start toilet training? Is it all right if he sits on the toilet?
- When should I stop taking him to the women's toilets (I don't want to give him an identity complex)?
- Is it okay if he sees me naked?
- Is it okay if he still sleeps with me? At what age should he sleep separately?
- He likes to touch my breasts; is this normal? Is this okay? At what age should I stop it?
- Should I find a male to tell him about sex, or get his father to do it?
- How should I tell him about sex?
- What should I tell him about sex?
- When should I tell him about sex?
- Should I tell him about menstruation and about women's sexuality and body parts? When should I do this?
- Should I discuss sexual identity? What if he's gay? When should I do this?
- How will I deal with pornography, particularly when he's surfing on the Net?
- What will I do when he has 'wet dreams'?
- How can I help him to be respectful towards women?
- How can I teach him to see sex as something natural and not smutty?
- When should I tell my son about sexually transmitted diseases (STDs)?
- At what age should I buy my son condoms?

Circumcision

Except for religious and cultural customs, there is no reason to have your son circumcised. Circumcision is a painful and hygienically unnecessary procedure. Some families continue to have their son circumcised in the belief that he will feel more 'normal' if he looks like his father. Most boys, other than Jewish and Muslim boys, are not circumcised. Seek advice from a maternal and child health centre nurse or your doctor if you are unsure about this decision.

Toileting

You can easily teach your little boy to stand and hold his penis when urinating. It isn't such a big deal, and the majority of boys, even those raised by sole mothers, will observe other males toileting in the 'male' way. If your little boy is urinating sitting down, that's fine; he will eventually see other boys standing, and do the same. Or you can tell him that boys stand up to wee, and show him how to hold his penis. Easy!

Some mothers worry about whether to take their sons with them to female toilets. Unfortunately it can be risky to let younger boys go into a male public toilet alone. Some female public toilets have signs saying at what age you can take your son in with you. If he is too old, then it is best that you explain you will wait outside the male toilets and that he can yell out or quickly walk away if anyone does something that makes him uncomfortable or threatens him. It's important to brief your son on his 'early warning signs', and to reassure him that most public toilets are safe, but that sometimes there are 'yucky' people who may try and hurt him, or ask him to do unpleasant things. It is better to be realistic than to pretend these things don't happen. Always encourage boys to go to the toilets together if they are out without an adult. Most primary schools now have policies to ensure that children always go to the toilets in pairs.

Masturbation

Why do boys play with their penis? Because they can. A penis is a very obvious thing. It feels good to touch it and fondle it. Often boys will enjoy doing this in the bath, while watching television on the couch, or while they are reading, and lots of other times too! There is absolutely nothing wrong with this.

A mother's role in all of this is to teach boys to become a little more discreet about doing this as they get older. Men don't masturbate less, they just don't do it so overtly!

As your son gets older, say five or six, you might say to him that it's okay to touch himself and you know it feels nice, but that it's something to do in private, like in the bath or in his room. Some people may say that boys masturbate because they get too much love and attention from their mothers, but never let such unfounded beliefs get in the way of being physically affectionate to your son. There is a vast difference between affection and nurturing, and sexualising the relationship with your son.

You may worry that your son yanks and twists his penis, and wonder if he will injure himself. A penis is a strong organ, think of what it has to experience! A boy will not purposely hurt his genitals. If you are worried, speak with a doctor or a maternal and child health centre nurse.

Mother/son boundaries

In some cultures sons sleep with their mothers or both parents until the boys are adolescents. This differs from ideas in Western society, which usually aim to separate a boy's sleeping patterns from his mother's as soon as possible. Boy babies are often physically separated from their mothers by putting them in a bassinet or cot sooner than girls. In addition, girl babies seem to be breastfed longer than boy babies. There is no right way to decide how old a boy should be when he stops sleeping with his mother. At times of stress it may be comforting for your son to crawl into Mum's bed, but obviously this is more appropriate to occur at age seven than at age fourteen. Don't worry that physical closeness and prolonged breast-feeding is unhealthy or will feminise your son.

One way of deciding about mother/son boundaries is to ask yourself who most enjoys having a sleeping, warm body beside them, you or him? How might your decisions about boundaries impact on your son, and at what age is it appropriate for boundaries to shift? Your son may enjoy your naked body when he is a baby, but when older may feel embarrassed or uncomfortable with seeing you naked. He may love putting his hand down your dress to feel your breasts when he is two, but this behaviour would be problematic if it continued at age eight.

Laurel says:

> Sole mothers struggle more with letting their sons go off into the world, especially if there is only a mother and her son. It is a huge temptation for a mother to draw in her son to become a partner. At times it's very hard to resist putting him into that space; for example, to have him sleeping in your bed.
>
> Sole mothers need to give up wanting their son's touch — to let them go. Even now I want to rub my son's gorgeous tummy, but I know that's not appropriate. Sam regularly slept in my bed until he was eight. Even if he gets sick now I might lie with him in his bed for a while — but I think that is caring, not at all a sexual or wrong thing to do.
>
> Dealing with him leaving home will be a challenge. It will be interesting to see how he goes about moving out and establishing himself.

At times your son will ask you questions. Then it is relevant for you to answer them with as much complexity as is age appropriate. Generally speaking, give simpler information to a younger boy, up to the age of ten, but ensure that he knows he can ask more in-depth questions and seek further information, as he needs it.

Not talking about sex will not mean your son is shielded from sexual issues. He will pick up knowledge about sex from the media and from his peers. Similarly, not talking about contraception or safe sex will not mean he won't have sex; it just puts him more at risk. And talking about sexual identity or homosexuality will not make him gay — after all, think about all the gay men and lesbians raised by heterosexual parents.

It might be helpful for you, as his mother, to sort out your own ideas and attitudes about men and sexuality. The following ideas are myths which may impact on a mother's role in shaping her son's sexuality:

- Men need to have sex more than women do. This may vary in individual relationships, depending on the age of the adults and their individual attitudes to sex. Most women love sex — there is just intense social stigma in admitting it.
- All men love pornography. Pornography varies in degrees — some men like it, others, particularly those who are respectful of women, find hard-core pornography distasteful, especially that which humiliates women and suggests abuse and violence.
- Men don't need affection or caring in sex, they just want straight-out sex. This is another macho myth — men, like women, enjoy sensuality, affection and intimacy. The male peer group may frown on men who express their vulnerability but men need love and affection, as do women. Some men need to be trained to be sensual, erotic and to see sex as more than just penis/vagina contact. Both women and men experience lust, and sex for sex's sake.
- A mother is not important in shaping her son's views of women, relationships and sexual identity, only another man can do this. Mothers are in an excellent position to offer their views on relationships and sexuality, particularly in helping their sons experience physical closeness and open communication.

If mothers hold these ideas, then they may feel that they cannot offer their son much in the way of sexual development. Both fathers and mothers can impact on their son's sexual development. It is great if your son has another trusting male to talk to, but do not think that you are not able to fulfil this role!

Eroticism versus pornography

Many mothers rightly fear the harmful effect pornography may have on their sons, particularly if it is violent and sadistic. Melanie tells of one incident, and how she was able to use it in a constructive way to explore her sons' ethics and attitudes in relation to pornography:

> I remember vividly when I moved in to a house that had been tenanted, and the previous tenants had left some explicit pornographic magazines in the garage, which my boys found. I was very distressed when I found the boys hovering over them laughing, and then asking me if this is what people do when they have sex. At the time they were only five, seven and nine years old. Of course, they had lots of questions, and I went about answering them as best I could. Because they saw pictures of oral sex, group sex, sex using objects, etc., I was put in a position of having to explain the difference between loving, intimate sex between two people who cared about each other and pornography.
>
> Naturally they shared their experience with as many people as they could tell, which helped to add to my anxiety. However, although they were exposed to this at a very young age, and I really wish they hadn't been, they were no doubt going to confront it at some stage, so at least they were at an age where I knew about it and had an opportunity to have my say.

Some of the ideas you may have about men's sexuality, and indeed your own experience of male sexuality, may inadvertently influence your expectations of your son's sexuality and sexual development, and the way you should talk to your son about sex.

Men have been just as socialised into believing and acting on myths about male sexuality. Many men are now challenging these ideas and seeking to incorporate both intimacy and physical sex into their sexual identity. These men prefer sexual relationships based on respect, trust and equality rather than power, and the lack of emotional intimacy. Many men in today's society speak of the difficulty of having to live up to stereotypical ideas of male sexuality. The idea that they need to be star sexual performers (as evidenced in the huge sales of Viagra), that performance is more important than intimacy, and that 'scoring' women is a priority for men, actually get in the way of men being able to establish nurturing and close relationships with women.

The difficulty men have in expressing their emotional and sexual vulnerability, and the need men have, but often find difficult to express, for intimacy, sensuality and physical closeness, as well as sexual fulfilment, are issues that many men are confronting in today's society.

There is a difference between pornography and eroticism. Heterosexual men are attracted to female bodies; they are aroused by nakedness. They do enjoy masturbation and fantasies, touch and smell. This is all natural and normal, as it is for women to feel the same about men, or indeed other women! At times it may be difficult to distinguish between sexist thoughts, attitudes and behaviours and those that are part of adolescent sexual development and normal healthy eroticism. It is important not to be tricked into believing the myths of male sexuality while at the same time attempting to guide your son in a direction of having a sexuality that fits with self-worth and confidence.

Sole mothers and sexual relationships

Sole fathers generally find it easier than sole mothers to develop sexual relationships.[1] Some mothers forgo their own sexual needs in the belief that it may be harmful for their children to know they are having a sexual relationship.

Your son need not be privy to your sexual exploits. This is a private matter for you as an adult. It is important to be open in discussing sexuality, but not in giving examples in real-life experience. If your partner stays the night and your son is home, keep your bedroom door closed, and respect your son's feelings if he seems confused and surprised. At the same time, tell him that you care about your new partner and that he will be staying overnight with you.

Help your son develop a healthy sexual identity

- Encourage him to be close to you. Don't stop cuddling him; give each other a massage (although perhaps just shoulders, rather than full body!), have fun dancing or running with him.
- Help him find ways to express all aspects of himself, sexual and otherwise, through sport, cooking, dancing, painting, art, sewing, scientific experiments — whatever it takes.
- Talk with him about his day-to-day life, his hopes, dreams and fears.
- Tell him he is attractive and gorgeous, that you just love the shirt he chose, that he smells good with aftershave — all of this makes him feel good about himself.
- Listen to him when he talks about girls; he may sound cute, but you need to acknowledge the depth and passion of his feelings.
- Encourage him to have friendships with the opposite sex, and to bring girl friends home or to ring them.

You are in an excellent position to give your son an understanding of how to relate to women in a way that is respectful, fun and caring. You can help him to show his feelings, and to have conversations, which are seen as valuing and interesting to women. Sons of sole mothers may well have the key to what women like in men — make sure you pass this on in order to unlock your son's sexuality from stereotypical and outdated male ideas.

Chapter 13

Dealing with Adolescent Boys

This book does not have a direct focus on adolescence, but it is worth spending some time contemplating this stage of your son's development. While adolescence is generally referred to as the physical and psychological signs of maturity that signify development from a boy into a man, adolescence also encompasses changes in cognition, attitudes, beliefs, emotions and behaviours. These changes may appear long before your son physically changes. Adolescence is occurring earlier than ever before, and we are living in a culture that pushes pseudo-maturity and adult 'acting out' before children are mentally and emotionally ready and capable. Thinking about how you parent and how you and your family will approach the period of adolescence can be helpful in assisting your son through this somewhat challenging and confusing stage of his development.

Parents seem to hold a great dread of adolescence, and most have some kind of horror story about it. Sole mothers, in particular, report that people cringe or offer their condolences when they tell them they have an adolescent son. Parents often say that thinking about adolescence is synonymous with thinking about drug and alcohol abuse, rampant sexuality, vandalism, car crashes, suicide, and a whole range of scary things. Sole mothers in particular are targeted for advice about how their son will change from a gorgeous little boy to a testosterone-driven monster and delinquent, particularly if there is not a male present in his life. The implication is that he will no longer care about you or your relationship with him and will instead be off to the world of boys and men.

Certainly adolescence is a time of great change, but it doesn't have to be disastrous. It may be taxing, confusing and challenging, but it is also a time when you can appreciate your son's intelligence and maturity and the fact that he is growing into an adult in his own right. Don't heed the messages of disaster — instead think about what will help to lessen the tensions of adolescence and increase the attachment between you and your son, while at the same time enabling him to explore an independent identity. An adolescent needs his mother, but he may express this need differently or seem to not want a connection.

Jane, mother of twin boys says:

> With adolescence it's as if someone has taken my beautiful, compliant little boys away. They get very cross at times, and can cop a real attitude with me.
>
> I think it's important to keep a sense of humour with adolescents, it gets you through and stops you holding grudges. I love the humour — it's the family's way of looking at the world — it's a bit absurd. The boys are quite irreverent. One thing I love about our family is that we always apologise to each other if we have an argument. I apologise to them too if I yell at them — it's something we put in place earlier on.
>
> They still talk to me. They talk about books and games; they want to tell you the whole lot but they don't want a dialogue with you. I can get frustrated, but at the same time we have lots of family conversations. I think boys tend to be more black and white in their view of the world, whereas girls are more interested

in people's motivations. I think we are still pretty close, but it's different. I'm no longer the love of their life, but I think that's great. That's how it should be.

What happens in adolescence?

The psychologist Erik Erikson in 1965 posed that the developmental task for an adolescent is to achieve a sense of identity.[1] If this is not successful, he predicts the adolescent will have a sense of dislocation and meaninglessness, which he named 'role confusion'. He highlighted the need for others' approval by adolescents — not just by their peer group, but by parents and other adults too. He writes that the clannish behaviour of young people is about the fear of identity confusion, and wanting to be with people who accept and approve of them. Being marginalised and isolated by a peer group is very traumatic for an adolescent.

Adolescence is characterised by a whole range of physical and physiological changes — children grow at an amazing speed; hormones surge through the body, affecting the brain and other organs; and physical signs of puberty are manifested. A child who once seemed happy to obey orders and conform to parental standards may start to challenge and argue. Whereas he once sought his mother's company and talked about his day, he may now withdraw and spend more time in his room listening to music or talking on the phone. He may seem no longer interested in coming to the beach or a movie with you, instead preferring the company of his friends.

An adolescent is often faced with situations where he has to make many difficult decisions — to get a ride home with a drunk driver, to drink alcohol or smoke marijuana, to use condoms, to have sex, to wag school. He has to deal with the ready availability of drugs, and sexually transmitted diseases. A range of consumer items cry out 'Buy me': video games, DVDs, computers, scanners, sportshoes, clothes, CDs, motorbikes and cars.

Adolescence can be a challenging and worrying time for

both the adolescent and his parents. Perhaps, more than ever before, adolescence is a time where there are more choices for a boy to make — a generation ago he would leave school and either go to university or straight to work. He would probably get married and have children. Now he may not even get a job — more and more young men remain unemployed. An adolescent son may expect to live at home with his mother for a longer period of time, as financially it may not be possible to 'go it alone'.

Adolescence has always carried its share of risks, but today seems a very precarious stage of development that you must see your son through. It is normal for an adolescent to exhibit emotional change and moodiness, a greater concern for the approval of peers, a worry about being 'normal' and new ideas about authority. He may also take a high moral ground and seem more inflexible in his view of the world.

Hannah talks about her son Danny, who is fourteen:

> Early in the year I went through a hard time with him. It started by him not doing his homework but I didn't find out until the parent/teacher meeting. It would have been helpful if the school had notified me earlier. We negotiated with the school, and he was supposed to catch up over the school holidays. One day I came home in the afternoon and he wasn't there. He'd taken $40 from my wallet and gone with a friend to Luna Park, but at the time I didn't know where he was.
>
> It got late, and eventually I phoned the police. He came home at 11:30 p.m. The police could have helped more by giving him a bit of a lecture or warning, but they didn't. They didn't seem to care. After that he started to manipulate me, and say if I didn't give him things he would run away. In the end I stood my ground and didn't give in. That was hard to do, because I was scared that he would run away, but he hasn't since nor does he say he will.
>
> At school he has friends and is popular. He still doesn't apply himself, but does make sure he catches up. In many ways he is a typical teenager — personal hygiene is out the window and he

won't brush his teeth for days. He loves snuggling up on the couch in his doona.

I think he would feel confident to ask me questions about sex. He has told me that there's a girl at school whom he likes.

The benefits of being a sole mother are that you have an independent son. He goes to and from school by himself. Even though we are mother and son, we are also like friends. Things have settled down now and we joke around and are mock sarcastic to each other. He's a great kid.

Adolescence is not just a time of arguing, messiness and waiting up late for your son to come home, it is also a time of appreciating your son's growing body, his interest in what he wears, his growing political and social awareness, and his ability to have mature and stimulating conversations. Adolescents tend to develop very strong values and codes of ethics, and a strong sense of right and wrong, and he will enjoy being questioned in an interesting and non-judgemental way about his beliefs and attitudes.

Enjoy taking him out for dinner, showing interest in his homework, attending his sports matches, music nights or arts shows or whatever pursuit he is interested in. You are vitally important for helping to shape his identity as a person and as a man, and the sense of self-worth that goes with this. As a mother you have a great deal to offer your son in his developing connections with young women and as a model for conducting male–female relationships.

Most mothers say they find a balance between being loving and affectionate to their sons and leaving their sons space to become individuals. It is a normal stage in adolescent development for your son to impose personal and physical boundaries that include increased privacy. You cannot depend on your son to gratify your need for closeness and affection. He will often decide for himself that he wants greater privacy, or doesn't like seeing you walking around unless you are fully clothed. He may wish to make all his phone calls in his room.

Encourage him to close the bedroom door when he is getting dressed. The need to encourage privacy may be more important if there are other siblings in the house, particularly girls.

Peer connections

Much has been written in the media about the influence of peers on adolescents. Some research has 'proved' that the peer group is more important than parental influence for adolescents, some the reverse. Other research has indicated that boys from sole-parent families may gravitate towards their peer group more than boys of two-parent families. Whatever the case, boys will develop peer group friendships. You can have a great degree of influence in helping your son develop ideas about what he will look for in his friendships, as well as what he can offer as a friend. You can explore with a younger son why he likes a particular boy, and why someone else is not so worthy of a friendship.

Ask questions like:

- What is it about Harry that you appreciate in him as a friend?
- Do you think those things are important in friendships?
- What else do you think is important in a friend?
- What do you think Harry likes about you?
- What does he notice about how you treat him that makes him want to be your friend?
- When you get older do you think these things will still be important, or will other things matter too?
- What is important for you in friendships now you are at secondary school?

Your son may vacillate about his friendships in early secondary school. In his first few years he may feel insecure and lacking in confidence, and hang out with boys of whom you do not approve. But don't despair, as he may also change his friendships. You can also ask the school to place him in a different form if you are particularly worried about the impact of a particular group of boys on him. It is better to encourage moving *towards* more suitable groups of boys than moving *away* from his existing peer group.

You can also encourage your son to form attachments with suitable boys and girls by inviting particular children around, involving him in activities where he is more likely to meet boys and girls with similar values to your own, and getting to know other children and their parents through involvement in your son's primary and secondary schools.

If your son has friendships of which you do not approve, it is not a good idea to criticise these boys. In fact, this may drive him closer to them. What you can do is to put limits on when he sees them, attempt to make sure that he only spends time with them that is supervised by an adult, and keep in touch with his school about any ramifications on his behaviour and schoolwork. In addition, rather than attempting to push your son away from these boys, it may be more helpful to encourage him to bring them home, where at least you can keep an eye on him and them. You could most encourage the boy whom you view as the least detrimental, or who has a parent with similar parenting values to your own.

Your son is less likely to gravitate towards a gang and irresponsible or risk-taking peers if he feels he has a solid home foundation where he is loved and appreciated. It is important that you keep tabs on where your son is, who he is with, and set limits on where he can go and when he'll be home. Adolescents still have to be accountable. The more involved you are in his life, the less likely he will be to stray.

Testosterone

Testosterone is a hormone that is present in boys and men, and to a far lesser degree in women. A number of authors have highlighted the role testosterone plays in boys' development. 'Testosterone provides energy and focus. A boy with high levels of the hormone makes good leadership material. Early in the school years, teachers often notice a certain kind of boy who will either become a hero of the class or a complete villain.'[2] And 'Some girls have a lot of testosterone but, on the whole, it's a male thing — and needs our understanding, not blame or ridicule. Testosterone equals vitality, and it's our job to honour it and steer it into healthy directions.'[3]

Some writers seem to suggest that testosterone is the most important element in a boy's development. The implication is that testosterone produces qualities in boys that are therefore missing in girls. Pollack argues that this kind of biological determinism feeds into the myth that boys' behaviour is shaped by hormonal, rather than other, influences. He writes that 'based on the "myth of toxicity", boys at school are often perceived as "little (testosterone driven) monsters" whose "aggression" must be controlled and disciplined, rather than as vulnerable little boys who must be nurtured and encouraged.'[4]

He believes that testosterone does contribute to a boy's natural patterns of behaviour, but is not necessarily the major factor in determining a boy's behaviour. It may well predict a certain type of energy in boys — and this can vary in its expression from boy to boy — but the way this energy is channelled lies in the hands of parents.

A concern with overemphasising the role of testosterone is that any out-of-line boys' behaviour may be attributed to testosterone: 'Oh, it's just the testosterone'. Indeed many mothers say just that, particularly those with boys who have a diagnosis of ADD/ADHD or who are seen as 'problem children'. It seems the false importance placed on testosterone leads mothers to believe that a boy's behaviour cannot be shaped. The way parents care for their son has a powerful effect on a boy's behaviour, at least as strong as any biological influences. As Pollack writes: 'How you treat a boy has a powerful impact on who he becomes. He is as much a product of nurturing as he is of nature.'[5]

Testosterone is only one of the many influences in boys' development. There is no research that has isolated the role of testosterone as contributing more than do other influences. Certainly boys are different from girls in many ways, but this does not mean that testosterone should be privileged or that boys' behaviour cannot be shaped and guided.

Sexuality

Boys in our society are flooded with sexual images — sexy men and women are shown to be the 'winners' — they are the ones who get what they want in life. Boys hear about sexual atrocities such as rapes and murders and stalking. They see sex as being about attractiveness and brashness when they watch the nightly soapies. They see and hear about paedophilia. And they see images of gorgeous women looking their seductive best.

You may be confused about how to impart the kind of sexuality you hope for your son. You don't want to encourage a premature interest in sex, yet you want him to know the facts. You want him to develop positive attitudes and beliefs that give a context to how he will act sexually.

The issue of sexuality is still contextualised differently according to a child or person's gender. Safety is still emphasised as being important for girls, as well as how to prevent pregnancy and sexually transmitted diseases (STDs). Safety is not emphasised so much as an issue for boys — the emphasis is on using condoms so as not to get a girl pregnant, and to avoid STDs. Girls are encouraged to think about the timing and readiness of their sexual encounters, but this is not nearly as common an issue with boys. Unfortunately this means that the emphasis on sex education for boys is very narrow — how to buy and use condoms, information on the facts of life, and that is about it. Meagan raises the dilemmas that responsible mothers face with other issues pertaining to their son's sexual development:

> I found out that Alex (15) had a girlfriend who was 18 and had a car. Her parents had a caravan, and they would go there supposedly to listen to music. I felt very uncomfortable about this — she was so sophisticated and so much older. I talked to Alex about his choices, and how he would make decisions about having sex. I didn't really know what was going on.
>
> One night he didn't come home at the time we agreed. In fact, he stayed out all night, and I was worried sick. We eventually found him asleep, on his own, in her caravan. But it does raise issues about talking to boys about safety, and I would have talked to the girl's parents if the relationship had continued because I didn't think it was appropriate that a fifteen-year-old boy went out with an eighteen-year-old. Luckily the relationship only lasted two weeks, and now he has an age-appropriate girlfriend.

Boys, like girls, need a broad sex education that encompasses relationship and communication, safety — both their own and their partners' — and value clarification.

It may be important to clarify your own beliefs, particularly those that relate to gender and sexuality.

Ask yourself, and discuss the following with your son:

- What do you think about boys who call girls names or make fun of their appearance?
- What attitudes and values about women's sexuality leads to men calling women 'slut', 'whore' and 'moll'?

- What is it that makes boys so worried about being called a 'poofter'?
- What do you think it is about male culture that encourages boys to brag about their sexual conquests (real or otherwise)?
- Why do you think boys find it easier to talk to their friends about what they do, rather than how they feel?

Such questions may be helpful in initiating a curious conversation with your son, and sharing and clarifying your ideas about sex.

There are no hard and fast rules about when to tell your son about sex and discuss sexual issues. Other people may also discuss sex with him, but as the main carer in his life it is appropriate that you do most of this. You can read a book with him, talk about issues that are raised in television shows (soapies are great for this), or just chat over dinner.

What seems to get in the way for mothers is the idea that being a woman means knowing nothing about male sexuality. You may not know how he feels, but you do know the facts of life and what happens for a man. You can tell an older boy that when he gets to puberty he will grow hair, have wet dreams and erections. These are matters of fact! You can let him check out condoms and try one on if he wants. These approaches mean that sexuality doesn't become a smutty, secretive thing, but is open to conversation and seen as part of everyday life.

Laurel says:

> We talked about sex from an early age — it was never taboo. My friends were also open in talking about sex. Before he reached puberty he would ask me questions about sex and I would answer him honestly and openly. I'd also go to the library and get him books to read. I think mothers have to consider the sexuality between the mother and the son. They need to respect their son's need for privacy.

Sam (16) hasn't had a girlfriend, and I don't know if he's had sex. We've gone shopping together and I've asked him if he wanted me to buy him condoms. I've addressed it in a matter-of-fact way.

Being gay

Sexuality is not always a fixed entity, but can change across time and circumstance. Some people may be attracted to the opposite sex for a period of time, others may feel attracted and fantasise about sexual encounters but never do anything about this attraction, others maintain a particular sexual identity from a young age.

There is a difference between sexual identity and sexual orientation. Sexual orientation relates to the object of sexual desire. Sexual identity is about how a person identifies themselves sexually — the 'Who am I?' question. So a man may identify himself as heterosexual, but occasionally have sex with men. It is often the process of establishing and recognising one's own sexual identity that can take time and prove difficult and painstaking for adolescents, particularly if they are gay or lesbian.

Sexual identity is not just about with whom you have sex. It is about whom you are predominantly drawn to in both a romantic, intimate and sexual way; who you wish to have an intimate relationship with. Sexual identity is often complex, unclear and confusing, particularly with the onset of adolescence. Such is the stigma of homosexuality that it takes a lot of courage to 'come out', even to your mother. Approximately 5–10 per cent of the population are gay or lesbian.

Although attitudes towards homosexuality have improved over recent years there is still a lot of fear and distrust in the general community. Many sole mothers express a fear that without a male role model their sons have more risk of growing up gay. They may fear their sons being gay because this is in opposition to their own heterosexual identity, but also because they recognise that being gay in a homophobic society is a great challenge. They worry that their sons will not get the sense of self-worth, approval from others, and inclusiveness that heterosexual men get. They worry that their son may be teased or bullied, or ostracised, and fear that being gay means their son will be at risk of contracting the HIV/AIDS virus. They may also have hopes and dreams for their son's future that fit with a heterosexual orientation.

For some people, homosexuality is a choice they have made; for others it is not so much a choice but a reality, the way they are 'made'. In recent times there has been much media publicity from scientists who claim to have isolated a homosexual gene, and that this gives strong scientific evidence that being homosexual or lesbian is genetic. This remains to be proven outright. This claim has both negative and positive repercussions. For some, it legitimates homosexuality — and challenges ideas that it is 'caused' through environmental influences. In addition, if homosexuality is seen as genetic, it may be more accepted as a naturally occurring phenomenon. On the other hand, there may be repercussions in the face of genetic engineering that are alarming. For example, could this mean that prospective parents would screen their foetus for a gay gene?

Most gay men feel comfortable with their sexuality, and do not want to be any other way. It is more often the difficulties gay people have in living in a homophobic and heterosexist world that makes life problematic. If you discover that your son is gay, you may wish to search for answers, often in the misguided idea that if you locate the reason your son is gay you can solve the 'problem'. Essentially this is a waste of time. If your son is gay, he is gay because he is gay, and there's nothing you can do about his sexual identity. What you can do is give him the love and acceptance to deal with society's negative attitudes towards homosexuality and gay adolescents and men.

While heterosexual adolescents may spend time talking to their parents, and especially their peers, boys who feel confused about their identity or attracted to other boys may keep silent, and keep their confusion and fear a secret. One of the most important needs for adolescents is to feel included as part of a group, and this fear of difference is what may keep gay adolescents silent, often with dire consequences.

Boys who either disclose their sexual identity, or are viewed by others as gay, may experience teasing, bullying, and even violence. The greatest fear for these boys is rejection on a number of levels — from their family, wider relationships, friends, school, community and society. It is a huge burden to face.

Because gay boys and men are often ostracised or discriminated against, and because they are still seen as different or abnormal, they may experience deep feelings of shame, guilt, self-loathing and isolation. This experience can be all the more profound when they feel there is no one to confide in, or if they fear the people they love will reject them. Although there are no conclusive studies, it is estimated that, particularly in country regions where there is less support and perhaps a stronger macho ethos, many boys who commit suicide are boys with issues relating to their sexuality. It would seem that a significant number of gay youth is represented in the Australian youth suicide statistics. Other gay adolescents seek solace by numbing their pain in drug and alcohol use. The lack of support for gay boys may also explain school dropout and failure, depression and anxiety.

It is impossible to tell if a boy will or won't be gay. You may worry if your little boy likes to dress up as a girl, wear high heels and put on Mum's make-up. He may prefer playing girls' games to playing with his male peers. This is creative play — let him enjoy this. It does not mean he has tendencies towards being gay. In fact, gay men are stereotyped as being effeminate when there are great differences in gayness — some love clothes and cooking, others like football and car mechanics. It is interesting just how many boys do love dressing up and applying make-up. Why wouldn't they? It's a fun world of fantasy, the realm of every child.

There is variation among the gay community as much as there is with the straight community. If your son is exhibiting 'female' behaviour then he is lucky enough to be able to try out all his interests rather than having to limit himself to specific 'boy' interests. Let him explore his world and develop his creative and communicative side. If he is gay, not letting him do these things won't stop his sexuality; on the contrary, it will make it harder for him to have an open and sharing relationship with you. He may go on to develop other broader interests, or incorporate existing interests as his life experience develops, or he may go on to be a chef or makeup artist.

The phobia about homosexuality is so strong that it encourages people to discount anything else that is positive or worthwhile in a person. It's a little like racism, where people are judged by the colour of their skin or appearance rather than 'what's inside'. Sole mothers can naturally feel scared and dismayed when they discover their son is gay. Many instantly examine their parenting to find traces of what they did wrong! Sole mothers, in particular, are inclined to blame themselves for not providing a male role model or not fostering a strong-enough relationship between their son and his father. They worry they were too overprotective, or that their son was too mother-bound. None of this is true. If it were, gay sons of close-knit heterosexual parents would not exist. And they do, despite the prevalence and strength of heterosexism. Being gay has nothing to do with the mother/son relationship.

You may worry about what people will think, and have a genuine concern for how your son will fare in a homophobic world. You naturally want your son to have a healthy, happy life, and may be worried that your son's homosexuality will cause him pain, suffering and rejection. These days there are many supports for gay people; it is a matter of finding them, and in general the gay community is strong and protective.

If you have an open, honest and respectful relationship with your son he should be able to discuss issues relating to his identity, of which being gay is only a part. It is important that he understands that you value him raising these issues, and that you will accept him and love him no matter what. It is okay to raise your difficulty or surprise with his telling you he is gay, but he needs the reassurance that he is loved and accepted. The more he feels you are with him on his journey, the less likely he will need to use alcohol or drugs to submerge his feelings. If there is at least one person who accepts him for what he is, then the prospect of depression and suicide is much reduced. See the list at the back of the book for organisations that can be helpful.

Many mothers of gay sons express concern about the HIV/AIDS virus. The virus affects both gay and straight people. All adolescents are at risk of contracting sexually transmitted diseases, including hepatitis, if they have unprotected sex.

Having a gay son may be confronting for you at first, but to lose his love and contact through misunderstanding and prejudice is a high price to pay when there is so much that you have already enjoyed in him. In fact, having a gay son may open you to a world of other supportive parents and a diverse and close community. There is much you can do to assist your son in discovering himself and developing his self-appreciation and self-value.

Being 'straight'

Not only can you provide your son with the information about sex and his sexual development, but you can shape his attitudes. If he uses a derogatory comment about a girl — for example, the term 'slut' — ask him:

- Do you know what that means?
- Why do you think it is that girls and not boys are called sluts?
- Do you think that's fair?
- If you were a girl and were called that, how do you think you would feel?

You might question some of the schoolground practices, like the way boys 'score points' over sexual conquests, or how boys may harass girls sexually, or feel entitled to make sexual comments to girls. You might also wish to explore some of the ways that girls are encouraged to behave when boys are around, and how difficult some girls' behaviours and attitudes make it for boys. Discuss what he might wish to do in order to take a stand against any heterosexist practices that he make him uncomfortable.

Have conversations with him about his ideas in relation to responsibility for safe sex and contraception, about how he might make a decision about having his first sexual experience (with luck it will be a decision!), and how he will know when he is ready to have a sexual relationship. Although boys may appear to have bravado and sexual confidence, they are just as vulnerable and confused as girls. Sharing some of your experiences with him (if you can bear it!) may provide a humorous and relaxed introduction to talking about sex.

There is a myth that boys are so testosterone geared that there is no need to talk to them about the decisions they might make relating to their first sexual experience. On the other hand, girls are constantly spoken to about having sex too early, who they will have as their partner, how they will know when they are ready, how will they guard against pregnancy and STDs. Boys need and value the same kinds of conversations. Many men report that their first sexual experience was based more about the need to appear manly in front of their friends, and to pass through some kinds of rite of passage, than actually about sharing an intimate and close experience with a special person. Many adult men regret that their first sexual experience was, in fact, like this.

Mothers are in an excellent position to discuss how sons will know it is the right time to have sex, how they will make that decision with their girlfriends and how they would want the experience to occur.

Adolescents and the media

As your son reaches his teens, he will start to move towards wanting to be part of the adult world. This may raise a dilemma for you — how to help your son do this and to facilitate him choosing his own way, but how to also steer him towards more wholesome activities. Many mothers are concerned at the amount and type of sexually and violently explicit material to which their sons are exposed.

It has been estimated that children spend approximately 49 per cent of their leisure time engaged in the use of the electronic media (videos, computer games, listening to music and computers).[6] While the media has a place in teaching skill development and educational learning, you may be worried that it has more harmful effects, such as undermining family life and exposing your son to moral and ethical practices that are contrary to your own beliefs and attitudes. It is not only directly violent videos that you may be concerned about but programs such as the news, 'real-life television', and even the effects of advertising.

Melanie says:

> My boys spend every second weekend with their father. He has become an indoors person, and has discovered that hours of Sky television, watching sport, computer games and playstation games occupy most of the time he has the boys, with little effort on his part. The result is when they come home they sometimes bring the playstation with them on special occasions. This I have to put limits on. I find after half an hour of it they become aggressive and go into another surreal world. To counter this, they have to read to earn time on the playstation. Sometimes I ban it if their behaviour becomes antisocial. I explain to them why, and the other repercussions of spending too much time on these games, i.e. eyesight problems, RSI later in life, poor concentration, and aggression. They don't like being banned, but they do listen to what I say.

An adolescent may be at particular risk if he is spending time alone; for example, after school, when he is unsupervised and has access to the internet, where pornography is freely accessible. Although there is no definitive research on the harm of adolescents viewing pornography and violence, it is generally agreed that there are some parallels between watching this material and antisocial or violent behaviours.[7] Another study has demonstrated that viewers exposed to pornography become more callous towards sexual exploitation and more tolerant of rape than non-viewers.[8]

Communication

If your son knows there is nothing so bad that he can't tell you, that you will listen and hear him out and still be there for him, you will have lowered the risks markedly. Not only is it important for him to know you are there but also for you to be able to gauge whether he is withdrawing from you or dealing with hard issues that could do with some outside intervention. For example, if he was feeling confused about his sexual identity, you may consider approaching a counselling service that is familiar with and skilled at dealing with such issues.

Many boys become withdrawn when they have experienced bullying and alienation, yet fear that they would be 'dobbing' if they disclosed this. They fear that if their parents or teachers were notified things would only worsen. Unfortunately some schools still hold the 'survival of the fittest' attitude, but bullying should never be underrated in its impact on children's lives. It is important that your son knows that this behaviour is wrong, that he deserves to have something done about it, and that you can be his advocate in this.

An adolescent boy often won't respond as well to direct communication, but responds better to communication through doing. It may be less confronting to your son if you speak with him while he is fixing his bike — make him a cup of hot chocolate and sit down beside him. Make a once a fortnight or month dinner 'date' with him, so the two of you can sit and talk. This is especially important if you have other children — as an adolescent he will need some special individual time with you. Go rollerblading, bikeriding, or do ball practice with him, and use this opportunity to talk. You may find that the time driving to and from school or to sports events is an opportune time for talking; in many ways your son is a captive, and you can use this time to initiate conversation.

It is important that your son knows that you love hearing about his successes, but that unhappy times and things he has failed to accomplish are also important to discuss. Let him know that life can be tough, and that society can be hard on both girls and boys for different reasons.

> ***Ask your son:***
>
> ◆ What ideas have you heard about how men should be?
> ◆ Do you think any of these ideas are hard to achieve, or might make it hard for a boy growing up?
> ◆ What do you think of these ideas?
> ◆ How might these ideas make things hard for you, growing up from a boy into a man?
> ◆ What do you think you can do about that?
> ◆ Do you think these ideas can be challenged?

Depression

Depression and anxiety are two mental health conditions that are increasing across the industrialised world. More and more adolescents are being diagnosed with, and treated for depression. Adolescents may experience depression for a number of reasons. It may be because they lack a sense of their place in the world and have a sense of not connecting or being part of something greater than themselves. It may be because they lack a sense of self-worth and confidence in their own uniqueness and abilities. It may be that they feel powerless to change their life experience or the world around them.

Depression can often be a short-term or intermittent state that characterises adolescence. It may be part of hormonal changes or the rapidity of change in adolescent development. When it deepens to such a point that it is affecting your son's day-to-day functioning or is associated with suicidal thoughts, then it is of concern to you.

You may blame yourself for your son's depression and any associated consequences. Yet even your most exhaustive attempts may not always help your son to find a solution to his sadness or life dilemmas. Some things may just be too private or too torturous for him to share. This may be particularly true if a boy is experiencing a situation where he feels shameful, guilty and unable to protect himself or others around him. Boys who are either directly being abused, either sexually, emotionally or physically, or are witness to others being abused, may be more prone to depression and less able to break through the secrecy imposed by the abuser.

Key signs of depression include:
- waking early in the morning or during the night and being unable to get back to sleep
- changes in appetite, either putting on or losing considerable weight
- not wanting to be involved in activities that once gave him joy and interest
- sleeping in or staying in bed for long periods of time
- withdrawal from friendships and family
- seeming worried and negative
- using drugs and alcohol
- unexplained changes in school and home behaviour
- truanting and poor school performance

These alone may not be signs of depression, and similarly your son may be depressed without exhibiting any of these symptoms. However, if you suspect that he is depressed, it is worth talking to him about your fears and seeing if he will open up to you. Sometimes depression can be caused by changes in his life or environment, a changed family structure, or an incident that is distressing or traumatic. Sometimes depression can be linked to biological causes such as a chemical imbalance, and have little to do with what is happening in his life. Depression may also run through family generations — it can be a 'learned' pattern that is passed from parent to child.

If you feel concerned about your son and he will not talk to you nor allay your fears, then you should approach a health professional such as a counsellor, school welfare co-ordinator, doctor or psychiatrist for advice and support.

Suicide

Australia has the third-highest youth suicide rate in the world. A number of factors are attributed to this, such as high youth unemployment, family breakdown and social isolation. Boys are far more highly represented statistically than girls, and many families whose children have died say they had no inkling that their sons were depressed or feeling suicidal. It is estimated that the overall suicide rate may be 40 per cent higher for indigenous communities compared with the non-indigenous population.[9]

Boys who suicide come from a variety of cultures and family backgrounds. One thing that stands out is that these boys have a sense of failure and meaninglessness. It is not so much that they are socially isolated, but that they are disconnected from anything meaningful in their lives. They may be great athletes, or excel at school, they may have loving parents but within themselves feel a void or lack of connection.

The society in which we live does not espouse the value of community, religion and family. This means that a parent or parents may have to play a greater role in giving their son a sense of his purpose in the world. Whereas the community once played a significant role in the wellbeing of children, now parents find that they alone bear this responsibility.

Many parents of boys who suicide say they had no idea that anything was wrong. They look back and see that their son was achieving, he had friends at school, he seemed happy, and was involved in a number of extracurricular activities. Adolescents are vulnerable to suicide because of the mood swings that accompany hormonal changes, but also because boys more than girls are often not given an opportunity to show their feelings openly, to talk about hurting, about being bullied, about not coping, about being stressed or depressed. They are expected to 'soldier' on, tough it out, and cope.

What seems clear is that a number of complex, interwoven factors contribute to this high suicide rate, and that we should look at these factors, both how the structure of our society may lead to suicidality, and how to assist boys who are dealing with depression and alienation.

Drugs and alcohol

It would be rare for an adolescent not to be offered drugs or alcohol. Most adolescents will try some form of drug, and most will try it at least once. Often parental patterns of drug and alcohol use affects whether children will go on to use them; for example, children whose parents smoke are more likely to smoke themselves (despite being told not to!).

The drug that most parents fear their child will use is heroin. Heroin is certainly a devastating drug, but only a fraction of adolescents go on to use heroin. The numbers of adolescents who try heroin is increasing yet most still do not try it. There is now more scientific research about patterns of drug and alcohol use, and, despite heroin being highlighted as the most worrying drug, other drugs also have serious implications for adolescents' health and wellbeing.

There is more and more information about the harmful effects of seemingly minor drugs and alcohol. For example, adolescents who binge drink, even occasionally, can still do great harm to their bodies and minds; binge drinking can lead to a reliance or dependence on alcohol. In addition, being drunk contributes to the greatest cause of death for young people through car accidents. Boys who are drunk may often make unwise choices, which can put their safety and that of others at risk.

Many mothers will have smoked marijuana, perhaps in copious amounts, in their youth. Marijuana was once viewed as a harmless drug that increased spiritual awareness and had no detrimental side-effects. Marijuana today is much stronger, more readily available, and smoked by people at a much younger age than the previous generation, who probably first tried it at university or once they had left secondary school. There is strong evidence that there is a link between marijuana use and psychosis for those adolescents who may already have a predisposition to mental illness. Marijuana use has also been linked with school dropout rates and lower academic performance. Although marijuana use does not necessarily lead to the use of more serious drugs, it may be easier to obtain such drugs if you are already in a 'marijuana circle' of friends. In the previous generation marijuana was not viewed as being a drug of addiction, but drug and alcohol and health services are now finding that people are coming for counselling for marijuana dependence.

Adolescents may use drugs to be part of the scene. They want to keep up with their peer group or impress others by risk taking and behaviour that is in contradiction to the adult world's ethos. They are more likely to be pulled this way if they are not connected with family or community, if they see in their peer group a togetherness and acceptance that is lacking in their family life. This does not mean that if your son uses drugs and alcohol that you are to blame. It is a myth that adolescents who use heroin, for example, come from 'damaged' families. Your son's peer group has immense influence, and in many ways it often a matter of fate whether your son will choose to abuse drugs and alcohol.

A boy may often use drugs or alcohol in order to deal with painful or difficult feelings, particularly if he feels unable to express them safely. Being intoxicated may be the only way he feels he can be vulnerable or open, or a way of suppressing painful emotions. The problem is that the shroud of being 'out of it' becomes so enticing that occasional using turns to addiction.

Harm minimisation

Most drug and alcohol organisations accept that adolescents will experiment with drugs and alcohol at some time in their lives. Rather than give a message of abstinence, they encourage adolescents to use drugs and alcohol in ways that maximise safety and minimise risk taking. They may advocate using clean syringes and needle exchanges, not using drugs when alone, making sure the adolescents know who they are buying drugs from and choosing where and with whom they use the drugs.

You cannot keep your son from being exposed to drugs and alcohol, but you can offer him discussion about what choices he will make and how. Ask questions with curiosity, questions that open up dialogue about drug and alcohol use rather than close conversations down. Let him know that you will be available to talk about his choices, to support him, and to be open to hearing his experience. You can also provide him with information about drugs and their effects. Giving him information won't encourage him to use drugs and alcohol, but may help him to make decisions in choosing what he may use and in how to use it safely. If he does use drugs or alcohol, it is important to be there for him, to let him know that you love and support him, and to let him know you are there for him to talk to. If drug and alcohol use becomes too great a concern, pushes your parental boundaries too far or is linked with aggression, then seek professional help.

Ask your son:

- Do you think most kids try alcohol and drugs?
- So is that something kids just do today?
- Do you think there is a reason kids use alcohol and drugs?
- How will you make the decision about whether to use or not?
- Do you talk with your friends about it?
- What do they say?
- Are there some drugs you might consider trying and others you won't?
- What would influence your decision?
- What will you do if some kids offer you drugs you don't want to try?
- What if they tease you about not wanting to use?
- Do you think we'll be able to talk about it?
- Who would you go to if you felt that drugs or alcohol were becoming a problem for you?
- What do you think might help a kid decide not to use a particular drug?

What might be helpful?

When family therapists Olga Silverstein and Beth Rashbaum wrote *The Courage to Raise Good Men,* they discussed their therapeutic practice where so many men had disclosed their grief at adolescence when they had noticed their mothers starting to move away emotionally from them. This grief and feeling of loss had continued for the men throughout their lives and impacted on the way they developed, as well as on their relationships with women. They explored how often mothers feel it is a necessary and helpful thing that they emotionally distance themselves from their sons. In fact, these now-grownup men reported that what they had really needed at that time was to feel their mother's comfort and security.

Many of the strategies used to parent younger children are useful with adolescents, but some additional ones stand out.

- **Give guidance**

Although your adolescent son may act and argue as if he is mature and grown up, he still needs guidance. Rather than telling him what he should do or bringing up past mistakes, give him guidance by exploring the options. For example, say 'Remember last time we had that mix-up about where to pick you up? How do you think we could do it better this time?' or 'I wonder what is the best way to work out what clothes we should prioritise to buy?' or 'What do you think is a reasonable time for a thirteen-year-old to come home from the disco?'

Adolescence is a time when your son needs much support and encouragement. Often he may experience a crisis in self-confidence and face self-doubt and indecision. This can sometimes be over what seems a trivial thing, like a too-short haircut or not having the right brand-name sportshoes, but it is important not to minimise his experience and to accept the meaning this experience has for him in order to help him work through it.

- **Place more responsibility on your son**

An adolescent is more sensitive to criticism and judgement, even though he may seem more judgemental himself. Rather than jump in and disagree with him, ask questions, and explore with him his view of the world. He needs to learn that he can solve his own problems, and that you believe him capable and responsible enough to do this.

Another myth that mothers of sons, especially adolescent sons, are vulnerable to is the myth that boys should be sent to their fathers at adolescence. This myth implies that there

is 'secret men's business' that only fathers can advise and educate their sons on. There is also an implication that mothers will not be able to handle their son's behaviour at adolescence, and that male power and authority is needed. These myths are disempowering to sole mothers, and are not at all proven. Sole mothers may have to be firm and assertive to a greater degree than in their son's earlier years, but to believe that you have to rely on a male's influence can lead to disconnection of a son from his mother and a world view that women are not as competent as males. Many men who have been farmed out to their fathers at adolescence deeply regret the loss and disruption of the close relationship they had with their mother and her community.

Meagan, a mother of two adolescent boys, advises against sending sons to live with their fathers if their behaviour becomes difficult:

> I strongly advise sole mothers against telling their sons to go to their fathers if the mothers are having difficulties with their sons. I think boys can get the feeling they are no longer loved, and also that their mothers lack an authority that only males can provide. They may also think that you don't want them to be around — a dreadful message for an adolescent to receive. It's like ostracising them, and admitting defeat. You have to accept sixteen-year-olds will push their mothers before anyone else. It's the easiest mark to hit.
>
> If things are tense, I can see the benefit of 'time out' — giving both parties space. But it has to be severe for that to happen. Adolescence is about a clash of wills. If you send them off to their fathers you won't get through it with them. They need to know that they pushed the boundaries too far, but that you can handle it.

Of course, it may be prudent for a son to choose to live with his father at varying stages of his life — perhaps he can access a higher standard of education from his father's location, perhaps his father can help him in an apprenticeship or trade, perhaps he just wants to see what life is like with Dad. There is a vast difference between family members making choices about with whom they will live and sons being shunted off to their fathers because of poor behaviour.

- **Help with decision making**

Adolescents need to be able to explore the world and broaden their experience but they still need formal limits to do this. As your son begins to want to venture further, negotiate ways in which you can both make decisions, and what expectations you as a parent will have of him. It is important that he knows what is and isn't acceptable behaviour. It can be helpful to prepare together a written document on his privileges, limits and responsibilities, as well as the consequences when he doesn't stick to these.

Living happily together

Some mothers almost literally count the days until their son moves out. It doesn't have to be like this. Your adolescent child will respond much better to negotiation, through feeling he has a say in decision making rather than submitting to authority and a high degree of parental control. Indeed, it is often in families where parents have been controlling and hierarchical that things go wrong when their children reach puberty.

One way of encouraging a happy life is to have regular 'check in' meetings, a bit like house meetings, where you and your son can discuss issues that arise and negotiate what needs to be changed. It is better to do this very early in adolescence so that it becomes a normal part of your life together. Often it helps to record minutes of these meetings. You can note in advance how the two of you are going to make decisions about money, going out, curfew times, homework, house duties, and so on. You can talk about your need to know he is safe, and negotiate how you will be assured of this; for example, that he always lets you know where he is staying the night.

A word about the proverbial bungalow

Because many parents believe that with adolescence comes a desire to separate from their family members and for an adolescent to have his own privacy, they often go to great lengths to create a separate space for their son away from the rest of the family. They believe that giving him this space will affirm his maturity, and give him the peace and quiet needed for study. Sometimes they build on an extra room with its own special entrance; others move their adolescent into a bungalow.

But there are a number of negative consequences of this. First, it means your son is distanced from the normal run-of-the-mill family activities such as chatting, preparing meals, and hanging out with other siblings. Although you have not provided the space with the aim of getting him out of the way, this is how he may see it. And so, inadvertently, it becomes an alienating process. Second, it means that you are not able to connect with him so easily. Rather than being there and available, you or he has to make a special effort to have talk or do things together. It is an effective bar to communication and intimacy. Finally, having his own space mean that it is not as easy to supervise or account for him. Friends can come and go; he can choose whether to play loud music or study; he can more easily hide the fact that he is smoking, drinking or using illicit drugs.

It is interesting that parents do not have the same concerns about giving a daughter her space. Perhaps this is indicative of the push to have girls relate, but boys to separate.

Ask yourself:

- When you were an adolescent, were there any adults — family, teachers, friends, etc. — whom you look back on as people who positively influenced your development?
- What was it about the way they responded to you that encouraged this positive regard?
- What were some of the important principles you held close to your heart?

- Did these conflict or coincide with those of your parent(s)?
- How important was it that these principles and beliefs were acknowledged and respected? What difference did the way your parents and other adults responded to these principles make to your own sense of identity and development into an adult?
- What did you learn about expressing your opinions and feelings? Was this helpful? What impact did this learning have on your present way of expressing these opinions and feelings?
- What did you learn about conflict? Did you learn that it was to be avoided at all costs, or that it was an acceptable and normal part of life? How has this learning impacted on the way you handle conflict as both an adult and a parent?

Ask your son:

- When you think about yourself and who you've grown up to be, is there anyone whom you think has really had a big impact on shaping your identity?
- What was special about your relationship with this person? (It could be you!)
- If I asked that person what was appreciated most about you, what do you think that person would say?
- Is that person's view for your future identity similar to, or different from, the view you have for yourself?
- What is the best thing about becoming an adolescent?
- What is the hardest thing about becoming an adolescent?
- How can I best help you through the hard times?

> - What do you think is important in the way we set rules now you are in secondary school?
> - How can we work out how to let you have more freedom but ensure you are safe?

Adolescence is a time of great change, both for you, your son and the relationship you have already shared. While it may sometimes feel like an emotional rollercoaster, it is vitally important that he knows you are there with him, no matter what he is experiencing. Make his home a place of nurture and safety, and strengthen your relationship with him so that you can enjoy the opportunity adolescence offers for connection, growth and shared enjoyment. Adolescence is not the end but the beginning of a foundation for the closeness and connection that will continue when your son becomes a man.

Chapter 14

How to Recover from Domestic Violence and Prevent Child Abuse

It is estimated that domestic violence occurs in about 10–30 per cent of Australian households.[1] Domestic violence is said to be a 'gendered crime' because 90 per cent of the violence is by men against women. It is usually women and children who flee their homes to women's refuges, hotels, family and friends to feel safe. The effects of experiencing domestic violence for both mothers and children can be profound and long-lasting.

What is domestic violence?

The term domestic violence applies to a wide range of behaviours, including:
- physical abuse and assault, such as kicking, slapping, punching, shoving, grabbing, or using a weapon
- emotional or psychological abuse, such as threats, putdowns, constant criticism, giving 'the silent treatment', and psychological warfare

- social abuse, such as isolation, criticising family friends or relatives or behaving so badly that they no longer come to visit, putdowns in public, or monitoring your social life
- financial abuse, such as controlling all the money, giving you a small allowance and expecting you to provide for all the family, or expecting you to hand over all your pay
- sexual abuse, such as rape, forcing you to do sexual things you do not wish to do, or making derogatory sexual comments

It is a myth that domestic violence is about men's anger. Domestically violent men often use this excuse themselves, and give their partners reasons for their violence: 'You keep nagging me' or 'Can't you see I'm stressed at work' or 'You just can't control the kids'. Domestic violence is not about anger. Most men who are violent do not show such behaviour to other people. On the contrary, many may seem charming, caring and fun to be with in public.

Many men who are violent say that their partners should change so they won't be violent. They argue that if their wife were slimmer or a better cook or more understanding they wouldn't need to be angry. Many women keep trying and trying, but no matter how hard they try their men do not change.

Change will only occur if the man is prepared to acknowledge he is responsible for his behaviour. If he gets involved with the law, he is forced to look at his behaviour. Domestic violence is a crime and a man who appears before the court on an intervention order or for assault may be required to undertake counselling and attend a men's behavioural change program. A man may find that, when his partner leaves him, usually with the children, and he is faced with an ultimatum of changing or permanently separating, he decides to take some action towards responsibility.

Domestic violence is about power and control. It occurs in a context where men, traditionally, have more rights and power in our society. Despite the gains of feminism, many men still believe that women should be subservient to men. Men use violence to maintain their control and power in their relationships. They do this by creating an atmosphere of uncertainty and trepidation. Women who are in situations of domestic violence often experience a range of symptoms including nightmares, anxiety, depression, weight loss or gain, nervousness, and a sense of guilt and failure. Women speak of 'walking on eggshells' always feeling worried that abuse or violence may occur, or thinking ahead about how to prevent it (you can't!).[2] Many women who have mental health disorders, such as anxiety, depression and post-traumatic stress dirorder, have experienced domestic violence directly or witnessed it as a child.

There is a perception that domestic violence only occurs between adults, and not enough attention has been focused on the impact of domestic violence on children. Another misconception is that, as long as children are not physically hurt or do not directly witness the violence, they are not harmed by their mother's experience. More and more research is proving that the impact of living in a family where their mother is beaten or abused is highly detrimental to children.

Some mothers are unsure about what domestic violence really is. The media tends to focus on examples of extremes of violence such as serious assault and battery, but all forms of domestic violence have serious consequences. Women often tend to minimise their experience. This may mirror their partner's words that 'It isn't that bad' or 'It's only a scratch.' The following questions cover a definition of domestic violence.

Ask yourself:

- How do you and your partner argue? Does it feel like an equal discussion? Do you feel that you can be 'heard'? Do you listen to each other? Is your arguing respectful?
- Does your partner raise his voice, yell, make verbal threats?

- Does he interrupt, contradict, and use criticism or sarcasm to undervalue you?
- Do you worry about what you say to him — that he won't believe you anyway, that what you say will get you into trouble, that he will be resentful of your time without him, or jealous if you spend time with other people, including family and friends?
- Does he always seem to find a reason to criticise your friends, family, and workplace?
- Does he want you to do sexual acts that make you feel degraded?
- Has he ever physically hurt you — pushed or shoved you, kicked or hit, pulled your hair or pinched you?
- Has he ever threatened to use violence, including use of a weapon, against you?
- Do you feel scared of him?
- Are the children scared of him?
- Does life with him feel totally unpredictable?

The effects on children

Children who grow up in households where their father or another adult is violent can experience a range of problems similar to those of their mothers. Research indicates that some form of mental or behavioural disturbance is four times more common for children living in domestic-violence situations than for children in non-violent homes.[3] The effects can differ according to the gender of the child, how long the child has been exposed to violence and abuse, the frequency of the violence, and the child's developmental age. It is also important to remember that men who are violent to their partners are often violent towards their children, and use very harsh physical punishment. Some men who are violent may also sexually abuse their children.

0–2 years

Babies in the womb have been found to react to their mother's stress, and may be more unsettled at birth or have feeding difficulties. After birth, babies exhibit poor feeding, sleeping and behavioural patterns. They may seem whingey, irritable or clingy. Toddlers may withdraw, scream with fear, try and shut themselves away, or try and stop the abuse.

2–8 years

Children at this age are exploring the world and learning whether it is a trusting and safe place. They are very egocentric and believe the world revolves around them. If they witness abuse or violence, they may believe it is their fault. They may try and distract their parents, or act out as a response to what they observe. They may react to witnessing violence by being fearful of others or bullies themselves, not wanting to leave their mothers, and having difficulty settling to one activity, particularly schoolwork. They may also seem hyper-vigilant. Children at this stage of development may exhibit low self-esteem, poor coping skills, and a belief that violence is acceptable and that men should be controlling and dominant. Feelings of low self-worth and confidence continue and intensify throughout childhood, if the children continue to be exposed to violence.

8–12 years

If abuse has been long term, children may feel they can do nothing to stop it. They may give up and become resigned to their fate, and schoolwork and social connections suffer. They may withdraw or become aggressive. They may not want other people or children to know about the bad secret at home; this means they may become isolated and secretive. Boys in particular may act out the violence and be aggressive towards other children and their own siblings, particularly girls. They may also use violence and abuse towards their mothers, and become rebellious and out of control.

12 years and over

At this age children may openly blame their mother for not stopping the abuse and protecting them. They may feel embarrassed, angry, lonely and powerless. Their relationships with peers reflect the beliefs that violence and aggression are acceptable, and that it is important to be controlling of, and powerful over, others.[4] Adolescents raised by violent fathers often have very traditional ideas about how men and women should behave. These ideas reflect the view that men should be dominant and privileged, and women passive and nurturing.

The violence can impact on the children's development so that they learn that the world is an unsafe place, that their needs do not matter and will not be met, that adults and relationships are not to be trusted, that their family has a dark secret. They learn that violence is an acceptable way to deal with conflict.

Some other effects on children include:
- guilt that the violence is their fault
- guilt that they should have protected their mother or stopped the violence (more common in boys)
- confusion because they love their Dad but hate his behaviour
- turning to drugs or alcohol in order to escape the abuse and the feelings it manifests
- feeling over-responsible
- being aggressive (especially boys)
- developing behavioural problems, such as truanting, bedwetting, stammering, etc.
- poor academic performance — not paying attention in class, not wanting to try, feeling depressed, apathetic and confused or tired from being awake in the night
- being physically incapacitated — nervous disorders such as headaches, stomach aches, asthma, digestive upsets or skin disorders may appear

There are differences in the ways that boys and girls

respond to growing up in domestically violent households. Boys are more likely to:
- become verbally and physically aggressive
- believe girls and women are inferior and do not deserve respect
- turn to substance abuse — alcohol, marijuana, glue, and other substances
- exhibit behavioural problems, such as running away from home
- truant from school
- fail academically — slowed developmental capacities as a result of a feeling of lower self-worth, and loss of abilities for academic growth and development
- be socially isolated — moody, wanting to spend time alone, having difficulty relating to peers, and poor conflict management skills

Fathers who are violent are often absent from home, take little responsibility for their children, are more inclined to use physical punishment, more inclined to abuse alcohol or other drugs, and show less affection and nurturing. All of these factors also hinder a child's opportunities for a healthy development.

Parenting after domestic violence

It is extremely difficult for you to parent effectively when you are living with a violent partner. This is not because you are intrinsically a 'bad' mother, but because the effects of the violence are so profound. Many mothers feel let down and dismayed that the man they expected would be a loving parent has turned out to be so irresponsible and self-interested. Many women report that the first act of violence occurred when they were pregnant. This may be because it is with the pregnancy that the man feels he has gained control over her, or feels jealous of this new 'rival'.

Many men use violence or the threat of violence to the

children to subjugate their partners. This is another method of control. They may manipulate the children to take sides against their mother in order to undermine her role as an intelligent and caring parent.

Because the effects of violence are so severe, you may be depressed, stressed, highly anxious and feel a sense of hopelessness in your role of parent. You may be so focused on providing for your partner's needs or avoiding another violent episode that physically and emotionally you cannot be there for the children.

The effects of the violence may even be manifest in psychiatric illness, such as clinical anxiety or depression. At times this can develop to such an extent where the child protection system is notified and the children are removed from their mother's care. In general, the child protection system tends to hold the mother responsible for her children's welfare, and if she continues to live with a violent man they may remove the children.

Many women try, without success, to attempt to manage their partner's violence. They hold on to the belief that if they try hard enough or do the right thing he will no longer need to be violent. This can mean that there is a constant focus on pleasing him and making things right, that the children's needs are subsumed to those of the father's. Mothers may also attempt to manage his interactions with the children, and believe they can shield their children from knowing the truth or can make up to them for the experience of witnessing the violence.

Despite the evidence of the harmful effects of living in violence, many mothers still hold onto ideas about the importance of a male role model. Many mothers cite this idea as being one of the strongest in preventing them from leaving — 'But he wouldn't have a father'. You can challenge this myth and the hold it may have in stopping decisions that would move towards safety rather than violence. A violent father is not an appropriate role model, and the sooner a boy is removed from witnessing his mother's abuse the greater the chance he has of not growing up like his father. Boys do not need fathers who are violent and abusive.

Even after leaving, it may often take a long time for you to recover from the effects of violence. You may have legal and family law matters to deal with. You may face the fear of abuse during visitation handovers. You may feel guilty that you have broken up the family or deprived your children of a father. You may try to compensate your children by letting them act out or by indulging them.

Sally, mother of three-year-old Christopher and four-year-old Carly, says:

> I find it difficult and draining since leaving. I try and compensate for the loss by allowing Christopher to have his dummy longer than other mums would. I am more sensitive to their needs — I think that because they've been exposed to violence (a situation most kids aren't exposed to), I put in more time. Living in violence undermined my parenting; it felt like everything I said or did was wrong. I was constantly criticised. It made me feel incapable, and that I always had to check with someone else. There were no boundaries set with the children. He'd let them stay up late. If I'd send them to their room, he'd go and cuddle them — he'd undermine me.
>
> I carry the guilt of being a sole mum — of feeling I've broken up the family; my ex-partner saying it's my fault that the kids haven't got a father strengthens this guilt.
>
> I felt I had dealt with this after leaving, but now the guilt has moved to different areas — it's guilt that I can't give them what they want financially.
>
> But it's positive that I've broken the cycle of violence. When we were together he'd always disagree with me and work against me; now I can set boundaries for the children, and parent more closely. When you are on your own, you're more conscious of the way you parent. Since I've left, the kids are more respectful to me — it's teaching them a different way. The kids used to use smacking and hitting to get their own way, but I'm changing that.

After leaving, they were both naughty and unsettled, but then their sleeping settled down — it seemed they thought they were safe. It took longer for the feelings and emotions to come out in my son — I think he was confused, and didn't understand.

I think it's important to teach boys to respect women, and view people with equality. Removing myself from the situation was a big step in teaching respect.

Recovery — what makes a difference?

Women often fear that their sons will follow in their father's footsteps and be violent. You may also fear, or may experience, your son's violence and abuse of you or other family members, even when your son is still very young. You may worry that if you attempt to constrain his behaviour he will choose to leave and live with his father (he may also be threatening to do this). You may worry that to challenge your son's behaviour is unfair, given what he has already experienced. Most mothers hope that their son will be different from his father, and want to encourage non-violent attitudes in their sons, attitudes in which women are respected, and responsibility and caring for others is emphasised.

There are many things that you can do to begin the recovery from the experience of domestic violence:

- **Consult a counsellor**

Counselling can be helpful in starting to address the ideas and attitudes that resulted from the violence. It can be helpful to try and get in touch with who you were before the violence, what the violence has done to your self-identity, and what you wish to reclaim and strengthen. Living with violence can make you confused and self-doubtful.

A good counsellor can help you work through this so that you can make choices that are right for you and your children. A counsellor can help you arrange the necessary changes to your life such as contacting a lawyer, getting an intervention order, or linking your kids into counselling services.

- **Attend a domestic violence support group**

Many women who have experienced domestic violence think that the violence only happens in their family and that they are to blame. Attending a group for women who have experienced domestic violence helps you to break through the isolation of the experience, and gives you the opportunity to

gain support from other women. There are also some groups for children. Your local community health service is a good starting point to access these groups.
- **Take one day at a time**

    Healing takes time, and may seem slow. Plan carefully, and don't expect too much from yourself. Remember, you and your children have been exposed to a highly abusive and traumatic experience.

    Take some time to relax. Get some childcare, even if it is only for a few hours a week. Go for a walk; try yoga or meditation; take up a sport or hobby. Create time for yourself.
- **Recognise that life will be tough for a while but it *will* change**

    You may have less money, or have moved house. Recognise that any change, even change for the better, is stressful. Give yourself permission to grieve, to feel tired, angry, relieved, whatever. These often-conflicting feelings are normal, and to be expected.

    Let your children know that you appreciate their strengths and capacity for change. The children will be readjusting too.

What helps children recover?

All children are affected by witnessing or directly experiencing domestic violence. A number of things make a difference:
- how long they lived with the parent who was violent, generally the longer the exposure to violence — the more harmful the effects
- being supported by another person who will listen to them; having close contact with another adult means that there is another role model for clear and respectful communication, conflict resolution, and someone special who cares about them

- if you take action and leave the situation, this gives the children the message that you are strong and decisive and that no one deserves or has to live with domestic violence
- being able to talk about the 'secret'
- clear acknowledgement that the abusive behaviour was wrong
- having a sense of personal achievement; for example, through education, sport, art or music
- being able to feel safe again, both physically and emotionally
- having access to good housing, finances and other resources
- being linked to a community and feeling part of it

What if my son is being violent or abusive?

If your son has witnessed violence, you may find him copying his father's behavior. Even mothers of young preschool boys may experience disrespectful language, having objects thrown at them, or being hit or spat at. Do not tolerate this behaviour; if left unattended it can become more serious and harder to address. Although behaviours may be associated with grief, sadness, confusion and a range of other emotions, these feelings cannot be an excuse for such behaviour. Your son must learn to express his feelings in other ways than through disrespect and abuse.

You may feel at a loss in tackling your son's behaviour. At times even a little boy can wield immense power and physical strength. Remind yourself that such power in the hands of one so young does not foster trust and security, but is in fact, a scary and out-of-control feeling for him. He will actually feel safer when you take control and exert your authority. It is important to decide in your own mind if his behaviour is abusive or violent, or whether it is 'testing' behaviour. For example, most children try swearing. This in itself is not abusive (but you may still wish to tackle it). If your son swears *at* you, or calls you derogatory names, then it is abusive.

Write a list of the behaviours and attitudes that make you uncomfortable, and sift through which ones needs a tighter parental approach and which constitute abuse or violence.

If you have recently experienced violence, it can sometimes be hard to name the violent or abusive behaviours. This is because a violent man may convince you that such behaviour is normal and acceptable so that you begin to doubt your gut feelings and be unsure yourself. Consult a friend or a counsellor to sort this out.

If your son is behaving abusively, then another set of tactics is necessary to deal with his behaviour and it would be advisable to seek counselling. It is a much more difficult process to address the behaviour of a boy who is bigger than you are and sees himself as a grown man. Women do not deserve abuse and violence from their partners — or their sons!

Here are some tips to deal with a son's abusive or violent behaviour:

- Never use violence or abuse yourself — smacking your son may mean that as he grows older he will smack you. Remember the saying, 'Violence breeds violence'. Use firmness, assertiveness, and parental care and love.
- Make sure he faces the consequences of his behaviour — if he purposely breaks or damages something, deduct the cost from his pocket money or allowance; he should help to clean up any mess or destruction he creates, and could forgo TV that night, or you can impose a similar consequence.
- Use time out — carry him into his room if necessary, and explain why he is there and that such behaviour will not be tolerated. Younger children soon pick up the message if the response is immediate, clear and consistent. If your son is bigger than you, and will not respect your boundaries, it is important to gain professional help.

Talking to your son

Sometimes, particularly if you are under stress, it is easier to pick up on the not-so-good qualities in your son. It is important to note these qualities, both for yourself as his mother and for his recovery. Your son may have some behaviours like his father's, but he is also more than his father.

Ask yourself:

- What are the qualities I most appreciate in my son?
- How did he come to develop those qualities?
- How can I best nurture and encourage those qualities?
- Are those qualities ones found in me, my ex-partner, or ones he has developed himself?
- What is it like to discover that qualities once liked and admired in my ex-partner are now exhibited by my son?
- How can I best deal with the likeness of son to father, without being disrespectful or undermining of my son?

It can be difficult for your son to deal with the knowledge that his father is violent. Some sons, particularly those who have grown up with violent fathers, may follow in their father's footsteps; others may abhor violence, and pledge to behave differently. Some boys feel guilt or shame that they are their father's child. It is important that your son does not feel tarnished because of his father's behaviour. He may feel torn between loving his father but hating his actions, but he may also side with his father and blame you, his mother.

These are very difficult issues to deal with. Recognise that there are some valid qualities that your son may appreciate in his father, but that his father's behaviour was not acceptable, and was not to be tolerated. For example, his father may have been a great sportsman or a computer whiz

— this doesn't make it okay to be violent, but it does mean he has something valid to offer your son.

You may wish to explore these questions with your son as he grows more emotionally mature.

> ### Ask your son:
>
> ◆ What are the things (if any) you like about your Dad?
> ◆ What's the hardest thing for you to miss out on in not living with your Dad?
> ◆ What are the things you wish were different? (Acknowledge that this is hard.)
> ◆ What parts of your Dad would you like to develop in yourself?
> ◆ What parts would you like to be different?
> ◆ Do you think you'd like to be different if you become a dad? How would you make sure this happened? What might be an early warning sign that things were getting a bit too much like doing things Dad's way?

Being exposed to domestic violence means a boy has to deal with a huge range of issues he may not otherwise have had to think about. Children are also extremely resilient and make amazing recoveries. Many boys who have experienced domestic violence grow up to be loving, caring and open men who choose life paths that are completely different from that of their fathers. Many boys come to terms with their father's violence, and as they get older manage to have a relationship with them, despite the past. Mothers play a vital role in helping boys through this difficult time. A warm, understanding and supportive relationship with one parent can help counteract the negative effects of violence. It's worth it!

Child abuse

Unfortunately those who advocate finding a male role model for boys rarely mention the possibility of paedophiles seeking out young boys. Many mothers fear that in attempting to find a male role model for their son they could inadvertently help a paedophile. The fear of paedophiles is not an exaggerated one! It is estimated that one in seven boys is sexually abused, usually by another male, most commonly one the boy knows and trusts. It is a myth to think that these abusers are gay; on the contrary, most are heterosexual males in seemingly 'normal' relationships, with their own children or as part of the community. Paedophiles often target those children whom they think they can easily befriend, or offer to help a mother whom they perceive is vulnerable or could do with additional support.

Sometimes perpetrators are fathers, uncles, grandfathers, other siblings or new partners, and this can make the situation fraught with anxiety and difficulty, and more difficult for a child to speak up.

Paedophiles often do not act immediately, but bide their time and wait until they have won the boy's and the mother's trust. The first instances of abuse are often relatively 'minor', but gradually over time they become more serious and more abusive. Paedophiles are clever at convincing children it is their fault, that they wanted the abuse, that no one would believe them, or that something dreadful will happen if they tell.

Incest is sexual abuse occurring within a family. It is usually not a one-off occurrence — for 30 per cent of children abused by a relative, the abuse continued for more than one year.[5] Incest is more likely to be disclosed when children are between the ages of 4 to 5 years and 13 to 14 years, respectively. Often there is no medical evidence of sexual assault, but this does not mean that abuse has not occurred. Although the vast majority of perpetrators of incest and sexual abuse are men, there are also women who sexually abuse children. It is a myth that children lie about being abused. Often the idea that someone we know could be abusing our child is too horrific to bear thinking about, but it does happen. It is best to believe your son and investigate his concerns, rather than dismissing them outright.

The effects of childhood sexual abuse are traumatic and longlasting, for both boys and girls. For boys the macho ethos makes it perhaps even more difficult for them to disclose the abuse, and many do not until they are adult men, or perhaps never do. Boys, more than girls, may feel they could have done something to prevent the abuse, but the shame is too great! Many parents are shocked beyond belief when they discover their son has been abused, at times by highly respected members of the community — politicians, clergy, schoolteachers, sportspeople or family members. The hardest thing for you to learn is that there is no way of telling whether or not a male person in your son's life is a paedophile.

This does not mean you should be so protective that you do not allow your son contact with men; this would be extremely detrimental to his development. The vast majority of men are appalled at paedophilia, and take a strong stand against such behaviour. It does mean that you should be aware of some of the indicators that a child has been abused, and that you should teach your child protective behaviours.

How child abusers operate

The stereotype that child abusers are older men in long brown overcoats who offer a child lollies is a myth when it comes to profiling child sex offenders. Although some sex offences may be one-off incidents, most child abuse is by people well known to the child and family, and most abuse continues over time. Many abusers are fathers, stepfathers, uncles, leaders of social and sporting networks, or others in positions of trust and responsibility.

Child abusers are well skilled in the ability to continue

their abuse without being found out. They use a number of tactics to make it extremely difficult for a child to tell and to resist their advances.

Most child abusers are male, though some are female. They are young, old, wealthy, poor, heterosexual, homosexual, married and single. Although some particular characteristics may stand out in the paedophile profile, there is no way of either picking an offender or discounting that a person may not be an abuser.

Many paedophiles make it their business to create a warm and trusting relationship between the child's family and themselves. This is done way before any attempts at abuse take place. Some abusers 'choose' their children — they may target those who may be socially isolated, having difficulties at home, or would be less likely to be believed; others are opportunistic and take advantage of the sole-parent family living nearby, or the child who likes to look at their motorbike or play with their puppy.

Sole mothers may be more 'at risk' of being targeted by paedophiles because they are stressed are not as physically or emotionally available to their children. They may inadvertently welcome the opportunity offered by the man next door to help James with his homework or take him to footy training. He may offer to babysit, take him camping or away on holiday.

Abusers take their time to 'groom' the child and form a close relationship with him. They give him affection, praise, special outings and gifts in order to encourage the child to depend on them, and be loyal to them.

They will often start a process of having 'special secrets'. At first these may be fun secrets, but later will become the secret of abuse. At each stage of the 'grooming' they will progressively test out the child's resistance to sexual intimacy. They will encourage the child to take responsibility for what is happening — the child will be confused between the strength of the growing emotional bond and the abuser's message that their relationship is special and secret, and one that demands the utmost loyalty. All this makes it very difficult for the child not to feel complicit in what is happening, to have any understanding of the dynamics at work, and very hard to tell anyone else.

Such grooming can occur for months without any explicit sexual abuse occurring. Often the abuser will be very open, playful and affectionate with the child, often in front of or with a parent. So the abuser may organise a picnic with mother, son and himself. If he is able to win the mother's trust, how much more successful will he be in ensuring secrecy and compliance from the boy?

Abusers are very subtle in moving from this playful and affectionate physical contact to sexual contact. Again, this may happen by degrees; at first they present this as accidental, then later are able to tell the child that he wanted this, as there was no rebuttal. This leaves the child feeling complicit and guilty, which in turn prevents him from telling for fear of punishment. These feelings may be even stronger if the child responds physically to the abuser's advances — for example, gets an erection.

It is important for sole mothers to know how abusers operate, and thus to understand the difficulty for children to disclose. Children need to feel confident that, at times, if they need to, they can disobey adults and assertively say 'No!'

Children rarely lie about abuse — perpetrators lie all the time! Giving your son love, affection, security and the opportunity to be listened to will help protect him from being targeted by a paedophile, and will mean that, if he is, he can tell you.

Signs of abuse

There is no clear way of gauging if a child has been abused other than if they actually disclose abuse. Most often a child's behaviour will change, often quite dramatically. So a gentle, easy-going boy may start distrusting, or swearing, or not doing his schoolwork.

Some of the symptoms of abuse can occur as a reaction to everyday changes such as puberty, separation and divorce, grief or life experiences and events. Some of the signs can also be seen in children who witness or experience domestic violence. Most professionals refer to such symptoms as 'indicators' — they are not definite effects of abuse but are indicators that abuse may have occurred. It is worth noting them so that if you feel at all worried or concerned you can ring a counsellor, social worker or child protection agency and raise these concerns, rather than feeling unsure. It is always better to be safe than sorry!

Some of the indicators of abuse include:

- nightmares
- difficulty going to sleep
- not wanting to have baths
- bedwetting
- regressive behaviour; for example, wanting a dummy
- tummy aches
- refusal to go to school
- troublesome behaviour at school
- crying
- marked change in behaviour
- depression
- fear of a particular person; for example, not wanting to go to Uncle George's house
- harassing younger family members
- not wanting to do the things he loved, such as sport
- self-harming behaviour and suicide attempts
- aggressive behaviour at school
- sexualised behaviour and 'acting out'
- using drugs and alcohol

Because the perpetrator is someone whom you know closely he may try and encourage you to think that your son's changed behaviour is due to factors other than abuse. He may tell you that your son is acting spoilt and needs more discipline, or that his changed behaviour is because of other changes, such as starting a new school or failing a school test. At the same time he may be telling your child that if he discloses what has been happening, Mummy may have a nervous breakdown, or he will be sent away from home, and that no one will believe him anyway.

The lies and deceit that perpetrators use are cunning and planned. Trust your own intuition, and if in doubt talk to someone outside your family.

Protective behaviours

Protective behaviour helps children protect themselves. This is particularly important, given that perpetrators are almost always physically bigger, stronger, and have more power and authority than the child does. This makes it harder for the child to resist their advances.

Some basic ideas to teach your son are:

- **Tell him he has the right to feel safe all the time**

It is necessary for him to learn to distinguish between feelings of fun and excitement as opposed to fear and danger.

- **Explain that his body is special**

No one has the right to hurt or touch him in a way that makes him feel uncomfortable or frightened.

- **Help him to identify 'early warning signs'**

It is important that he makes a link between what he is feeling in his body that indicates to him that he is not safe or comfortable. Ask him: What part of your body do you notice most when you are feeling frightened or unsafe? Even a very young child will be able to identity 'funny' feelings in his stomach; a faster heartbeat in his chest, or feeling 'yucky' all over. It is helpful for your son to identify these early warning signs, not just to help him with his intuition that things aren't right with grownups but also in relation to other risky and dangerous situations.

- **Help him to work out what he will do if he feels his early warning signs**

    It is important that he understands another protective message — nothing is so awful that you can't tell someone. He should know that he can talk about all sorts of feelings, including 'yucky' or scary ones, even those feelings that he thinks are supposed to be kept a secret.

- **Help him talk about secrets**

    Explain that there are good and bad secrets. Ask him to name good secrets, like surprise birthday parties, planning for breakfast in bed on Mother's Day, or someone special coming to visit. Bad secrets may be harder to name, but might include being hurt at school, seeing something disturbing happening, or being asked to keep a secret that makes you get an early warning sign. Tell an older child more directly that if anyone touches him in a way he doesn't like or makes him feel unsafe or uncomfortable, this should not be kept a secret.

- **Name a safe person**

Your son should ideally be able to name one person for each finger and thumb on one hand to whom he could talk about an unsafe feeling. Encourage your son to name you as the number-one person; the other four may include his dad, friends, relatives, teachers, and even a pet!

- **Persist with telling**

Tell your son that sometimes grownups are too busy to listen, or may not even believe him, so it is important to persist in telling the people in his network of safe people, or even other people, until he is believed. Tell him that teachers and police are particularly helpful in talking about early warning signs and feeling unsafe.

Teaching protective behaviour does not have to be like a formal lesson, but parts of it can be incorporated in day-to-day life. For example, if you are with your child and he has a fright, such as hearing a loud noise or being on an amusement ride, ask him where in his body he felt that fear. If he talks about fears in his life, such as when a big dog scared him, let him know that you appreciate him sharing his feelings with you.

Protective behaviour is a fairly simple concept, but it gives your son strategies to remain safe and protected. It also gives him the message that his feelings and his body are special and valued. Learning protective behaviour is no guarantee that your child will not be abused, or that he will disclose abuse if it happens, but it is a helpful start.

The vast majority of men who work with young people in sports and social agencies are not paedophiles but caring and committed men whose input would be most advantageous for your son. Don't let the fear of paedophiles prevent your son from enjoying these activities and a connection with other young people. Being with other adults and enjoying the connections and responsibilities that such groups bring are important for a boy's development. Just teach him to be aware.

What to do if you think your son is being abused?

If you discover your son is being abused, your world will be turned upside down. You may experience a huge range of emotions, including shock, grief, fear, sadness, guilt, anger, revenge, disbelief and shame. These feelings can last for a very long time, particularly if there are legal ramifications following your son's disclosure of abuse.

One of the hardest things to deal with if your son discloses sexual abuse is the recrimination that may follow from less-informed members of the community who may ask, 'Why didn't you prevent this?' or 'How could you not know this was going on?'

You may also put great blame and guilt on yourself for not knowing. Our society is also one in which mothers are expected to assume a great deal of responsibility for their children, and are blamed when anything goes wrong, despite mothers not being supported or acknowledged for the special role they undertake in our community.

But the mechanisms of abuse, which include secrecy and intimidation, mean that you could not possibly know that your partner or trusted person would abuse your son. There is an expectation that mothers of sons in particular should be able to trust those men around her who interact and support her son. Women who have been sexually abused themselves may find it difficult to interpret what seems like a genuine interest in their sons by another adult as a ploy to abuse them.

Ask your son:

- I've noticed that you don't want to go to the football with Uncle Frank anymore. I'm wondering if you don't feel as comfortable as you used to with him?
- I'm wondering what's taken away your pleasure from spending time with Ben? Does it make you feel sad or yucky when you're with him?
- I feel sad when I see a boy who was so interested in his school projects not seeming to care at all. It makes me think that something really upsetting must be going on in your life. Can we talk about it?
- I've noticed how much you stay in your room now, you just don't seem happy. You know nothing's that bad that you can't tell me about it. Is there something you want to talk about?

> - I've noticed you don't seem to like Dan any more. If you felt unhappy about him living here who would you tell? What would Teddy advise you to do?
> - Grandpa said you wouldn't sit on his knee any more. I just want you to know that that's your right, it is your body, but I wonder if anything's changed in the way you think about him?

Some professionals such as the police, as well as teachers and doctors, are legally required to notify Protective Services if they believe a child is being abused. If you talk to these people, the matter will be taken out of your hands in order to protect the child.

If your son tells you he is being abused, you need to talk to someone urgently about this. It is too distressing and confusing to try and deal with this on your own, and both you and your son need assistance. The sooner he receives counselling and an end is put to the abuse, the greater the chance is that the effects of the abuse will be minimised. See the list of agencies at the end of this book; it includes telephone services where you can talk and receive advice but still remain anonymous.

Chapter 15

Lesbian Mothers Raising Sons

The family is seen as the cornerstone of our society. Politicians, the media, religious groups, teachers and the general public talk about the family as if it is something that has an agreed-upon definition and understanding by all. The term is used as if 'the family' as we now know it has been with us forever, and has nothing to do with history or cultural or moral values.

Most understandings of the family seem to embrace the idea of a white, middle-class, heterosexual, two-parent, two-children-and-a-dog-stereotype. This, of course, discounts the majority of Australian families, such as those of Aboriginal people, extended families from non-English-speaking backgrounds, sole mothers, sole fathers, step-families, a couple without children, an older person and her cats, a group of friends, and lesbian and gay families.

Many people are starting to redefine the word 'family' and are choosing to live in different or alternative families and communities. This is becoming increasingly common with lesbians. More lesbians are now choosing to have children either with or without a partner. This may be because there is more tolerance to lesbians and other family configurations. It may be because there is more access to the means of artificial insemination, or that there is greater support and connection in the lesbian and gay community.

This socially and biologically driven phenomenon is producing a disproportionate number of male children within the current lesbian baby boom. Lesbians who choose to undergo donor insemination have at least a 65 per cent chance of bearing a son because of the need to predict exact ovulation times, the conditions of which favour a male embryo developing.[1]

One of the most often-heard criticisms of in-vitro fertilisation or artificial insemination for lesbian couples is that their children will not fare as well in life as children born to heterosexual parents. This is absolutely not the case. In fact, children of lesbian mothers are no more likely to suffer behavioural problems than children of heterosexual mothers. Research has found that children's development is not related to their parents' sexuality.[2] A study of fifty lesbian families, whose children were conceived through the resources of a sperm bank, showed that the children's normal social and emotional development was unrelated to variables such as parental sexual orientation or the number of parents in the household. The children in this study who did exhibit behavioural problems were those with parents who experienced higher levels of parental stress, higher levels of interparental conflict, and lower levels of love for each other.[3]

What makes lesbian parenting of any child special, let alone the lesbian parenting of a son? S. Pollack and J. Vaughan question the issues confronting lesbian mothers,[4] and pose a range of complex and multifaceted questions, including:
- How do these issues change as the children grow from infancy to childhood, from adolescence to adulthood?
- What are the needs of biological/non-biological lesbian parents?

- What is the role of the 'co-mother'?
- Are lesbian mothers just like heterosexual mothers, as some current comparison studies imply, or does the status of lesbians in our culture ensure that, to one degree or another, lesbian mothers *will* experience motherhood differently?
- How do children affect lesbian relationships?
- What happens when lesbian relationships break up?
- How do we deal with the health, legal, education and social service institutions?
- Do lesbian families treat boy and girl children differently?
- How to negotiate 'coming out'?

Lesbian mothers do not live in isolation, and their son's development will be influenced by a range of factors, other than the sexuality of his mother. Jan, a mother of four children — two of them boys, Joel (29) and Ben (24) — talks about her experience of 'coming out' as a lesbian, and how her two sons handled the experience in different ways:

> Joel was nearly fifteen and Ben was nearly nine when I had my first lesbian relationship. Of all my four children Joel was the least accepting, and didn't attend school for two weeks after I told him. At the time he had just moved to live with his father for a while. My lesbianism has always been an issue for him, though it's less now.
>
> In many ways I don't think it was so much a lesbian issue, as a blended family issue — he was the older male child, and we'd already had power struggles. He lived with his dad for two and a half years, and came back to a different family. My older daughter was now the oldest child, and my partner had moved in and played a parenting role. Joel resented her and resisted her position. I think his reaction would have been less had I been with a man, and also because my partner was only six years older than he was.
>
> When I tried to talk with him, he became agitated and angry. I wrote to him a couple of times and said that I believed I had the right to choose what relationships I had, and that I hoped he'd

get to a point of being able to respect that right. But he still hasn't taken it up with me.

My other son, Ben, was very different. He never lived with his father, nor connected to men as a young person. I guess my father was the most significant man in his life. This meant Ben had a special relationship with women. He was more sensitive and emotionally open. He accepted my partner into his life.

He was a good athlete but a slow learner, and suffered at school for this. As a teenager he got into drinking and smoking, and we worked hard with him to move him beyond his peer group. He came through that extremely well. He's likeable, easy to be with, and is currently looking to establish his own business. He's focused, motivated and a clear thinker. For him my lesbian relationship provided him with the family he had never had (I was pregnant when I left his violent father). He's quite comfortable with me being a lesbian, and when we all lived together was the happiest time for him.

Research on sons raised in lesbian families indicates that they may have to deal with teasing and feeling different, and they may experience feelings of isolation and rejection, but this does not mean that they cannot grow into thriving adults, adults who are tolerant and accepting of difference. Much of the way that sons deal with having a lesbian parent is a reflection on how their mother feels about her sexuality and how people to whom she is close relate to her.

Lesbian mothers can face more discrimination than do heterosexual mothers. They are discriminated against not only by their relationship status (unattached to a man) but also because of their sexuality. If heterosexual mothers are undermined by myths about the fate of boys in sole-mother families, how much more difficult it must be for the lesbian parent or parents raising a son? For lesbian mothers the difficulty is not so much in the parenting of a son but in dealing with the marginalisation and discrimination that results from the promulgation of heterosexist attitudes.

Some of these attitudes include:
- that lesbian families are not 'real' families
- that lesbians should not have children
- that a child, and more so a male child of lesbians, will not grow up 'normally'
- that a son of lesbian parents will 'turn homosexual' simply because of the parents' sexual orientation
- that lesbians shouldn't have access to artificial insemination

These attitudes isolate and marginalise both lesbians and their sons. They can make it difficult for lesbians to access the medical and other helping professions for fear of stigma or prejudice. It can also make it difficult for lesbians to feel okay about attending mainstream parenting groups and accessing mainstream parenting services. There are few parenting resources specifically for lesbians, although these are now increasing in number.

Some of the issues raised by lesbian mothers raising boys include:
- dealing with homophobia and heterosexism — at preschool, school and beyond
- wondering how much to be 'out' — will this make things difficult for my son?
- wondering where to be 'out' — should I tell the preschool, the school, and, if so, how?
- wanting my son to develop an 'alternative' masculinity, one that is not based on stereotypical ideas of maleness
- dealing with my son's questions: Where is my Dad? How did I get to be born? Why are you lesbian?
- understanding the needs of a boy
- dealing with family members
- wondering how to link my son in with other men
- dealing with some aspects of the lesbian community, which may want to exclude older boys from women-only events

In addition, a lesbian mother can feel uncertain of how to respond to the myriad of questions from other adults in

her life. Many of these questions may contain inherent value judgements or heterosexist attitudes:
- people wanting to know how you became pregnant, or if your son has contact with his father
- people asking you about the provision of male role models for your son
- people assuming you would not want to be part of a heterosexual community
- people assuming there must be a partner hidden away somewhere
- people assuming that you and your partner both take on the label of 'Mum'
- people assuming that you and your partner take on strict heterosexual-gendered roles
- people assuming you and your partner are co-parenting
- people asking who is the 'real' mother if you have a partner

These can be very tricky issues when trying to find a path between being true to yourself as a lesbian and not feeling you have to answer to other people's expectations and curiosity. You may want to be direct, but feel concerned that direct answers may impact negatively on how people respond to your son. You may want to share and be open about your life, but in a way where this is accepted and not under scrutiny.

Probably a good starting point is to challenge some of the myths about lesbians and lesbian parenting that even lesbians themselves get pulled into! Perhaps one of the most harmful experiences for children is to grow up with parents who feel ashamed, embarrassed or guilty — this is the same for a son of lesbian parents. It is much more helpful for him to grow up with parents who have a healthy, strong and sure belief in the choices they have made and their ability to bring up a son than for him to feel their sexuality or relationship is something that needs to be hushed up and a secret. Of course, as a lesbian mother you will need to plan what and when you tell your son, the same as does any parent, but, generally speaking, the younger your son comes to accept his family experience as normal the more secure he will feel. Chances are he will experience prejudice, but you can help him by talking about how he might deal with this, and respond to it.

Although there are many issues that can be of concern to lesbian mothers, it is also worthwhile to consider that lesbian households are raising a new generation of men who will differ significantly from those raised by heterosexual parents. Lesbian parenting generally incorporates strong feminist principles, which offers a great potential to challenge those myths about how men should behave and how relationships should be enacted. Many sons in lesbian households see women holding a vast array of non-traditional jobs, such as politicians, bus drivers, lawyers, engineers, architects, film makers and corporate consultants. The fluidity of gender roles is one of the most important contributions to lesbian parenting.

Who is my father?

Some research has cited 'the father question' as one of the most concerns in raising a son.[5] Some difficulties relating to father origins are:

- Should I tell my son the truth, that his father was a sperm donor?
- What if he wants to know how I got the sperm, and how he was conceived?
- At what age should I tell him that his father donated sperm?
- How can I tell him in a way that emphasises how special he is to us?
- How can I explain the choice to become a lesbian after being married and having children?
- My son doesn't know I'm a lesbian — should I tell him, and at what age?
- Does it matter that he doesn't see his father?
- Should I tell him his father is gay?

It is important for children to know something of their origins; this helps create a sense of their own personal identity. If you were previously in a heterosexual relationship and your son still sees his father, you can explain that after (or maybe before) you separated you discovered or decided that you were more interested in sharing your life with a woman. You can tell him that you and his father decided to have a baby, but that not being with his father and you being a lesbian does not mean he is not special. On the contrary, he is the most important person in your life. You can tell him that the most important thing is to feel okay and happy with who you are, whether lesbian, straight, or a bit of both!

What and when you decide to tell your son will depend on your own values and ways of doing things. It does seem to be helpful for children to know their origins from a very young age rather than having a 'bombshell' dropped on them later. Some mothers have told their sons that they came into being 'because Mummy really, really wanted a baby' so she decided to have one through a different way. You could explain to a younger son that you made the baby with your eggs in your body, but used the sperm of someone other than your husband. You can tell him how special this makes him. An older child is more able to deal with the complexities of artificial insemination.

Ask yourself:

- Have heterosexist ideas undermined your self-acceptance and your parenting of your son?
- How might these heterosexist ideas try to convince you that your mothering isn't as good as or up to scratch as that of heterosexual mothers?
- Are there times when you have been able to resist these ideas?

- If you were to resist these ideas, what difference would it make to your mothering?
- What are the important ways of being for you as a mother? Do they fit with the heterosexist ideas? If not, how are they different?
- How will you maintain your own individual idea of parenting?

Lesbian mothers may feel concerned about how living in a lesbian household will impact on their children. Don't let your concern get in the way of acknowledging that often children of lesbian or 'different families' show a greater tolerance and appreciation for diversity in others. In fact, research has indicated that children raised in lesbian households are more accepting of diversity and open to a range of ideas about lived experiences. It is more helpful for your son to see that being lesbian is no big deal to you — that you see being lesbian as being just as normal as being heterosexual; it is just a preference you have made. Being 'out' and giving him direct and honest answers leaves him more easily able to deal with homophobic behaviour in the schoolyard. As your son gets older he may be more sensitive to living in a lesbian household, but this can also be a reflection of adolescence, where most parents are rigidly scrutinised and found wanting. Adolescents want to conform and yearn for sameness, so this may mean you will have to revisit some of the issues and dilemmas you had thought he had dealt with at an earlier age.

Your son may go through a number of 'stages' as he develops and intellectualises being the son of a lesbian mother. If he feels he may at risk of being stigmatised, he may utilise a number of strategies to avoid this.[6] These strategies may include staying closeted or coming out very selectively about his mother. He may go through a period of not wanting to bring friends home in case he is 'found out'. He may explain your partner as an aunt or friend; he may investigate who is safe to tell and who isn't; or he may come out about his family and confront those who stigmatise him. He may respond passionately, and at times aggressively, to people who challenge him or make fun of his family. This may seem disconcerting to you if you have tried hard to encourage your son to feel proud and confident about having a lesbian parent. Boys who act in this way need to find constructive ways of dealing with their feelings without taking it out on others. It is important to continue to talk and listen to your son and accept what is happening for him.

Many lesbian mothers reduce their son's and their own sense of marginalisation and isolation by joining with other lesbian mothers in social activities or in a lesbian-parenting group. They may also be active in seeking out lesbian-friendly preschools and schools, and by promoting school policies that emphasise 'no tolerance for bullying' and appreciation for diversity and difference.

Your son may not want to participate in lesbian functions, particularly as he gets older, but again this may be a reflection of adolescent rather than anti-lesbian behaviour. If you are clearly 'out' in the community and politically active, he may lean towards conservatism or 'straighter' ways of behaving in an attempt to feel more integrated with the rest of society. This difference to your way may feel alarming, but is also part of his development as an individual and making his own choices. He will hope that you will accept this difference in him and the decisions he is making for his own life.

Jessica Wells writes that lesbian parents have all the earmarks of an oppressed group breaking new ground.[7] They are subjected to appalling injustice at the hands of the courts; forced to educate other people everywhere they go, including places that are traditionally relied on for nurturance, such as doctors' offices and schools, and may selectively hide their family structure for fear of recrimination, thereby struggling with the mixed messages sent to their children. Often lesbian mothers are saddled with pressure to see themselves as being as good as their heterosexual counterparts in raising traditional children rather than acknowledging the inherent differences in their children. Despite this, they are frequently able to overcome all the obstacles and create close and loving households.

A lesbian mother is just like any other: you want your children to grow up strong and happy, you struggle with their parenting, you organise shopping, socialising, helping your son with his homework, and you share affection, joy, sadness and pain.

Four potential benefits to a son reared by a lesbian mother:

- He learns to respect, empathise with and tolerate the multicultural environments in which others live.
- He has the opportunity to experience flexible interpretations of gendered behaviour and the freedom to value equality in personal and intimate relationships.
- He comes to understand that families are based not only on biological relationships but perhaps more so on love, self-definition and choice.
- With the emergence of intentional and visible gay cultural activities in recent decades, the son of lesbian parents observes and experiences strong ties in the gay community that have the potential to support and enhance his family relationships.[8]

Being a lesbian parent means you probably have made a deliberate and conscious choice to have a child (even if you were heterosexual before you were lesbian). Let your son know that. It means having the courage to venture into uncharted territory, and the excitement of being able to recreate and challenge definitions of family and networks.

Chapter 16

Conclusion: Sons of Sole Mothers Speak Out

When we read in the media about the trouble boys are in in our society, we, as mothers, may feel overwhelmed by the dire predictions made about boys, particularly those raised by sole mothers. It is very rare to hear about boys who have been raised by sole mothers, without a male role model, who have 'made it'. It is also unusual to hear about the struggles that young women in our society face — struggles that Dorothy Pipher has documented so well in her book *Reviving Ophelia*.[1]

Many groups in our society are in trouble. Our society is becoming increasingly troubled as a result of an economic and political structure that leads people to be thought of in terms of products or dollars. Consequently, those who do not produce or are unable to consume (or buy) are rendered insignificant. In this system, the heterosexual middle-class family unit is the cornerstone of consumerism — think of TV ads and how 'the family' is represented. Other family forms, or those not in family relationships, are marginalised and denied access to resources.

Depression, anxiety, unemployment, homelessness and substance abuse are all increasing as a result of the troubled society in which we live. Men are struggling to find their place in a post-feminist world. Relationships are struggling, with more couples ending the struggle than staying together. Girls are expressing their frustrations through attempted suicide, substance abuse, anger and self-harm. They experience anorexia and domestic violence and sexual assault. Although some statistics may show girls are attaining higher academic results, many are falling through the gaps and dropping out. It is also important to consider that, even if girls do achieve academically, they still have to deal with 'the glass ceiling' and the dominance of men in the professional world. It is a myth to say that boys are in trouble and girls are doing fine.

Research findings inevitably reflect the bias of the researcher, and this appears to be exemplified by those who represent the needs of boys and men. There is much research of the detrimental effects of family breakdown; there is also research that clearly demonstrates that children do far better when families separate rather than continue in loveless and conflictual relationships.

It is mere conjecture to suggest that boys cannot thrive without a male role model. There is absolutely no proof. Some of the proponents of the male-role-model theory — and it is a theory — may have particular barrows to push but it is vital that sole mothers recognise that these are simply ideas, and to form your own opinions and practise wisdom about what is right for your son and for you.

This last chapter contains the stories of some adult men who have grown up in homes without a male role model or father. It also gives their mothers' viewpoints. These stories will hearten and inspire you!

Andrew

Andrew, 32, is a dentist who grew up in country Victoria:

> Mum and dad separated when I was three. They tried to get back together a few times but finally divorced when I was six. I lived with mum but both parents were always civil to me and mum encouraged me to see my dad, although I only saw him at weekends every couple of months. I didn't like going there

because my dad was so different from my mum. Looking back I didn't really get on with my dad until my early 20s. Now I can see that he really loved me but then I experienced him as distant.

Any difficulties I experienced as a child were more a reflection of the divorce — we had to move house and I changed school a few times. I think that made me feel insecure, I didn't like being left alone.

I think my mum gave me everything I needed. I felt incredibly loved by her but she wasn't overprotective. It was freely given love. My mother has taught me a respect for all people and to accept people as they are. That all people are important. She is a Uniting Church minister and has strong social justice values, which she passed on to me. I also have her stubbornness. She was a fighter!

I attribute growing up okay to being raised by such a loving mum, and having a very close-knit extended family. My mother made a really concerted effort to give me as many opportunities as she could.

She started reading sex-education books to me when I was about five. And when I was a teenager she'd always make it easy for me to bring friends around after school, or would take me swimming. She was conscious to get me involved with other people.

I came out as gay when I was 26. My mum was very loving but I think she found it a bit hard as she had a kind of 'sacred sex' attitude shaped by her Christian beliefs. But she absolutely did the best she could and I felt no sense of rejection. She just didn't have the same understanding about male sexuality as me.

When I was young I didn't realise how much mum sacrificed for me. Now I can see that she pushed hard for me and I now realise the sacrifice.

Tom

Tom is in his mid-thirties and grew up in Canada. He is a social worker:

Conclusion | 273

My dad died when I was thirteen. My grandmother had moved in when I was ten and she was a strong presence in my life. My mother worked and it was my grandmother who took on the caretaking role. We are Chinese and Gran was very traditional and maintained the Chinese ideals. For example she would always insist on family rituals like eating together. She was always there when I would get up in the morning and made sure my household routines were carried out like getting washed up, having breakfast, and putting on clean clothes. She helped us to remember our culture and language and also spoke Chinese to us (she didn't speak English).

When my dad died it did not greatly affect me because my mum and grandmother were such strong influences in my life. My father was less involved in my life as I got older, whereas my grandmother had always been 'hands on'. Both my mother and grandmother were protective and sheltered me from the emotional upheaval I could have experienced from my father's death. Grandmother was the one I got my approval from and I accepted that she was head of the family.

Having a strong and supportive family and being so linked to my Chinese origins has helped me deal with the elements of racism I did experience growing up — there were incidents of physical and verbal assault — and even though I looked physically different I did not feel alone and felt okay about myself.

I think being raised by two women and with my sister meant the male/female roles were not so staunchly ingrained. My family's influence has made me open to diversity in male and female roles; for instance I appreciate the duties and responsibilities of housework and do a good job. As an adolescent I learnt about male roles from the media, wider culture and TV but not having a dad made no difference to knowing how to grow up male.

I loved my dad but I think not having him did not really affect me because the female role models were so strong. Not everything was rosy. There were tough times when I really missed my dad, and when I rebelled against my family's expectations. It's more important to feel loved and cared for than having a male role model. I'm happy being who I am, I'm not your average male bloke, I'm more sensitive to things and I think I turned out okay.

Rob

Rob is 19 and is studying town planning at university. His mother Ann also speaks in this book. Rob says:

> I was two years old when my dad left. I have thought about it a lot. The hardest thing was feeling embarrassed when your father wasn't around and everyone else's was. I felt this most in secondary school with sport. I think it was because I felt different from the other kids.
>
> Now I look back and I don't think not having a dad made a difference. At the time I think it took me longer to learn how to be a man — to interact socially with my friends but that's okay now. I did have some men around me — my grandfather who died when I was twelve and my best friend's father, Charles. I guess only having one adult perspective was hard — but I suppose it wouldn't have needed to be a man, just another view when I wanted to discuss things.
>
> Growing up with two women (my mother and sister) did teach me patience! They used to argue with each other a lot. I'm happy with the way I grew up — I feel clear about who I am as a man. It may have been because really I have never known my dad, perhaps if he had left when I was ten or older it would have been harder.

James

James, 19, is the son of Kaya, who also speaks in this book. He is studying professional writing at Deakin University and wants to write fiction. He has an older brother and younger sister:

> When I consider it, I didn't really long for a dad. You don't long

for what you haven't had; there was nothing to compare it with because I never had my dad living with me. When I look at the guys at school who did have dads I see that some of them were pretty messed up. Mum and my father split up before I was born. My older brother came over from New Zealand when I was ten years old. He's seven years older and I guess I used to hang out with him.

Mum always treated me as an adult and never as a stupid adolescent boy. She gave me a sense of confidence in myself, listened to me and treated me with respect. Mum has always been against making gender distinctions in relation to mothers and fathers. She'd tell me she was both my mother and my father. Anyway what does a father do for his son other than taking him to sporting activities? I never felt I needed a father to be disciplined.

I think growing up with my mum and a sister made me more sensitive to women's issues. I notice that I get along more with women than some other guys, I don't feel intimidated by them, and it's never been an issue for me to relate to women. I've been in a relationship for four years now. I do feel different from other males but not in a negative way.

Other men can't express themselves emotionally or else they have to get aggressive to do it but my mum is emotionally expressive — she shows what she feels and I've picked up on that. I can show emotions like fear or intimidation or vulnerability. It doesn't frighten me to show these emotions like it does other men. I've always tried to talk with her and have voiced my feelings and emotions. Mum is very strong and she's a very lateral thinker. I've picked up on that and also her creativity.

Mum was pretty open about sex and sexual relationships. We just talked about it as something normal. She'd also give me books and she had boyfriends around. She'd say 'It's not bad, it's just making love.'

I did have a feeling of being marginalised because mum encouraged us to feel that way because of her schizophrenia. She'd compare us to how she thought families 'should' be. She's always had schizophrenia — that's the way she is. When I was a year old she was in a psychiatric institution for ten months and I went to live with nuns. But I can't remember that.

I've never told anyone she has schizophrenia. People don't understand. I can't remember her explaining it to me either, it's just something I've always known. People say to me that I have gone through so much and ask, 'How have you made it?' but it's been no big deal to me.

I enjoyed school and pushed myself. I made myself succeed. Both mum and my sister's father, who was living with mum, encouraged me to do well at school. I've made good friends with both men and women teachers — in fact I'm going out to dinner with my secondary school female literature teacher tonight!

I have talked to my father on the phone — he lives in Adelaide. I've only seen him a couple of times. It's not a full on father/son relationship but we get on well. I know he does regret not being there for me.

Because there was no man in the house my mum made me one. Some people would say that was bad. She'd ask me to help her do administrative things like pay the bills. I'd also help her make important decisions and she'd ask me for advice. I owe a lot of who I am to my mother — her strength and the way she treated me with respect and equality. We still talk and see each other although I now live away from home.'

David

David is 29 years old and is studying an arts degree at La Trobe University.

I didn't know my father — I lived with him until I was two and then my mother left him. He died when I was five. My mum had a few boyfriends but they didn't have much to do with me. When I was young I used to think it was a good thing not having a dad because I had so much freedom. But at times I wish I was disciplined — I had too much freedom. When I was thirteen I started to use drugs and get in trouble with the law. My family disowned me when I was about fifteen and then my stepfather kicked me out of home. I haven't had much to do with my mum since then until about a year ago.

I think I got into trouble because I was allowed too much freedom. I didn't have enough discipline and could do whatever I wanted. In some ways the freedom was positive — she let me form my own view of the world. My life has been hard.

The above stories testify to the resilience of children — they can undergo hardship and they can also come through it. The five men in this chapter — all raised by sole mothers — have a strong sense of social justice and empathy for others because they have, in their own way, experienced a sense of marginalisation and a need to push themselves just that bit farther because they were children of sole mothers.

The mothers may have wished that some aspects of their parenting was different but the closeness of the bond they have with their sons sustains their sons' belief in themselves and their abilities.

These stories illustrate that sons do get on with their own lives and prove their experience in their own ways, ways that can be positive and of benefit to others in the community.

As well as being raised by sole mothers, all the men interviewed experienced other degrees of marginalisation — being gay, being Chinese, being the son of a mother who had suffered mental illness, being the son of a violent father and being in an environment without clear boundaries. Yet each man reports that, despite some hardship and suffering, they were able to move forward in their lives in very positive ways.

Attempts by lobby groups to make divorce more difficult, to cut back social security benefits to sole mothers, or to reduce maintenance paid by non-custodial fathers, add to the burden carried by these sole parent families. Yet the men in this chapter talk more about marginalisation and feeling different as their greatest concerns and obstacles.

Our society tends to isolate people, rather than strengthen

community bonds. When we are looking to help boys raised by sole mothers, we need to look at providing a higher degree of validation and support to sole mothers. We need to address the financial stress and poverty that often arises from being a sole parent. But even more importantly we need to look at helping mothers to link in with communities — be it in preschool, school or a working community. We need to make those institutions that deal with parenting and children more relevant to changing and diverse family structures.

Schools need to consider that the majority of children may be from step- or sole-parent families and how this can both be acknowledged and such family structures strengthened and valued. Welfare agencies need to think about running specific parenting courses for sole mothers, and to set up support mechanisms for sole mothers and their children. And workplaces need to acknowledge the difficulty of sole parenting and to allow some flexibility in order to support sole mothers. No sole mother should ever need to apologise or feel guilty.

Helpful Contacts

Check the front pages of your local telephone directory for useful helplines.

- Parentline (national/NSW): 132055
  ACT Parent Helpline: 132055
  NT Child and Family Protective Services: 08 8962 4399
  Qld Parentline 1800 77135
  Parent Help Line SA: 1300 364 100
  Tasmanian Parent Helpline: 1800 001 219
  Parentline Victoria: 13 2289
- Community Health Services: ring your local council
- Men's Responsibility Groups: ring your local council or community health centre
- Domestic Violence: 1800 015 188, 1800 810 784, or ring your local council or community health centre
- Kids Help Line: 1800 55 1800
- Child Abuse Prevention: 1800 688 009
- Sexual Assault: 1800 806 292
- Family Drug Support: 1300 368 186

Notes

Introduction

[1] O. Silverstein & B. Rashbaum, *The Courage to Raise Good Men*, Viking, New York, 1994.

[2] M.J. Dudley, N.J. Kelk, J.T.M. Florio, J.P. Howard and B.G.H. Waters, 'Suicide among Young Australians, 1964–1993', *Medical Journal of Australia*, vol.169, 1998, pp.77–80.

1 The Experience of Being a Sole Mother

[1] Australian Bureau of Statistics, *Children, Australia: A Social Report*, ABS, Canberra, 1999.

[2] ibid.

[3] *Herald Sun*, 1999.

[4] R. Weston & B. Smyth, 'Financial living standards after divorce', *Family Matters*, no.55, Autumn 2000. It is estimated that income levels for women drop by two-thirds after separation. Males on average earn more than women. Research has indicated that when women have children their opportunities for employment, further education and income-earning capacity drop markedly. Many sole mothers may spend long periods out of the workforce — only 43 per cent are employed, 23 per cent are in fulltime work, and 20 per cent in part-time work. Children from sole-parent families are twice as likely to live in poverty as those in two-parent families.

[5] Australian Bureau of Statistics, *Australian Social Trends 2000*, ABS, Canberra, 2000, p.149.

[6] Weston & Smith, op. cit.

[7] Australian Bureau of Statistics, *Children, Australia: A Social Report*.

[8] ibid.

[9] S. Biddulph, 'Healthy masculinity starts in boyhood', *Australian Family Physician*, vol.24, no.11, November 1995, p.2050.

[10] P. J. Caplan & I. Hall-McQuor-

quodale, 'Mother blaming in major clinical journals', *American Journal of Orthopsychiatry*, vol.55, no.3, pp.345–53.

2 Questioning Gender

1. S. Biddulph, *Raising Boys: Why Boys Are Different, and How to Help Them Become Happy and Well-balanced Men*, Finch, Sydney, 1997, p.81.
2. R. Brannon, 'The male sex role: Our culture's blueprint of manhood and what it's done for us lately', in D. David & R. Brannon (eds), *The 49% Majority: The Male Sex Role*, Addison-Wesley, Reading, Mass., 1976.
3. C. Hughes & K. Weiss, 'Perpetrator Programs, An Insider Witness Perspective', *Domestic Violence and Incest Resource Centre Newsletter*, Winter edn, 1999.

3 Encouraging Good Communication in Boys

1. Dale Spender, *Man-Made Language*, Pandora, USA, 1999.

4 Talking about Feelings and Emotions

1. W. Pollack, *Real Boys*, Owl Books, New York, 1999, p.57.
2. P. Mitchell, 'Valuing Young Lives', *Evaluation of the National Youth Suicide Prevention Strategy (1995–9)*, Australian Institute of Family Studies, 2000, p.24.

5 Setting Limits and Boundaries

1. J. Newsom & E. Newsom, *The Extent of Physical Punishment in the UK*, Approach, London, 1989, p.106.
2. ibid.

6 Attention Deficit Disorder and Attention Deficit Hyperactivity Disorder

1. C. Green & K. Chee, *Understanding ADD: Attention Deficit Disorder*, Doubleday, Sydney, 1994.
2. ibid.
3. W. Pollack, *Real Boys*, Owl Books, New York, 1999, p.255.

7 Helping Your Son with School Life

1. W. Pollack, *Real Boys*, Owl Books, New York, 1999, p.236.
2. M. Evans & L. Kelly, *Children, Australia A Social Report*, ABS, Canberra, 1999, p.23.
3. S. McLanahan & G. Sandefur, *Growing Up with a Single Parent: What Hurts, What Helps*, Harvard University Press, Cambridge, Mass., 1994.

8 Dealing with Your Son's Anger, Understanding His Grief

1. R. Taffel, 'Discovering our children' *Family Therapy Net-worker*, 1999.

9 Separation: Residence and Contact

1. E. Gallagher, *Children and Divorce*, unpublished, 1996.
2. K. Funder, 'Changes in Child Support', Family Matters, no.48, spring/summer, 1998, p.37.

10 Creating Connections and Negotiating New Relationships

1. S.E. Khoo, *Repartnering After Divorce: The Formation of Second Families*, Child Support Scheme Evaluation Study, Australian

Institute of Family Studies, Melbourne, 1989.
2. Australian Bureau of Statistics, *Marriages and Divorces*, ABS, Canberra, 1999, p. 77.

11 Combining Sole Parenting with Paid Employment

1. S.R. Zubnick, S.R. Silbum, A. Garton et al, *Developing Health and Wellbeing in the Nineties*, Western Australian Child Health Survey, ABS & ICHR, Perth, 1995.

12 Being Open about Sexuality

1. M. Grose, *Great Ideas for Tired Parents*, Mandarin, Port Melbourne, 1996.

13 Dealing with Adolescent Boys

1. E. Erikson, *Childhood and Society*, Penguin, Harmondsworth, 1965, p.252.
2. S. Biddulph, *Raising Boys: Who Boys Are Different, and How to Help Them Become Happy and Well-balanced Men*, Finch, Sydney, 1997, pp.46–7.
3. ibid, p.47.
4. W. Pollack, *Real Boys*, Owl Books, New York, 1999, p.243.
5. ibid, p.55.
6. 'The Effects of Television and Multimedia on Children and Families in Victoria', Family and Community Development Committee, Parliament of Victoria, Melbourne, Aug.1998, p. 271.
7. K. Browne & A. Pennell, *The Effects of Video Violence on Young Offenders*, Home Office, Her Majesty's Stationery Office, London, 1997.
8. D. Zillman & J. Bryant, 'Pornography and the trivialisation of rape', *Journal of Communication*, vol. 32, Autumn 1992.
9. J. Harrison & J. Moller, Injury Mortality amongst Aboriginal Australians, *Australian Injury Prevention Bulletin*, Issue 7, 1994.

14 How to Recover from Domestic Violence and Prevent Child Abuse

1. J. Mugford, *Domestic Violence*, National Committee on Violence, Australian Institute of Criminology, Canberra, 1989.
2. M. Condonis, K. Paroissien & B. Aldrich, *The Mutual Help Group: A Therapeutic Program for Women Who Have Been Abused*, Redfern Legal Centre, Sydney, 1990.
3. E.N. Jouriles & K.D. O'Leary, 'Interpersonal reliability of reports of marital violence, *Journal of Consulting and Clinical Psychology*, 1985, no.53, p.297.
4. A. Blanchard, 'Violence in families: The effect on children', *Family Matters*, Australian Institute of Family Studies, no.34, 1994, p.31.
5. Dymphna House, *Facing the Unthinkable: A Survival Guide for Mothers Whose Children Have Been Sexually Abused*, Dymphna House Inc., Haberfield, NSW, 1990, p.9.

15 Lesbian Mothers Raising Sons

1. J. Wells, *Lesbians Raising Sons*, Alyson Books, New York, 1997.
2. C. Patterson, 'Families of the lesbian baby boom: Parents' division of labour and children's adjustment', *Developmental Psychology*, vol.31, 1995.
3. R. Cahn, B. Raboy & C. Patterson, 'Psychosocial adjustment among children conceived via donor

insemination by lesbian and heterosexual mothers', *Child Development*, no.2, April 1998.
4   S. Pollack & J. Vaughan, *Politics of the Heart: A Lesbian Parenting Anthology*, McNaughton & Gunn, New York, 1987.
5   K. Cortez, 'My two moms: Issues and concerns of lesbian couples raising sons', *Progress: Family Systems Research and Therapy*, vol.5, Encino, Calif., 1996.
6   C. Allison, Children of lesbian mothers: Negotiating stigma in a homophobic world, University of California at Santa Barbara, work in progress, p.323.
7   J. Wells (ed.), *Lesbians Raising Sons*, Alyson Books, Calif., 1997.
8   K. Allen, 'Lesbian and Gay Families', in T. Arendell (ed.), *Contemporary Parenting: Challenges and Issues*, Sage, New York, 1997.

16 Conclusion: Sons of Sole Mothers Speak Out

1   M. Pipher, *Reviving Ophelia*, Doubleday, Sydney, 1996.

Bibliography

Allen, K (1997), Lesbian and Gay Families in Arendell, T (ed) *Contemporary Parenting: Challenges and Issues*, Sage, NY

Allison, C *Children of Lesbian Mothers: Negotiating Stigma in a Homophobic World*, work in progress, University of California at Santa Barbara

Bennett, Dr D. (1987), *Growing Pains: What to do when your children turn into teenagers*, Doubleday, NSW

Biddulph, S., 'Healthy masculinity starts in boyhood', *Australian Family Physician*, vol.24, no.ii, November 1995

— (1997) *Raising Boys: Why boys are different and how to help them become happy and well-balanced men*, Finch Publishing, Sydney

Blanchard, A (1993) Violence in Families. The Effect on Children *Family Matters*, The Australian Institute of Family Studies, no 34

Brannon, R (1976) 'The Male Sex Role: Our Culture's Blueprint of Manhood and What It's Done for Us Lately', in David, D & Brannon, R (eds) *The 49% Majority; The Male Sex Role*, Addison-Wesley, Reading, MA

Browne, K and Pennell, A. (1997) *The Effect of Video Violence on Young Offenders*, Home Office, Her Majesty's Stationery Office, London

Cahn, R, Raboy, B and Patterson, C, (April 1998), Psychosocial Adjustment among Children Conceived via Donor Insemination by Lesbian and Heterosexual Mothers, *Child Development*, no 2

Condonis, M, Paroissien, K and Aldrich, B (1990) *The Mutual Help Group: A Therapeutic Program For Women Who Have Been Abused*, Redfern Legal Centre Publishing, Sydney

Cortez, K 1996 'My Two Moms:

Issues and Concerns of Lesbian Couples Raising Sons, *Progress: Family Systems Research and Therapy*, vol 5, Encino, California

Dallos, R and Urry, (1999) *Abandoning our parents and grandparents: does social constructionism mean the end to systemic family therapy?* The Association for Family Therapy, GB

Dymphna House (1990) *Facing the Unthinkable: A survival guide for mothers whose children have been sexually abused*, Southwood Press, Australia

Erikson, E *Childhood and Society*, Penguin, Harmondsworth

Family and Community Development Committee, Parliament of Victoria (August 1998) *The Effects of Television and Multimedia on Children and Families in Victoria*

Flanagan, C and J (1988) *Working Parents: Happy Families*. Angus and Robertson, England

Freedman, J & Combs, G (1996) *Narrative Therapy: The Social Construction of Preferred Realities*, Norton, New York

Gallagher, E (1996) *Life in a War Zone*, unpublished paper

Gallagher E (1996) *Children and Divorce*, unpublished paper

Goldstein, R (1994) *Stop Treating Me Like A Kid*, Penguin, USA

Green, C and Chee, K (1994) *Understanding ADD: Attention Deficit Disorder*, Double Day

Grose, M (1996) *Great Ideas For Tired Parents*, Mandarin, Victoria

Harrison, J and Moller, J (1994) Injury Mortality amongst Aboriginal Australians, *Australian Injury Prevention Bulletin*, Issue 7

Henwood, B (1995) *The How-To of being a Working Mother*. Angus and Robertson, Australia

Herald-Sun (1999) Millennium Survey, Melbourne

Howard, J (1998) *Bringing Up Boys: a Parenting Manual*, Australian Council for Educational Research, Melbourne

Hughes, C and Weiss, K *Perpetrator Programs, An Insider Witness Perspective* in DVIRC Newsletter, Winter Edition, 1999

Ives, S, Fassler, D, Lash, M (1985) *The Divorce Workbook*, Waterfront Books, Vermont, USA

Jouriles, E.N., Murphy, C.M., and O'Leary, D.K. (1994) Interspousal Aggression, Marital Discord and Child Problems, *Journal of Consulting and Clinical Psychology*, vol 57 (3)

Kidd, J and Kidd J (1990) *Sibling Rivalry*, Doubleday, Australia

McLanahan, S and Sandefur, G (1994), *Growing up with a single parent: What hurts, what helps*, Cambridge Mass, Harvard University Press

Mugford, J (1989) *Domestic Violence*, National Committee on Violence. Canberra: Australian Institute of Criminology

Newsom, J and Newsom, E (1989) *The Extent of Physical Punishment in the UK*, Approach, London

Patterson, C.J. (1992) Children of lesbian and gay parents, *Child Development*, 63

Patterson, C.J. (1995a) Families of the lesbian baby boom: Parents' division of labor and children's adjustment. *Developmental Psychology*, 31

Pollack, S and Vaughan, J (1987),

Politics of the Heart: A Lesbian Parenting Anthology, McNaughton and Gunn, New York

Pollack, W (1999), *Real Boys*, Owl Books, New York

Serfontein, G (1990) *The Hidden Handicap: How to help children who suffer from dyslexia, hyperactivity and learning difficulties*, Simon & Schuster, Brookvale, Australia

Silverstein, O and Rashbaum, B (1994) *The Courage to Raise Good Men*, Penguin, USA

Spender, D (1999) *Man-made Language*, Pandora, USA

Taffel, R (1999) Discovering Our Children, *Family Therapy Networker*, USA

Webber, R (1994) *Living in a Stepfamily*, Australian Council for Educational Research, Melbourne

Wells, J (1997) *Lesbians Raising Sons*, Alyson Books, New York

White, M (1984) Pseudo-Encopresis: From Avalanche to Victory, from vicious to virtuous cycles, *Family systems Medicine*, 2

— (1986) The ritual of inclusion: an approach to extreme uncontrolled behavior in children and young adolescents, *Dulwich Centre Review*

— (1988) Saying hello again: The incorporation of the lost relationship in the resolution of grief, *Dulwich Centre Newsletter*

— (1991) Deconstruction and Therapy, *Dulwich Centre Newsletter*, 3

Woolfson, Dr R (1995) *Starting School*, Thorsons, London

Zillman, D & Bryant, J 'Pornography and the Trivialisation of Rape', *Journal of Communication*, Autumn, 1992, vol. 32

Zubnick, S.R., Silbum, S.R., Garton A. et al (1995) *Developing Health and Wellbeing in the Nineties*, Western Australian Child Health Survey, ABS & ICHR, Perth

Index

Aboriginal xi, 257
ADD/ADHD 15, 87-93, 96; domestic violence 89, 92; testosterone 202
adolescence 131, 195-229
anger 107-124, 131
anxiety 4, 21-2, 56, 58, 111, 209, 216, 237, 270

Biddulph, S 28
blended families 169
boundaries 65-86, 93, 186, 189-91, 225, 238
breast feeding 189
bullying 83,98, 100-4, 207, 209, 215
bungalows 226-7

child abuse 246, 246-256
childcare 126
child protection 237
child support 126
circumcision 187
communication 39-52, 53, 54, 98, 99, 112, 215
consequences 86, 169

contact 125-55
depression 4, 20, 31, 58, 216-218, 270; abuse/domestic violence 21-2, 235, 237, 250; anger 108; homosexuality 209, 211; men 56, 159; suicide 219
discrimination, 14, 260
divorce 9, 67, 126-7, 135, 138, 250, 272, 277
domestic violence 29, 102, 111, 133, 141-2, 150, 154, 169, 230-246, 250
drugs 69, 196, 211, 217, 219-22, 235, 250

emotions 53-64
employment 173-185
Erikson, E 197

Family Court 126, 133, 139, 142
feelings 53-4
feminism 231, 263
fighting 80-3
financial hardship/stress 9-12

gender 27-38, 56, 131, 159, 275;

287

communication 40; separation 128; stereotyping 54, 105
grief 120–124, 128-30, 132, 171, 242; mothers 129; separation 67, 145
guilt 123, 151; ADD/ADHD 90, 92; anxiety/depression 21–2; child abuse 254; domestic violence 232, 235, 238, 244; homo-sexuality 209; limits and boundaries 71; paid employ-ment 174–5, 182; separation/divorce 31–2, 67, 71, 127; stress 183

homosexuality 206–11

incest 246
internet 214
in-vitro fertilisation 7, 258
isolation 8, 16, 18; adolescents 209; boys 180; domestic violence 231, 240; homosexuality 209; lesbians 259, 260–7; suicide 218

Koori, xi

lesbians 257–268
limit setting 22, 49, 52
loneliness 17–20, 159

male role models 156–7, 159–60, 167, 269–70, 274; being gay 207; lesbians 262
masculinity 32–5, 159, 164, 261
media 213, 273

Pipher, D 269
pocket money 79
Pollack, W 90, 202–3
Pollack, S and Vaughan, J 258
pornography 192, 214
post-traumatic stress disorder and ADD/ADHD 89; domestic violence 232
poverty 11, 29
problem solving 118
protective behaviours 251–53

Rashbaum, B and Silverstein, O 1, 222
relationships 156–172
residence 17, 125–55
Ritalin 92

school 94–106
self control 118
separation 125–55
sexuality 186–203
siblings 80–1, 119, 148, 172, 200, 227
Silverstein, O and Rashbaum, B 1, 222
smacking 84
Spender, D 40–1
stress 5, 16, 17, 56, 129, 183, 218; ADD/ADHD, 89
suicide 30, 56, 159, 196, 218–9, 250, 270

Taffel, R 115
temper tantrums 117
testosterone 55–6, 66, 112, 161, 196, 203, 213; ADD 202
time out 116–7
toileting 188

Vaughan, J and Pollack, S 258
violence 15, 31, 43, 66, 84, 88–9, 91–2, 102, 108, 111–2, 115, 125, 133, 141–2, 150, 154, 169, 191, 209, 214, 250

Wells, J 267
work 7, 9, 17, 126